Ronald L. Sutphin

LEE DANA

To: Lee Danna

Enjoy —

Ron Sutphin

Venture Management

Venture Management

The Business of the Inventor,
Entrepreneur, Venture Capitalist,
and Established Company

William H. Shames

The Free Press
A DIVISION OF MACMILLAN PUBLISHING CO., INC.
NEW YORK

Collier Macmillan Publishers
LONDON

The Free Press
A Division of Macmillan Publishing Co., Inc.
866 Third Avenue, New York, N.Y. 10022

Collier–Macmillan Canada Ltd.

Library of Congress Catalog Card Number: 73-17642

Printed in the United States of America

printing number
1 2 3 4 5 6 7 8 9 10

Library of Congress Cataloging in Publication Data

Shames, William H
    Venture management.

    1. New products. I. Title.
HD69.N4S485   658.4   73-17642
ISBN 0-02-928400-7

Passages and diagrams on pages 73-102, 132-135, 137, 196-199, 222-226, and 231-237 pertaining to Metrodyne Corporation and Sibany enterprises used by permission.

Passages on pages 138-144, 145-147, 177-186, and 213-218 pertaining to Identimation Corporation used by permission.

Quotations on pages 274-276 from *The New York Times.* © 1971 by The New York Times
Company. Reprinted by permission.

Contents

Preface

Venture management is the branch of business management that deals with new business ventures, including start-up companies, new subunits of larger organizations, and new products and services. Thus, with venture management an estimated $40 billion for annual research and development, in all forms, is managed and new product and service needs of 215 million Americans is started and implemented.

A new venture is a joint effort by people who are *investors* of time and money in order to make a tangible and intangible *profit* for each of them. These investors include inventors, entrepreneurs, and other employees; vendors of products and services; the families of the new venturers; and individual and institutional venture capitalists.

The tangible and intangible profits are the measure of the success of the new venture, and in a new venture, a very fragile institution, indeed, the judging of success is necessarily immediate and continual. The investors and key players in a new venture define success in different ways from a variety of viewpoints. Worthy goals for judging success are not inherent, but rather are individual to the viewpoint of each of the key players, the entrepreneur, inventor, venture capitalist, and executives of established companies.

Of these players, individuals who expect success solely on the basis of tradition, science, logic, and rationale have difficulty in the venture management business, in new ventures. As Donald A. Schon wrote, in *Technology and Change:*

> Both invention and innovation are widely misunderstood, because, although they are essentially irrational and uncertain in nature, many business executives tend to idealize them as essentially rational, deliberate processes in which success is assured by intelligent effort.

Venture management is not a science but a practical art. The venture capitalist studies economic trends and the business plan of the entrepreneur/inventor and, finally, bets on his judgment of the *people* involved in the new venture. To the entrepreneur and the inventor, the new venture is the food of life. The lack of signposts is the challenge that makes it worthwhile.

This book, for example, is a new business venture of the Free Press. For a publisher, each book is a new product. Although there are established patterns in publishing books—in particular, business books—Free Press must finally make an intuitive judgment after considering perhaps six possibilities: "This new book will *certainly not* succeed"; "This new book will *probably not* succeed"; "This new book will *possibly not* succeed"; "This new book will *possibly* succeed"; "This new book will *probably* succeed"; "This new book will *certainly* succeed." The same possibilities apply to any new business venture.

Since venture management is an established industry, with thousands of players and billions of dollars, prestige, and egotism in the balance, there probably is *a* market for this book.

Case Histories

To add reality and clarity to this book, examples are drawn from the experience of setting up still-thriving businesses. I was president, entrepreneur, and co-founder of Sibany Manufacturing Corporation, a company that has been engaged in new business ventures for twelve years. I am now president of Risers' Venture Management Company, also in the business of starting new companies, and have been consultant to a number of established companies and new business ventures. I believe a successful business is *primarily* people effectively communicating with each other.

Without the rubbing, cross-fertilization, real communication, and, on occasion, outright battling between entrepreneurs, venture capitalists, and inventors, and the fruits thereof, a venture manager would not become an increasingly better decision maker; a venture management company would not survive. My experience with the start-up of a dozen companies, which includes many mistakes as well as proper choices, and with several dozen new products and services, provides the knowledgeable (though often trial-and-error) basis for the attitudes that are expressed in *Venture Management.* The point is I once felt it appropriate to tell a new controller, "Protect the company from my excesses in dreaming and fantasizing. On the other hand, remember, that without dreams and commitment to things that are unprovable, you and I wouldn't have our jobs."

The role of the independent inventor and the sale or license of new business opportunities to outside companies is covered in the first two chapters. The early days of Sibany as an inventor and innovator of new products and its evolution into the venture management business are discussed, as an example, in Chapter 3. Venture management is a continual cycle of planning (Chapter 5), implementation (Chapter 6), and shakedown (Chapter 7), in context of venture capital, which is itself the subject of Chapter 4. The most important functions in the new venture are marketing and finance, which are explained in the next three chapters—8, 9, and 10. The "bottom line" (judging the success of the new venture) is the subject of both Chapter 11 and Chapter 12. The relatedness of the established company to venture management is woven throughout the book.

Preview

It is the thesis of this book that each key player in venture management is,usually, inadequately aware of the aspirations, attitudes, goals, and problems of the other players. Thus, for example, the treatment here of the role of the entrepreneur or the independent inventor is intended not only for that player but for other players as well, so that they can understand him better, communicate with him better. Communication, to be meaningful, can take place only in the terms of the person to be communicated with.

It is suggested that the three *most tenuous judgments* of the venture management business are:
- choosing between the new ventures which will be successful and those which will not
- deciding when to stop instead of persisting
- finding the right product or service

It is also suggested that the four keys to the success of the new business venture are:
- the chief executive officer
- the plan and carry-through of marketing and sales
- the financial plan and its implementation
- a controlled cash flow and budget

You will *not* find in this book, however, a step-by-step plan for what to do with and about new ventures. There are no complete plans; decisions must be based on the specific evidence in front of you.

You *will* find emphasis on experience, evidence, rules of thumb, insight, and on the dreams, motivations, and foibles of venture managers—including my own. For myself, this book has already opened a new dimension to my life. It has helped to provide me with the courage to continue writing, as part of my business career and just for fun. Every word in it is solely my responsibility.

Other people have been important, though, in the writing of this book: Herb Nagourney bet on an unpublished writer; Ed Barry, George Rowland, Ellen Simon, and Bob Wallace, of the Free Press, and Georgia Kornbluth helped me to better focus and direct the material. My wife, Diane, and Maxine Novak typed the manuscript and were patient with my frustrations and my frustrating ways. My children, Jeffrey, Erica, and Jonathan, usually answered my cry for more coffee. Most important, Auren Uris and Larry Dolan put the writing of the book on the track to begin with. Many others, too numerous to mention, read, criticized, and made suggestions for various parts of the book or encouraged and benignly pushed me to keep going. Writing a book, like anything we perceive as being outside our ability, is greatly aided by friends who are willing to tell you what they believe, regardless of what you want to hear.

Venture Management

Chapter 1

The Independent Inventor

With the proper environment, we [in the United States] can haul off and invent and design almost anything we want.[1]

What is an invention? Who invents? How does inventing take place? What is really new? How do new products come to market?

Increasingly in recent years, both government and industry have conducted a widening search for answers to these and other questions about invention and innovation. The growing interest in these processes stems from the effects they have on major segments of industry, on individual companies, and on the United States economy as a whole.

While the gross national product has grown at an average annual growth rate of 2.5 percent during the past 20 years, some technologically innovative companies have grown at an average compound rate of almost 30 percent annually.

Innovation can be very profitable. Everyone wants the process to continue. But not everyone knows how to participate.

The greatest single stumbling block to innovation is not a lack of new ideas, nor is it even the problems involved in translating these ideas into

1. Robert A. Charpie, chairman of the Panel on Invention and Innovation, after a three-year study for the U.S. Department of Commerce to improve the climate for technological change. *New York Times*, May 14, 1967, pp. 1f.

1

production, marketing, and distribution. The major problem is lack of understanding, coupled with unrealistic ideas and false assumptions—in other words, the application to new ventures of the business practices that are successful in established companies.

What new products will people buy? At what prices? Is a certain company capable of making and selling a product it has never made before? How much is a company willing to spend on innovation? How and when must the money be allocated? *Is its management really prepared to break new ground?* How much of an investment is an invention worth? To inventors? To industry? And at what stage?

What is the innovative process?

The Source of Innovation

It is a curious and surprising fact that most genuine new-product concepts come not from the nation's giant research-oriented companies nor from government, but from "garage" and "basement" inventors. Xerography, jet engines, helicoptors, rockets, Polaroid cameras, vacuum tubes, air conditioning, zippers, FM radio, power steering, and automatic transmissions were all contributed by independent inventors. The accompanying list, taken from a Commerce Department report, includes many other 20th-century contributions of the independent inventor.

An appropriate question at this point is: What gives the independent inventor the edge in breakthrough innovation? His very independence is a significant factor in answer.

Inventors are individualists: Problem solvers generally are. In large companies, even large companies committed to innovation, inventors frequently are subject to committee decisions that may constrict them or conflict with their own inclinations.

A novel product, technically feasible and with the best marketing prospects, may still not fit corporate growth objectives. The company's manufacturing facilities may not be geared to produce it. Its marketing organization may judge the product unsuitable to present or future distribution capabilities. Or, according to a consensus of those required to make the decision, the investment required might be put to better use elsewhere.

Then, too, the lines of communication in many companies are not good. A lack of technical knowledge within a company about a product which may be outside the company's own particular field can be an impassable barrier to the product's acceptance by those who must approve its feasibility. Or, if a radically new design of an existing product would make expensive plant

SOME IMPORTANT INVENTIVE CONTRIBUTIONS OF INDEPENDENT INVENTORS AND SMALL ORGANIZATIONS IN THE TWENTIETH CENTURY

Xerography
Chester Carlson

Shrink-proof Knitted Wear
Richard Walton

Mercury Dry Cell
Samuel Ruben

DDT
J.R. Geigy & Co.

Dacron Polyester Fiber "Terylene"
J.R. Whinfield/J.T. Dickson

Power Steering
Francis Davis

Insulin
Frederick Banting

Catalytic Cracking of Petroleum
Eugene Houdry

Kodachrome
L. Mannes & L. Godowsky Jr.

Vacuum Tube
Lee De Forest

Zipper
Whitcomb Judson/Gideon Sundback

Air Conditioning
Willis Carrier

Rockets
Robert Goddard

Automatic Transmissions
H.F. Hobbs

Polaroid Camera
Edwin Land

Streptomycin
Selman Waksman

Gyrocompass
A. Kaempfe/E.A. Sperry/S.G. Brown

Heterodyne Radio
Reginald Fessenden

Penicillin
Alexander Fleming

Jet Engine
Frank Whittle/Hans Von Ohain

Ball-Point Pen
Ladislao & George Biro

Titanium
W. J. Kroll

Frequency Modulation Radio
Edwin Armstrong

Cellophane
Jacques Brandenberger

Shell Molding
Johannes Croning

Self-Winding Wristwatch
John Harwood

Tungsten Carbide
Karl Schroeter

Cyclotron
Ernest O. Lawrence

Continuous Hot-Strip Rolling of Steel
John B. Tytus

Bakelite
Leo Baekeland

Cotton Picker
John & Mack Rust

Helicopter
Juan De La Cierva/Heinrich Focke/Igor Sikorsy

Oxygen Steelmaking Process
C.V. Schwarz/J. Miles/R. Durrer

Source: *Technological Innovation: Its Environment and Management.* U.S. Department of Commerce, 1967, p. 18.

equipment obsolete, the temptation to avoid new design is understandable. It is easier, and safer, to assume that the way things are already being done is the best way to do them, and accordingly the response of these players to a new idea is often, "We thought of that already, and it won't work. What we're already doing is better."

Unable to evaluate most of these factors with any certainty and with their judgment often colored by decision makers' prejudices and fears, industrial managers are usually cautious about going into untried areas. The penalties for saying "no," if any, seem far less pressing than saying "yes" to a risk that may not pay off.

The individual inventor, on the other hand, is usually totally committed to his product conception, even though his commitment may be unrealistic. Usually, since he is not in the environment of a large company he will risk financial insecurity for years—and sometimes for decades—to prove that his invention is valid. Today, however, sophisticated companies are beginning to better understand the emotional need of such creative persons, and they seek to provide wide latitude for inventors within the company framework.

The key to the business of inventing and innovating is not so much original conception as good judgment about what is translatable into practical use —what someone needs and will buy.

What's New?

An invention is a new idea—a new product that performs an old function better, a break with the past that provides a product or service hitherto unavailable. It is putting ideas and things together to create something that didn't previously exist. Frequently, it is a simpler, more convenient, less expensive way of offering many people something that had been available only to a very few, at great expense. Or it may be a better alternative to products and processes we need or want, but would prefer in another form.

Invention is a zipper to replace buttons, a safety pin, an electric light, a motor, a thinking machine. Lots of people invent something during their lifetime. However, only a small proportion of such inventions reach the marketplace. Many are merely bright ideas. Some are ingenious, but too expensive; others are brilliant conceptions which depend upon materials or production processes that are beyond present-day technology. Some only their inventors can love, and no one else will buy, because they satisfy an individual preference rather than a general need.

It has been estimated that of thousands of new businesses formed every year to commercialize on technological innovation, more than half die during the first year. Fewer than 1 out of 100 survive three years.

How, Now?

How do you invent?

First, *find the right problem*. It is easier to invent a satisfactory solution than to determine what needs to be invented.

Second, *don't know too much about why it can't be done*. There are often good reasons why "we have always done it this way." Men who have devoted their working lives to existing products and processes have little patience with the assertion that there is a new and better way to perform the same function. As a result, much innovation comes from outside the conventional boundaries of an industry.

Successful inventing cannot be analyzed objectively. The reason that certain minds instinctively light on new ways to make things work often seems to be more in the realm of art than in the realm of science.

But the business of inventing *is* subject to certain rules:

- Know what should be invented.
- Believe that it can be invented.
- Challenge every assumption and limitation.
- Concern yourself not with what *is*, but what *can be*.

Wars have traditionally spurred invention. They provide urgent incentives to solve immediate problems quickly and effectively.

Commercial competition also is a satisfactory goal to creativity. Consider how quickly a multitude of ways are discovered to parallel something no one has ever done before, once someone finds a way to do it for the first time. Running the four-minute mile is an example: Once the old myth that it couldn't be done had been disproved by one person, many runners did it.

Insecurity is another effective prod to innovation. Shrunken profits have moved many companies to make commitments in new product areas. A saturated market for existing products demands invention of new products.

The healthiest incentive, however, for creation of new products is a desire for growth and progress, the excitement and refreshment of working in fresh fields.

Today's Idea Is Several Hundred Years Old

Inventions are often the work of many men, and many decades of research and discovery may result in a single invention.

One example is the genesis of television, which has revolutionized our society and required the work of thousands of inventors and discoverers. The first step in the invention of television was probably Musschenbroek's discovery of capacitance and invention of the Leyden jar in 1746. Then followed the work of several dozen individual inventors and scientists, which culminated in Armstrong's announcement of the development of FM broadcasting in 1933, and finally the corporate activities of AT&T, CBS, and RCA.

Invention and discovery are closely related. A discoverer reveals the existence of a natural phenomenon, as did Ben Franklin when he discovered negative and positive electrical charges. An inventor combines discoveries that is, (things) with ideas not previously utilized. In most cases, the ideas and the things have been around for a while but have not been seen or understood previously.

Sources and Ideas

Until the 20th century, most inventors worked alone or with a few assistants. The 19th century was the age of the inventor-entrepreneur. An individual, to get anywhere with his invention, *usually had to be both inventor and entrepreneur*. He had to know how to take his idea and make it into a business, and he lost his company if he managed poorly.

Most discussions of the subject of invention divide the process into the invention itself (i.e., the inventor's getting the idea, reducing it to practice, and acquiring the patent) and the innovation (i.e., the inventor's selling the manufacturing rights by license, and then the licensee's manufacturing the product and selling it). Fundamental to the invention process also is the *problem statement,* which is usually not specifically considered. The idea for an invention is the result of filling in a blank in a problem statement or answering a problem question: "If only there were a . . ." or "Does the processing of exposed film *have* to be done in a laboratory over a period of minutes or hours?"

Most problem statements and questions are the result of spotlighting nuisances in everyday objects. The computer, telephone, automobile, and television set stimulate many problem statements because of their prevalence. However, they also inspire thousands of other people and therefore add additional risk to the already insecure world of the independent inventor.

Commercially practical problem statements often derive both from *conflicts in terms* and from the *automation of common tasks.* Today's conflicts in terms often become tomorrow's definitions. They also have the advantage to the independent inventor of being incongruous, and therefore challenging. For example, it is well known that radio signals follow the earth's surface, but television signals tend to move in a straight line and therefore have to be transmitted by coaxial cable, reflection off a satellite, or by line of sight from one tower to the next. Thus the problem question arises, "How can television signals be transmitted with the characteristics of radio signals?"

The automation of common tasks has an important advantage in that the task is likely to continue regardless of the way our society evolves economically, socially, and politically. If you can automate a horse and buggy, every type of government or society will use your device.

Many inventions actually derive from accidents. After years of experimentation, Charles Goodyear, for example, accidentally dropped some crude gum rubber on a kitchen stove and thus discovered that heating rubber with sulphur would vulcanize it. Accidents can indirectly foster creativity because they involve an unplanned possibility. Once an inventor believes that he has exhausted the possibilities of a particular phenomenon, once he believes that he knows all the things that can be done and can't be done, he has lost his ability to be creative. In a sense, the independent inventor is an "accident" relative to the on-going company.

The Garage and the Research Facility

Increasingly, the independent inventor has become less independent. During the past forty years, inventions relating to television and other commonly used products have been owned and sponsored by large companies. In many instances government grants are made to large companies and to universities to sponsor invention and research. In addition, United States corporations spend billions of dollars annually on research and development. Although companies occasionally go outside their own organization for a new product idea, most are committed to developing their own new products and innovations. A few companies, however, are exceptions and, depending on the industry, should be sought by the independent inventor.

There is often a distinction between new-product ideas developed inside a company and those which come from outside. In the average case, companies are well equipped to develop their own *evolutionary* products. They are in a better position than outsiders to revise, improve, and update, whether their product is women's stockings, steamrollers, molding machines, or cosmetics.

However, it is becoming more and more apparent that companies have great difficulty in developing *revolutionary* products—that is, products that represent a major departure from previous items or lines. There are many explanations: Company employees from front line to R&D (research and development) are usually wedded to present items and ways of thinking that produce them; they're also all too familiar with "what can't be done." In addition, the climate of a stable organization tends to stifle the flights of imagination required to break with the past.

An independent inventor actually has an advantage in that he knows less about the specialties of a company or an industry than the in-company people. And while his lack of expertness means that he is naive in given areas, these very gaps in his experience somehow seem to make him more likely to generate the essential creative sparks than are the company or industry "experts."

The linking of giants such as RCA, CBS, and AT&T with invention can be misleading. On such a basis, one might assume that inventiveness is a special attribute of large companies or, conversely, that the efforts of the small company or the individual do poorly in the invention race. On the contrary, as indicated earlier, studies show that independent inventors and small technologically based companies are responsible for a remarkably high percentage of the *important* innovations of our time—a larger percentage than might be suggested by a comparison of their relative investment in money and manpower with that of large organizations. According to most studies, the contributions of large companies have been mainly in the area of improvement inventions.

A number of studies suggest the achievement of the independent inventor. Here are specific instances:

- Professor John Jewkes, *et al*, showed that out of 61 important inventions and innovations of the 20th century, which the authors selected for analysis, over half of them stemmed from independent inventors or small firms.
- Professor Daniel Hamberg of the University of Maryland studied major inventions made during the decade 1946–1955 and found that over two-thirds of them resulted from the work of independent inventors and small companies.
- Professor Merton Peck of Harvard studied 149 inventions in aluminum welding, fabricating techniques, and aluminum finishing. Major producers accounted for only one of seven important inventions.
- Professor Hamberg also studied thirteen-major innovations in the American steel industry. Four came from inventions in European companies, seven from independent inventors, and none were inventions of American steel companies.
- Professor John Enos of the Massachusetts Institute of Technology studied what were considered seven major inventions in the refining and cracking of petroleum. All seven were made by independent inventors.[2]

The Pluses and Minuses of the Individual Inventor

Still, it would be an exaggeration to suggest that the inventor or creative group in the large company is completely trapped by organizational flypaper while the individual inventor produces good ideas as easily and automatically as an apple picker in a lush orchard fills his basket.

The Bell Telephone Company (which is now AT&T), as an example, was one of the very first operating companies to organize invention when it set up a laboratory (now Bell Laboratories) in the late 19th century. Its first emp-

2. *Technological Innovation: Its Environment and Management,* prepared by Daniel V. De-Simone for the U.S. Department of Commerce, January 1967, pp. 16–17.

loyees were inventors hired to solve telephone problems and create new telephone problem statements.

There are advantages and disadvantages to both positions: (1) being an individual inventor and (2) having the responsibility for creative output in a large company. The small inventor can start on a shoestring. Labor makes up about 70 percent of the cost of product development in its initial stages, and so, when the small inventor provides his own labor, he has to invest only 30 percent in capital to get going. In addition, there is little problem with communications for the individual or for a company with a small staff. Compared with the large company with its red tape and complicated communications systems, the small inventor is highly efficient.

On the other hand, in large companies, approximately 50 percent of the R&D costs are underwritten by the federal government because all expenditures are tax-deductible. Another advantage of the large company is the talents of thousands of people immediately available from other parts of the company. For the individual inventor, operating expenses come out of pre-tax dollars and he is usually more or less on his own.

The average solitary inventor must work in linear fashion: he commits his resources to one idea, brings that as far along as he can, then goes on to the next. For the large corporation, however, where R&D is extensive and numerous separate ideas can be worked on simultaneously, profits of a single successful outcome can pay for the failures of the others. The lone inventor, therefore, is usually unable to average the risk, since nine out of ten patents issued never result in a marketed product. Nothing ever comes of them for any of a number of reasons, the most frequent of which is the impracticality or lack of commerciality of the idea. Perhaps the greatest problem the lone inventor faces is the need to be practical. Usually it goes against all his instincts.

Another, related attitude which differentiates the individual inventor from his corporate counterpart is his degree of commitment. The garage inventor often has a "calling"—an idea or concept that has set his imagination on fire. He is driven to push ahead, to develop the idea, no matter what—even in the face of failure. Despite his total commitment, the lone inventor is called upon to do his inventing with one eye on the marketplace. Almost by definition the inventor is a dreamer, and yet he is called on to be practical. It is a demand which few inventors are capable of meeting.

The corporate inventor, on the other hand, may not have to be very concerned with marketing or other forms of reality, but the department head is responsible for pushing his employees in the directions that will be most productive from the company's standpoint.

Usually there is no one to push the lone inventor in the direction of practicality. A disdain for marketing considerations is characteristic of the garage inventor. He will fall in love with an impractical idea just as deeply as with a practical one. He fails to make the modifications in approach that might steer his invention into worthwhile areas and bring it to the market. Lack of practicality involves three major hazards that lie between the independent inventor and his potential pot of gold:

- The tendency of the inventor to be so in love with his idea that he scorns realistic considerations.
- Ignorance of the marketing facts of life which would enable him to steer a more productive course in his development work.
- Inability to exploit his invention, or put it in the hands of those who can, and still retain a major interest.

Is There a Market for Your Idea?

Most inventors simply assume that there is a market for their inventions. More spcifically, they confuse the technical validity of the new product with the automatic presence of a large market. The sad fact is that very often there is no market—or at least not enough market to justify development, production, and marketing costs.

Many inventors fail because they delude themselves about the marketability of their inventions. To offset this tendency, inventors frequently attempt to ally themselves either formally or informally with a "businessman" or an individual who will help them assess and cope with the marketing problems associated with their invention. Two other good partners for the inventor who has something to offer and wants to get it to the marketplace are the engineer and the designer. More recently technology transfer companies have become available. These allies can take an inventor's idea and help develop it, shape it, and produce it in a practical form so that it will work. Despite an inventor's attempt to seek practical help, however, the impracticality of his idea or his approach still may preclude commercial development.

This thumbnail case history comes from my own personal experience. I recently received a phone call from a man who told me of a great invention he had. I suggested that he write to me and explain what his invention could do without disclosing how it was to be done. Later, he again phoned and said that he and his wife were in the area and asked if I would please see them.

I agreed to a meeting and we spent about an hour in a conversation that got nowhere. He did reveal that the product was a new type of fishnet that was lighter, cheaper, and easier to handle than those being currently used. I asked him whether he had tested his invention in actual practice and he kept changing the subject. I continued to press him about whether he had reduced his invention to practice and he continued to avoid answering.

"Reduction to practice" is a technical term used by the patent office to indicate that an inventor either has applied for a patent or has built a prototype or a working model (or has done both). Whether an invention has been reduced to practice is a critical question asked by a person or company thinking of investing in a new product because its answer defines the degree of commitment of the inventor. If there has been no reduction to practice, the inventor usually cannot or will not bring himself to put the invention to the acid test. Such a finding is usually a decisive factor for investors because, if the inventor is not willing to bet on his own invention with his time and money, few second parties will.

I next asked why the inventor thought his fishnet was an improvement. I was looking for one of three considerations used in deciding whether the inventor has something worthwhile: (1) The product is new and not previously available. (2) The product is presently available at a much higher price than the new one could sell for. (3) The product is available, but in a form that is generally less convenient, heavier, or in other ways physically and psychologically inferior to the new item. *The inventor never said anything that showed me he had a strong commitment to the invention.*

During the conversation, the inventor did all the talking while his wife nodded emphatically at each point he made. Despite this touching example of marital unanimity, it developed that the inventor knew little of the present state of the art. ["State of the art" refers to how the problem or situation is presently being handled by the products currently available.] The inventor's ignorance of the state of the art seriously damaged his credibility in my mind. Without knowing what is presently being done an inventor can have little basis for evaluating his idea or product.

This case suggests that potential investors or developers know almost everything. This is certainly not the case. Consider the inventor who for five years in the mid-1920s vainly sought to interest someone in his idea to use push buttons instead of a dial for radio station selection. Finally, in the late 1920s, he sold the idea to a radio manufacturer for a small sum—said to be $3,000, with no royalty rights. There is no need to point out the eventual wide application of push-button tuning. Without this one feature it is problematical whether automobile radios would have gained their present popularity.

The Premature Inventor

Perhaps the inventor with the push-button concept was somewhat ahead of his time. Certainly in the 1920s there was little need for this type of improvement when more basic problems confronted radio manufacturers and broadcasters.

Occasionally, an inventor fails not because he lacks marketing know-how or even business common sense, but because he is trying to exploit an idea whose time has not quite come. The prototype of such a premature inventor is Leonardo da Vinci (1452–1519). Da Vinci, perhaps the greatest mind in the history of Western man, was an inventor and innovator—and considerably earlier than the age of science. He invented a canal system, in the 15th century, with locks that are still in operation. Many of his other inventions were essentially useless and could not be applied in his own time. For example, numerous airplane designs and models; metal projectiles like modern bombshells that could be aimed more accurately than heavier stone balls; the propeller as a means of moving air backward to create thrust forward (and this was before the statement by Newton of his laws of dynamics); a machine gun; numerous mechanical musical instruments; a breech-loading cannon and an armored tank; parachutes; and various jet propulsion and hydraulic devices. Da Vinci is proof that inventions, like everything else, require the right timing.

The "Invention Killer" Myth

There is a belief current in some circles that companies either develop or buy inventions with good potential and then put them on the shelf. A whole range of "folk tales" have grown around this basic myth: for example, that there is a pill that converts a gallon of water into a gallon of gasoline, and a flashlight battery or razor blade that lasts forever.

Such myths have little foundation in fact. In our competitive economy there is little logic in the shelf theory. While the hoarding company was shelving its product, another company would probably be happily on its way to the marketplace with a competitive product. Another factor is that, historically, inventions seem to be made in more than one place at the same time. For example, in the 19th century, a vastly improved steel-making process was simultaneously invented in the United States and Europe. It is not likely that any one organization could buy up simultaneous inventions of the same thing and put them all away, to the detriment of the market and the deprivation of the public.

But the point should not be made too dogmatically. Somewhere, sometime, companies have surely held back inventions. There could have been many reasons, anything from excessive costs to poor timing, or even outright unwillingness to obsolete their product line. In an advanced and competitive economy, however, this practice seems to be outmoded.

Patents

One of the time-honored methods suggested to the inventor for his protection is to mail a disclosure of the product to himself. The sealed and dated missive supposedly represents legal proof of the inventor's achievement. This letter is supposed to protect him from two threats: first, the possibility that someone will steal his idea, and second, the possibility of a parallel invention coming at a later date. But authorities on this point say that this method is only better than doing nothing.

The inventor should not personally search out the patent possibilities of his idea. His first ally should be a competent patent attorney, and not necessarily the least expensive one he can find.

A competent patent attorney, like a doctor or dentist, can be worth his weight in gold. Where an inexperienced or inept patent counsel might have difficulties, a capable one can win contested points with the patent office. In some cases the prestige and reputation of a patent attorney will impress the company considering buying or licensing a new product. The company's legal advisers, in short, can be favorably influenced by the experience, reputation, and status of the inventor's counsel.

Contacting a patent attorney also may provide some useful feedback. If the attorney is not interested, the idea may not be patentable or marketable. If he is interested, the inventor immediately gains credibility and encouragement.

In some cases patent attorneys will trade services for an interest in the product; that's why it is desirable to seek out an *established* individual or firm. The reputable attorney will not take advantage of the inventor and will seek to work out a mutually favorable agreement.

As a rule of thumb, the typical patent law firm charges approximately $200 for a search of the state of the art with respect to a given invention, and $2,000 for the activities involved in making a patent application to the patent office.

Currently, the inventor is protected by an international patent agreement which includes eighty-three countries (the eighty-third country being the Soviet Union, which eventually gave up its hold-out status in order to protect itself and gain other benefits).

The international patent agreement gives an advantage to an individual who applies for a patent in any one of the eighty-three signatory countries. While he must actually apply for a patent in any particular country, he is granted, as a filing date, the earlier date he applies in any one of the eighty-three countries. For example, if an inventor applies for a patent in the United States on January 2, 1975, he has until January 2, 1976, to apply in any of the other eighty-two member countries. He will receive patent protection in each of these other countries as of January 2, 1975, along with that in the United States.

A widespread misconception is that patent protection starts on the day a patent is issued. Protection actually starts on the day the inventor reduces his idea to practice, whether by starting to build a model or by applying for a patent. For effective protection, the reduction to practice must be continuous, either in the development of a working model or in the pursuit of the patent, or both.

A thumbnail example: Bill Jones applies for a patent on a new basketball on January 2, 1975. Sam Smith, who had invented the same basketball on June 21, 1974, starts to build a prototype then but does not apply for his patent until January 2, 1976, a year after Jones. If Smith can show that he has reduced to practice his basketball idea in a continuing development, he will probably win the competition with Jones for the patent, even though he filed later.

Commercializing the Invention

Here is a typical series of steps for the inventor to follow:

- Conceive of a problem statement; invent an answer; consider it in detail so that it is refined and defined; start a laboratory notebook and keep careful notes of all the facts relating to the invention and its development.
- Make complete disclosure of the invention in your notebook and have each entry witnessed by at least two individuals—that is, signed with their signatures and dated. The development data also should be noted and the witnesses should indicate that the invention was explained to them and understood.
- The previous steps should be coordinated by consultation and disclosure to a qualified patent attorney to whom a written disclosure has been given.
- Next there should be a reduction to practice by applying for a United States patent and the building of a working model.
- An investigation of what is presently done in the area of the invention should be made through books, trade publications, and professional and other people in the field, including a search of the state of the patent art by a patent attorney.
- Finally, the product should be commercialized by the inventor through his company, a new company he forms, or the licensing or selling of the idea to another firm.

Models

Models go through various stages of development. The following terms are generally used, as models go from the drawing board into three-dimensional representations:

BREADBOARD   The first attempt at putting together a working unit —usually spread out, without too much concern about the relation of parts. More important is the convenience of the inventor and engineer to work on the subunits, make corrections and adjustments, and so on.

BRASSBOARD   A more refined and improved version of the breadboard, reflecting the solution of problems learned from the building of one or more breadboards. At this stage, commercial considerations are introduced. Such matters as availability of parts, nature of linkages, quality of materials, multiple suppliers, and the total cost of the product are considered.

PROTOTYPE   The arrangement of parts, subassemblies, and so on into a form as close as possible to the final commercial product.

PRODUCTION PROTOTYPE   This represents the design and production refinements that will make it possible to turn out units as easily as possible at a cost that is close to commercially feasible. Involved here are industrial design, production engineering, and the design and production models leading directly to a tooled manufactured product.

The Viewpoint of the Company

Peter Drucker, Theodore Levitt, and Dr. Richard Farson, dean of the School of Design, California Institute of the Arts, along with other business authorities, agree that the future of the average company—indeed its survival—often depends on its ability to innovate, develop, manage, produce, and market new products. Building this capability has become a major preoccupation of today's business managers. Product development is a way for the business manager to direct his company to growth and diversification, adding to a present line or going into fresh fields with new products.

Other roads to growth are buying a company, selling a company, or merging a company. The attitudes, risk factors, and judgments that differentiate new-product development from mergers and acquisitions are different, not necessarily better or worse.

New-product development is a long-term commitment. The dynamo-leader-pragmatist-politician who becomes head of the company is more comfortable personally commanding those matters where the results of his efforts are relatively short-term ones. He can see short-term results when he borrows money, goes through an underwriting, buys a company, or changes a manager. He knows it takes a long time from the idea to the commercial embodiment of that idea, and so he leaves new-product development to a group he has inherited or a group he creates. This function is called "planning," "corporate development," "product development," or "research and development."

Growth by Merger and Acquisition

Acquiring another company did not become a common practice among businessmen until the 1950s, but acquisitions have risks and pitfalls which inhibit many businessmen. However, the dramatic success of Litton Industries, one of the first of the modern conglomerates, institutionalized a new concept of business. The American economy would let thousands of businessmen with a flair for owning their own businesses spend a few years or a hundred forming their businesses. These founders would pick the people they want, the nature of their products, decide how they will make the products, how they will sell them, and how they will finance them; and they would make the thousands of major and minor decisions that form the pattern of an evolving business.

As tens of thousands of businesses change (most fail within a year; more fail within a second year, and thereafter; the rest attain various degrees of success and continuity) an acquiring organization can pick and choose those that are attractive.

Buy them, or sell your company to them, or merge with them. Put together a team to investigate how to do the same thing more often: a marketing man, a production man, an administrator, and an accountant.

But there are problems related to this approach. Not *all* are solvable.

A company is no longer the same when it becomes part of another company. A company, like a wife, cannot really be known until you live with it on a day-to-day basis, through good times and bad, through sickness and health, through the babies and teenagers, etc. Also, the man who starts a business has a tough time working for someone else. The management that stays may even lose incentive under new conditions. Suddenly they are working under rules and conditions established by someone else. It is no longer their baby.

There were other problems. The popularity and success of many mergers and acquisitions made it a common practice. Trade publications and the mass media spread the word. The "how-to" books explained success in six, more or less, easy lessons.

A new type of company was born: the conglomerate: the company whose basic business is to acquire ownership of other companies.

In 1969, the bubble burst. Many conglomerates had been unsuccessful after a succession of mergers. The stock market crash lowered the glamour of conglomerates, making if difficult or impossible to acquire other companies on a favorable basis.

Most important, the number of "lumbermen" had gone up, while the number of "trees" that were available after a hundred years of start-up and shake-out were fewer and fewer.

Growth by New Ventures

Those who planned early foresaw the dwindling of supply of existing companies and looked for other ways in which to grow. Venture management and venture capital as formal businesses were born.

During the period from 1958 to now, at least half the time, the entrepreneur and inventor were operating in a seller's market. There was more money to bet, and there were more companies looking to the outside for new products and other new ventures, than there were good things to bet on.

In these companies which are looking for new products, there are two opposing forces:

Force 1: Innovate or die.

Force 2: Innovate and lose your shirt.

And there's little doubt that many businessmen facing the prospect of pushing into new-product areas are beset by ambivalence: The desire for the fruits of innovation versus the fear of risks and headaches.

Of course, they're right on both counts. The man confronted by the choice of the two doors wants the lady instead of the tiger, and who can blame him?

Analysis of the forces pushing the executive toward new-product development can tell us something about the resolution of the dilemma. And seeing such dilemmas spelled out, one can understand the indecision, even confusion, exhibited by businessmen when called to act in the arena of innovation.

Executive indecision in this situation poses problems for several evaluators: senior executives, shareholders, a company's financial backers. Their questions: Is the decision maker confused by the complexity of the question? Does he have the ability to resolve the dilemma constructively?

Or is he balking because he feels the odds for success are against forward action in new products or other new ventures?

Forces for Innovation

Many proponents of innovation are vocal and highly placed, a strong presence on the business scene. These observers say that innovation is becoming the heart and core of business management. For example, economist, consultant, and management seer Peter Drucker writes:

> There is little doubt in my mind that entrepreneurial innovation will be as important to management in the future as the managerial function itself is currently. Indeed, it may be more important in the years to come. Unlike the 19th century, however, entrepreneurial innovation will increasingly have to be carried out in, and by, existing institutions, such as on-going businesses. It will, therefore, no longer be possible to consider it as lying outside management or even as being peripheral to management.[3]

Perhaps Drucker has knowingly folded his fist around a lead weight for added punch. Whether his thought is overstated is not easy to judge.

What *is* easily determined, though, is the nightmare reaction of the ordinary executive or corporate owner. As he sees it, he's got a tough grind just keeping his firm moving along on its traditional track. Now Drucker, a voice from a management Olympus, in effect trumpets, "Not enough, not enough!"

And to add to his worries, Drucker is not a lone voice. There is also Theodore Levitt, eminent innovation and marketing writer and consultant:

> We live in a business world that increasingly worships the great tribal god *innovation*, lyrically hailing it not just as a desired, but as a necessary condition of a company's survival and growth. This highly agitated confidence in the liberating efficacy of innovation has in some places become an article of faith almost as strong as the Natchez Indian's consuming faith in the deity of the sun. Man creates gods according to his needs. Significantly, the businessman's new demigod and the Natchez's more venerable and historic god make identical promises. They both promise renewal and life.[4]

3. Peter F. Drucker, *Technology, Management and Society* (New York: Harper & Row, 1969), pp. 35–36. Used by permission of the publisher.
4. Theodore Levitt, "Innovative Imitation," *Harvard Business Review*, vol. 44, no. 5, September–October 1966, p. 63. Used by permission of the publisher.

While Levitt's words have an ironic tinge, the uptight businessman is not likely to get the nuances. He is more likely to read Levitt straight, and take his outstanding writings on marketing and its new demands as implicit proof of the doom of the old, placid, and noninnovational ways.

The average businessman is also presented with abundent evidence that many who do innovate do well financially. The "big boys" thrive on an innovation diet; their new products are all around for the average onlooker to see.

Companies that depend on a diet of new products to help them grow and prosper also seem to be favored by the financial community. Investors pay a premium for ownership in companies that are oriented toward tomorrow. This premium results in a high price-earnings (PE) ratio (the price of the stock divided by annual per-share earnings). Stock of new-product-oriented companies often commands higher prices than the present earnings would justify, because future earnings are expected to be high. Whether the market is up or down, or times are good or bad, these companies seem to sell at a relatively higher price than their less venturesome cousins.

Furthermore, technological innovation is smiled upon and paid attention to at national levels. In 1964, President Lyndon B. Johnson directed the Department of Commerce to explore new ways of helping the development and spread of new technology.

Also, activity in the marketplace itself tells the businessman a great deal. Using a variety of figures, analysts make statements that indicate the rate at which new products appear. For example, the American Marketing Association conducted a study showing that in 1967, 55 percent of the groceries and frozen foods on foodstore shelves did not exist ten years before. Perhaps even more arresting for the businessman concerned about the life of his traditional product lines, 42.7 percent of the items offered in 1957 were no longer on the shelves in 1967.

Similarly, the director of marketing for Chevrolet recently made the prediction that 75 percent of corporate income in the 1970s would come from new products.

It is thus evident to the average businessman that today's high-growth companies are essentially innovative. The growth and success of organizations like IBM, Xerox, and 3M have made business history with a clear message that favors the new product.

And the climate in which the typical executive operates reflects a basic fact. Competition and the mood of the marketplace push him—often faster than he would like—toward new products. During the socio–economic revolution of the two World War II decades, and the resulting affluence, what used to be *aspiration* became *expectation*—and finally *demand*.

The Management of Ideas

In a speech delivered in New York City in 1970, Dr. Richard Farson, dean of the School of Design, California Institute of the Arts, said: "There is a belief current that creativity is rare, difficult and desirable. The opposite is true. Creativity is frequent, easy, and, being difficult to manage, troublesome."

In the context of new-product development, how relevant is Dr. Farson's generalization? Taking the points one at a time:

FREQUENCY? "Good" ideas *are* scarce; "mediocre" ideas, a dime a dozen.

EASE? While creativity may be prevalent in other areas—art for example—in the world of business, useful and exploitable ideas are not easily come by, and procedures for developing them are only indifferently successful.

DESIRABILITY? In this instance Dr. Farson is correct both in his statement of the general belief and in his contradiction of it. Yes, creativity is desirable—very much so in the business world. And yes, creativity is difficult to manage.

Of all the facets of new-product development, that of creativity—the production of ideas—is the least understood and often the reef on which the entire process founders. One basic problem is learning to distinguish between "good" and "bad" ideas. For example, one could say the Xerox copying machine is a good idea and the Edsel was a bad idea. But these evaluations are only true *after* the fact. As the history of these two products shows, the Edsel was considered an excellent idea and was given the full treatment by developers and marketers. The Xerox copier was held in low esteem by dozens of companies who rejected it, and only in the course of its development did it finally acquire the momentum to make its impact on the market.

Peter Drucker has other comments on the management difficulties in the production of ideas:

> Creativity, which looms so large in present discussions of innovation, is not the real problem. There are usually more ideas in any organization, including businesses than can possibly be put to use. Ask any company—including seemingly moribund ones—this question: "What in our economy, or our society, or our state of knowledge would give our business its greatest opportunity if only we could make it happen?" Dozens of responses will burst from management's lips. As a rule, we are not lacking ideas—not even good, serviceable ideas. What is lacking is management's *willingness to welcome ideas*, in fact solicit them, and processes, after all, are only the vehicles through which the ideas become effective. The specific future products and processes often cannot even be imagined.

For example, when DuPont started the work on polymer chemistry, out of which nylon eventually evolved, it did not know that man-made fibers would be the end-product. DuPont acted on the assumption that any gain in man's ability to manipulate the structure of large, organic molecules—a scientific skill at that time in its infancy—would lead to commercially important results of some kind. It was only after six or seven years of research work that man-made fibers first appeared as a possible major result area. [5]

But regardless of the doubts and difficulties surrounding the creative process in the new product context, there is no doubt that somewhere along the continuum of new-product development, in order for there to be an eventual success, there must be a creative phase which gives birth to an idea, a concept, and a product or service, and it must be well managed to result in a successful new business venture.

The exact position of the creative phase on the continuum may vary. In the "olden days" of production, the creative idea for a new product usually came at the beginning and started the new venture process. The electric light and the automobile, for example, were not preceded by marketing studies that established a need.

But as our economy became more sophisticated, the businessman learned that it was *not* necessary to sit around waiting for the lightning of an inspired new-product idea. As marketing developed and became a better-understood function, the businessman was able to analyze markets and consumer psychology to uncover *unexpressed* needs. With a need established, it then became possible for the new-product developer to set about creating a new product to fill the established or assumed need.

As satisfying a need became the objective of business thinking, creativity came to be equated with problem solving. And in the procedures used to stimulate creativity for new-product development, a usual sequence is for a company or agency first to establish a need, then to bring to bear creativity-stimulating methods that satisfy the need or solve the problem.

Creation: "In the Beginning . . . "

Most companies struggle for an objective means of determining good new-product ideas. One company with which we were associated used creative sessions as part of a line operation. Accordingly, the company rules that have developed for running creative meetings represent pretested and practical

5. Peter F. Drucker, Managing for Results (New York: Harper & Row, 1964), pp. 188–189. Used by permission of the publisher.

approaches, evolved over ten years, that can either be adapted to other companies or used for comparison with their present methods.

The following questions and answers outline this company's practices:

Q: How often are creative meetings held?

A: Approximately every ten days. This cycle is appropriate because that seems to be as often as the meetings are needed. And also, the time lapse seems ideal for the rest and rejuvenation of participants' mental processes.

Q: How many people participate?

A: The best number is the smallest possible group. This usually means three people. When more people are present, somehow the discussion goes down unproductive paths. Everyone begins to try to impress each other instead of creating. Two people, on the other hand, fail to ignite the creative spark; a two-way discussion lacks the stimulation quality of a three-man meeting.

Q: What kind of people should be included?

A: The people who do best in creative sessions aren't necessarily defined as being either "technical" or "marketing." People that fall into roles such as the following tend to boost results:

CATALYST   These are certain individuals who may not come up with the ideas, but have the ability to spark them in others by raising questions, suggesting refinements, and giving subtle direction to the discussion.

GOAL DEFINER   One person, sometimes the one who is also the catalyst, should lead the discussion. Sometimes he is the one most familiar with the problem under discussion and keeps the conversation on the track and oriented toward the goal. He must be able to do this skillfully, without unnecessarily limiting the flow of ideas and without offending or outpacing the others.

IDEA MAN   One individual—and possibly all the group members—should be able to contribute suggestions, recommendations, or answers to problems. This individual must have the qualities of naiveness, imagination, and ingenuity, and should be able to feed the discussion. Inventing is an art, and the prime requisite of the inventor is that he have enough technical and visualization ability to be able to look at things that have been given a name—such as a chair, a wheel, a can opener, and so on—on the basis of its integral and essential parts, rather than by its definition or by a name or word label. As soon as someone defines a chair as "that kind of object we all know," he loses his ability to be creative about a chair. The other requisite of the inventor or idea person is that no conception or statement of fact is on the face of it either a conflict of terms or an impossibility.

Q: Should a customer representative be present at a creative meeting?

A: Usually not. He brings with him preconceptions and prejudices that tend to derail the discussion. However, in some cases, it may help to have such an outsider witness a typical creative session to give him a better understanding of how the organization operates, and the nature of the brain-power the company can bring to bear on the customer's problems. Occasionally, there are extremely productive meetings where the customer is permitted to state the problem he would like solved and to describe it in some detail. Once he has answered and clarified questions, it is usually advisable for him to leave.

Q: How varied should the agenda of any one session be?

A: As varied as possible, usually at least one item for every thirty minutes of the session. Creative sessions tend to be erratic. Therefore, an alert discussion moderator can guide the conversation at any point either away from an unproductive course or into a different area of interest. Also, with several points to be covered the goal definer can quickly touch on all of the items early, then concentrate on the particular ones which seem to produce the brightest sparks.

Q: How long does a creative meeting last?

A: Usually half a day.

Q: How much control should the goal definer exercise?

A: This is delicate and intuitive. The sensitive moderator will exert practically no control and permit the discussion to be free-flowing. But he must *also* be quick to realize when a discussion is getting nowhere so that it can be terminated or steered into more fruitful channels. In some cases, early insights get lost in subsequent garrulity. In such a case the leader subtly, or otherwise, should go back to the promising bits of conversation and try to rebuild the discussion.

Q: How are ideas evaluated?

A: To begin with, creative sessions aren't the only times during which people are creative. Creativity is continuous and unceasing. A preplanned creative discussion may be the start, development phase, or conclusion of productive ideas. Ideas are constantly being evaluated, but it is highly effective if these evaluations, instead of being used as "stoppers," become milestones on the road to continuing elaboration, refinement, and improvement.

Q: Do participants in creative meetings get "worn out" over a period of months or years?

A: To the contrary. Meetings become more sophisticated as the participants develop rapport and learn to deal with each other's mental processes and attitudes. While the mechanical format stays the same, the learning and achievement curve turns upward and discussions become better. For example, meetings tend to focus more fully on specific, commercial goals, such as a current customer's needs. In less experienced groups, discussions often tend to be abstract and the ideas presented—however inventive—may lack the virtue of a more current commercial payoff.

Q: Would it be a good idea for other groups to copy this company's approach?

A: This approach seems to be a generally valid one, and could be duplicated by any group almost exactly, if the group were willing to keep the discussions open-ended and to be patient. Creative meetings often do not result in anything worth betting on. It takes a certain amount of mutual faith among the participants so that individuals can feel free to be creative in each other's presence. People must be willing to be naked in front of each other, to talk off the top of their heads without self-consciousness or fear of ridicule. Participants must be willing to accept not only creative ideas, but even what may seem like foolish suggestions. In order to speak freely in a group, individuals have to minimize the inhibitions of the participants and accept apparent lack of direction—even inconsistency. Being consistent often is the exact opposite of being creative.

Q: Are there any cautions for people in creative sessions?

A: They must be prepared to live with frustrations. A creative session is not an end in itself. An idea that sounds promising must then be tested for its commercial validity. And of course, even after that step there are many subsequent ones before anyone can make any money. This frustration must be dealt with on a personal as well as on a business basis. It is *inadvisable* to start the creative process unless there is willingness to cope with the drugery that may follow.

Another caution is not to become complacent about being more creative because you are an independent inventor or in a small company. It seems to be true that the systems and atmosphere of many large companies stifle creativity and initiative. However, they have developed resources, organizational strength, and know-how that facilitates their bringing a new product to commercial realization with less creativity and initiative.

Q: What is your relationship to a client?

A: It is a new-product program that consists of four stages:

Stage I. A period during which the inventions company and the client organization jointly explore and define the product or technology areas which are of most importance or interest to the client. The result of this stage is a priority list of areas to be explored in depth during Stage II.

Stage II. During this stage, creative meetings of the inventions company's staff occur for the purpose of generating product or technology ideas within the areas defined in Stage I. The goal of Stage II is a list of product or technology ideas that are rated by our staff on the following five scales:

1. *Technical Difficulty*— 1=easy, 10=next to impossible.
2. *Material Problems*— 1=none, 5=materials do not exist.
3. *In-House Capability*— 1=strong, 5=none.

4. Patent Position—1=strong, 5=nong.
5. *Time Cost of Working Prototype*–1=0 to 3 months, $5,000 or less; 2 = 3 to 6 months, $10,000 or less; 3 = 6 to 9 months, $15,000 or less; 4 = 9 to 12 months, $25,000 or less; 5 = 12 or more months, over $25,000.

Stage III. Meetings are scheduled with client personnel to become more specific about products or technologies to pursue further. The list generated during Stage III is classified into "no's" and "possibles." Stage III yields a list of possibilities which are then considered for Stage IV.

Stage IV. The list of possibilities is culled, and one or more ideas are selected for patent, technical, and marketing feasibility analysis.

Q: Can you illustrate a specific example of a typical invention cycle?

A: Yes. The problem statement is the interface with an invention or new idea. For various legal reasons it would not be practical to disclose an invention which is in process or one that is on the shelf. However, there is an example relating to optical character recognition (OCR) that should provide an appropriate illustration.

BACKGROUND   The inventions company has been working in the field of optical pattern recognition for several years. They have created a business and creative environment that seems to be productive in this area. Prior to one particular creative meeting, I sent a memorandum to the inventors of the company:

INTER–OFFICE MEMORANDUM

Subject: Simplifying the Problems of Optical Character Recognition (OCR).

Assumption: By and large, the cost of OCR equipment is a direct function of: (1) the number of variable letters and numbers to be read; (2) the amount of the deviation from a predictable fixed reading position; and (3) the amount, speed, and size of the paper to be handled and read. The problem statement in this memorandum attacks only the first two functions.

Assumption: If it had enough meaning to them, and a short learning curve, people would be willing to learn a new way to write by hand printing nonalphabet characters.

Assumption: We will continue using our (standard) font for numerics.

Assumption: The following schedule of letter equivalents requires an OCR device to read many fewer variables than the standard hand-printed alphabet. It would require significantly less electronic circuitry than our present reader:

A̅B	C̅D	E̅F
G̅H	I̅J	K̅L
M̅N	O̅P	Q̅R

Problem Statement: I believe the above schedule of letters was the basis for the Japanese code that was broken by American Intelligence in the 1930s. Could we have a $50 cost of goods for a reader *only* if people were willing to dictate a hand-written memo that says, "Miller, I love you!" as follows:

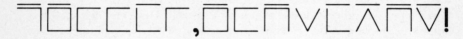

There was a discussion at the creative meeting, and general agreement that the problem statement could be technically answered by a relatively inexpensive reader. At the second creative meeting it was killed. There was competitive mark-sensing equipment that used analogous means. Our approach would not add significantly to the state of the art. Finally, it was decided that people would not be willing to relearn how to hand-print.

Management and the Creative Individual

The problem of managing creative people is a new one for many companies, entrepreneurs, and venture capitalists. Even in organizations where it is not new, it is often not solved satisfactorily. In fact there may be a contradition, even a conflict, between management and the creative person. The point becomes clear in the following dialogue:

INVENTOR: "Great news! I have just developed the world's first midget widget."

MANAGER: "Fine."

INVENTOR: "It's an unprecedented breakthrough in widgetometry."

MANAGER: "Excellent."

INVENTOR: "Do you realize what this means?"

MANAGER: "No."

INVENTOR: "How did you get to be a manager anyway?"

In this exchange, the two people are speaking different languages. The inventor is very clear and precise in what he has to say. He is full to overflowing with a message the manager completely fails to comprehend.

Disappointments and misunderstandings are inevitable both ways. Inventors must learn to communicate with managers with some degree of mutual understanding, and vice versa. It is logical for the inventor, scientist, and engineer to talk *technicalese*. It's just as logical for managers to listen in *managementese*. However, the problem, though difficult, is not insolvable. Establishing a mutuality of interest will usually do the trick. It may not be literally accurate or philosophically advisable to isolate creative people from all other corporate employees, as a separate and distinct group. But in actual practice, their work represents a kind of super-specialty, and they themselves tend to be non-organization-minded people. For example, many are more interested in following paths that intrigue them personally than in taking the roads of greatest value to the company. Unless they understand and accept the general focus of interest of the organization, their efforts, however brilliant, are likely to be off target. Several steps can be taken to increase the chances that "idea people" will operate in desirable areas:

First, stress the areas of company interest at hiring time. When a man is starting on a job is the time when the goal setting the company does will have its strongest impact upon him. The newly hired employee's understanding of and willingness to operate in specified directions may not be a complete guarantee of future behavior, but they are as good a guarantee as one can get.

Second, reinforce desirable efforts. Management can show—by praise, raises, stock options, promotions, and other rewards from the company treasure—its approval of desirable achievement.

Third, clarify the relationship of roles. When technologists fail to understand management's role, friction becomes as inevitable as taxes. An inventor should be taught to expect manager-mindedness as the context in which he will invent.

Fourth, strive for sympathetic entente. It's helpful if the manager gets to know some of the basic procedures and techniques of the people who work for him, and for the engineer to know some of the facts of life that create a working framework for his manager. Specifically, it would be constructive for an engineer or inventor to know facts like these about his immediate superior:

> His area of responsibility, including his title; his boss; his key subordinates; and the department, people, functions, and physical area in his charge.
>
> His information needs—how much in-depth background he wants, for example, in connection with projects.
>
> His preference in communications—telephone, face-to-face, formal or

informal meetings; and the writing style he prefers, including amount
of detail, type of outline, and so forth.

His standard of evaluation—for example, such matters as quality versus
quantity, observance of deadlines, caution versus daring, and so on.

How to get his approval on projects. Knowing his background may be a
key. For example, an ex-sales manager might be more concerned
with customer benefits; an ex-accountant, more interested in cost.

How to sell him an idea or influence his decision. A manager who
moved up from engineering is likely to respond more logically to
technical data and engineering benefits.

Similarly, it would be helpful to a manager to understand his scientist or
engineer subordinates, knowing specifically:

Is he a fast thinker or a slow thinker?

Does he prefer to think globally or in brass-tacks practical terms?

Does he prefer detailed discussions, the big picture, or both?

Does he like to take off on his own or would he be helped by a little
hand-holding from time to time?

Will his creativity be helped or harmed by continuing close contacts?

Fifth, create a common language. In the example given above, the scientist had developed a "midget widget." He knew exactly what it was. Clearly, the manager did not.

In many exchanges among scientists, engineers, and managers, as among others, technical concepts are unavoidable but their use can be made easier in two ways: Either the terms may be defined and clarified, or else they can be described in untechnical language. If the scientist says, "You know, a midget widget is an element that joins a moving part to a heating element," the manager then can follow the sense of what is being said.

To demonstrate the difference between effective and ineffective communication between inventor and manager, the earlier example can be changed to an effective dialogue:

INVENTOR: "Great news! I have just developed the world's first midget widget."

MANAGER: "Fine, but what is a midget widget?"

INVENTOR: "Glad you asked that question. It's the element that joins this moving part to the heating element. See, it's this thing I'm touching with my pencil right here."

MANAGER: "Uh-huh. What's different about it?"

INVENTOR: "Putting modesty aside, I must tell you that it is an unprecedented breakthrough. I have already had the legal department check, and I think it is novel enough to be patented."

MANAGER: "Excellent."

INVENTOR: "Do you realize the implications?"

MANAGER: "No."

INVENTOR: "I've been talking to a friend of mine who knows the market for this type of equipment. He says he thinks there is a $10 million a year market for midget widgets—and a good healthy profit for us."

MANAGER: "You're talking just like a manager."

INVENTOR: "I was hoping you'd say so. You see, you've taught me a lot. . . ."

MANAGER: "And vice versa."

Notice that the essence of the improved understanding illustrated by this dialogue is a communications exchange. "Communications" in this sense means a willingness to do two things—to ask questions and to answer them.

Realistically, this does not mean there will be an answer for every question, but at least freedom to ask questions should prevail. If, in addition to this freedom, there is an attitude of helpfulness and an intention to cooperate, two-way communications between creative people and management people will flourish, to the benefit of all.

Finding a company or a backer either to do something with an invention or to finance doing something with it is a major stumbling block to the independent inventor or the small new-products company. The problems of *selling* an invention or a new venture to a company will be discussed in the next chapter.

Chapter 2

Inventing as a Business

To an inventor his idea is an end in itself. He sees it as both a tangible extension of himself and a monumental improvement in the universe. It is his monument and will provide him with immortality. His idea is a contribution to society—if only "they" would accept his offering.

As the idea moves through its step-by-step course of destruction *(usually)* or fruition *(occasionally)*, the other players of business are rated by the inventor as inconveniences or enemies. In between fall nuisances, necessary evils, and short-term allies.

The rare players who warm to his idea or bet on it are heroes, and those who do not are deemed foolish and without imagination. Those who stop betting simply do not understand the problems. They were not qualified to judge in the first place, and only by accident had they decided to bet.

The inventor, like the mountain climber, loves his idea *because it is there* and *because he was the first to find it*. Most inventions are the creatures of noninventors and die at the finding stage: "I do not have the time because of my regular job." "I do not have the money because of the other bills I have to pay." "If the idea were any good, somebody else would have already thought of it." "I will do something about it next week." "I have tried it on several "experts"; they did not like it, and they should know." "Something will come along, and *then* I will be able to do something." "I have been turned down too often and I am sick and tired of trying."

Perhaps these reasons are valid, or maybe a little more patience or effort would win the day. Or perhaps more encouragement, acceptance, and investment by the other players in the business world would help.

One might conclude that the individuals in their "garages" are crackpots—after all, the "mad inventor" is one of our cultural stereotypes. But in those garages are also the modern counterparts of the inventor of the wheel and axle, bronze, and the first caveperson who noticed that wood floats.

In the motion picture *2001: A Space Odyssey*, written by Arthur C. Clarke and directed by Stanley Kubrick, a caveman inventor is shown at the time he discovers that his use of a bone as a club will make him able to control his contemporaries. He is shown testing his invention, and then in a burst of color the club dissolves into a space ship. The implication is clear: Once man learned that he was capable of controlling his environment, the space ship was inevitable. Although our society has become more sophisticated, complex, and geographically interrelated, the basic question of innovation remains the same.

For the investor and established company, the question is: "Who has found a better idea for controlling or using our environment and how do I make his interest and mine the same?"

For the entrepreneur and inventor, the question is: "I have a better idea for controlling or using our environment; how will I find an established company or investor and make his interest and mine the same?"

An inventor invents product ideas; an entrepreneur or innovator invents business ideas. An inventor is an artist. An entrepreneur is half artist and half businessman.

When the innovator deals in the world of technology and new products, he becomes the link between the inventor and the practical business world. Sometimes he works for a large company and is somewhat successful—but he is mostly frustrated by taking three steps forward and two back in his attempts to diversify the company.

Usually the entrepreneur starts his own business and attempts what is probably the highest risk of a business: taking an idea full cycle into a profitable business. Like the inventor, whether the entrepreneur is working for an established company or starting his own, he often fails, for many reasons. One of these reasons, however, is paradoxical: the half-artist side of his nature succumbs to the glamour of the idea as an end in itself.

The basic problem, as expressed by Theodore Levitt, is:

> The trouble with much of the advice business is getting today about the need to be more vigorously creative is, essentially, that its advocates have generally failed to distinguish between the relatively easy process of being creative in the abstract and the infinitely more difficult process of being innovationist in the concrete. Indeed, they mystify "creativity" itself. Too often for them "creativity"

means having great, original ideas. Their emphasis is almost all on the thoughts themselves. Moreover, the ideas are often judged more by their novelty than by their potential usefulness, either to consumers or to the company. . . . In most cases, having a new idea can be "creative" in the abstract but destructive in actual operation, and that often instead of helping a company it will even hinder it.[1]

The inventor of *our* discussion isn't "blown away" at the stage of finding an idea. He pursues it. He builds a model and applies for a patent. Step by step he is committed to changing the world, at least a little bit. While he does not agree with Levitt totally, he is practical enough to know that he must seek a series of alliances. His first alliance is normally with a patent attorney. His second alliance depends on variables: (1) whether he is either a casual or professional inventor, and (2) whether he believes he can actively participate in the process of getting the product to market. If he is a casual inventor and does not intend to participate in getting the product to market, he will turn over the invention to someone who will find a company to make and sell the product and pay the inventor a royalty. In recent years, the term "technology transfer" has been applied to bridging the gap between inventor and industry.

If the innovator is a professional inventor, he has determined that he will make his living, or attempt to do so, by continually inventing ideas and commercializing them. He is often his own innovator, either through a company he has founded or through an established company to which he has licensed it.

The opportunities and problems of exploiting an invention, a new product, or a service by starting a new company will be described in the Chapters 3 to 12. Much of that later discussion also applies to the innovation process of a single product. In particular, Chapters 4, 8, 9, and 10 deal with the two most important problem of any new business venture: marketing and financing.

Before discussing the technology transfer industry, and how it selects its prospects, qualifies them, and sells them a new product, we first should describe the licensing agreement, the most typical tool whereby the inventor and the established company become partners.

The Licensing Agreement

A license is an agreement to lease the right to make, use, sell, and usually sublicense, a patent, product, or process; it is made by the seller (the li-

1.   Theodore Levitt, "Creativity Is Not Enough," *Harvard Business Review*, vol. 41, no. 3, May–June 1963, pp. 72–73. Used by permission of the publisher.

censor) to the buyer, (the licensee). The agreement defines the rights and obligations of each of the parties. Occasionally, the seller and buyer agree to transfer title and ownership, and the agreement is an outright sale and assignment.

The agreement that follows is an abridgement of the substantive portions of several licensing contracts the author has negotiated and signed:

AGREEMENT FOR DOE ELECTRONICS
CORP. LICENSE

AGREEMENT, dated _____ between INVENTOR CORPORATION, a Delaware corporation (hereinafter called INVENTOR), and DOE ELECTRONICS CORP., a New York corporation (hereinafter called DOE).

WHEREAS, INVENTOR is in the process of developing a wireless link between two fixed stations which enables information to be transmitted and received without telephone lines or coaxial cable, and is the owner of the above-described invention, together with know-how, technical data, methods, and other information, regarding the manufacture, use and sale of such invention. The phrase "WIRELESS," as used in this Agreement, shall mean the foregoing, together with any future improvements thereon and future inventions related to, connected with or growing out of such invention, patentable or unpatentable;

WHEREAS, DOE has facilities and funds useful for the further development of WIRELESS; and

WHEREAS, INVENTOR desires to further the development of WIRELESS and to license WIRELESS and DOE desires to obtain such license;

NOW, THEREFORE, in consideration of the premises and of the mutual covenants and agreements hereinafter set forth, the parties hereto covenant and agree as follows:

1. INVENTOR's Organization, Good Standing and Authority. INVENTOR is a corporation duly organized, validly existing and in good standing under the laws of the state of Delaware, has corporate power to carry on its business as it is now being conducted, is duly qualified to do business and is in good standing in each jurisdiction in which the character of the properties owned by it or the nature of the business conducted by it makes such qualification necessary; and it is authorized to enter into and perform its covenants and agreements under this Agreement without breach of any obligation to any person or governmental body.

2. Definition of Research and Development. DOE
is a corporation duly organized, validly existing and in good
standing under the laws of the state of New York, has
corporate power to carry on its business as it is now being
conducted, is duly qualified to do business and is in good
standing in each jurisdiction in which the character of the
properties owned by it or the nature of the business
conducted by it makes such qualification necessary; and it
is authorized to enter into and perform its convenants and
agreements under this Agreement without breach of any
obligation to any person or governmental body.

3. Definition of Research and Development. The phrase
"Research and Development," as used in this Agreement, shall
mean the further development of WIRELESS, including:
improvement from all technological aspects; improvement from
all marketing aspects; industrial design; field tests; plans
for manufacture, use, and sale; market studies; patent
applications and trademark applications in the United States
and abroad; consideration of and, if appropriate, the taking
of legal action to obtain consent of any person or
governmental body.

4. Direction of Research and Development. Research and
development shall be under the overall direction and
control of DOE. Research and development shall be under the
immediate control of INVENTOR.

5. Research and Development. The initial phase of research
and development shall be the six months' period next following
the date of this Agreement. At DOE's option, research and
development may be extended for an additional phase or phases
of reasonable length, not to extend beyond the end of the
year next succeeding the end of the first phase, upon notice
to INVENTOR, given not less than 30 days before the end of
any phase.

6. Finance of Research and Development. During the
initial phase of research and development, DOE shall be
obligated to spend not less than $45,000 for the research and
development. During any additional phase or phases of
research and development, DOE shall be obligated to spend at
substantially the rate provided for herein for the initial
phase of research and development. DOE shall allocate all
amounts spent for research and development, in its
discretion, and disburse them in its usual manner as the
obligations therefore are incurred.

7. Employment of Jones and Shames. It shall be a continuing
condition precedent to those obligations, during the entire
research and development period, that Mr. Jones and Mr.

Shames continue in the employ of INVENTOR and devote
substantially all their working time, whether or not during
normal working hours, to research and development as defined
in this Agreement.

8. Definition of Exclusive License. The phrase "Exclusive
License," as used in this Agreement, shall mean the
exclusive right to make, use, sell, and sub–license,
throughout the United States and its possessions and
throughout the world, any invention included in WIRELESS,
all improvements thereon and inventions related to, connected
with or growing out of such invention for a period to end
with the termination of the last patent issued with respect
to such invention.

9. Definition of Net Sales Price, Sub–license Royalty, and
etc. The phrase "Net Sales Price," as used in this
Agreement, shall mean the sales or rental price, currently
being charged in bona fide arm's–length sales or leases to
others, for any product, which includes WIRELESS, F.O.B.
DOE's plant or warehouse; exclusive of amounts attributable
to any part of such product which is not attributable to
WIRELESS, including, but without limiting the generality of
the foregoing, shipping or packing charges, taxes,
quantity or other discounts. The phrase "Sub–license
Royalty", as used in this Agreement, shall mean the amounts
received by DOE under any bona fide arm's–length
sub–license to a third person, which includes WIRELESS,
exclusive of amounts attributable to any part of such
sub–license which is not attributable to WIRELESS,
including, but without limiting the generality of the
foregoing, costs and expenses incurred by DOE in or by the
granting or carrying out of such sub–license or the
collection of royalties thereunder. All royalties, and
other payments, which DOE may be obligated to pay to
INVENTOR hereunder, shall be computed quarterly for the
period ending with each of DOE's fiscal quarters. Such
computation shall include sales actually shipped and
invoiced, rentals actually invoiced and/or sub–license
royalties actually received during any such quarter. DOE
shall be obligated to make such payments not later than the
end of the 60–day period next succeeding the close of such
quarter. DOE shall maintain complete and accurate records
with respect to all of its payment obligations including
but not limited to its net sales prices, net rentals and
sub–license royalties, and shall report thereon to INVENTOR
not later than the end of the 60–day period next succeeding
the close of each of DOE's fiscal quarters. INVENTOR, or
appropriate persons authorized by it, may make reasonable
examination of such records; provided, however, that any
such examination shall be during DOE's normal working hours

and shall not be made more than once in each of DOE's
fiscal quarters.

10. <u>Payment Obligations</u>. DOE shall have an obligation to pay
for the exclusive license obtained hereunder as follows:

10.1 In the event that products including WIRELESS are sold
or rented by DOE, a royalty on such products, produced on
a commercial basis and sold while such exclusive license
is in effect, equal to 4.5 per cent of the net sales
price.

10.2 In the event that WIRELESS is sublicensed by DOE to
a third person, 50 per cent of the sublicense royalty
earned by DOE while such exclusive license is in effect.

10.3 With respect to WIRELESS, if no United States patent
is granted, after a reasonable time within which to
prepare and process appropriate patent application or
applications has elapsed, which United States patent is
sufficient to give the patent holder the sole and
exclusive right to make, use and sell, throughout the
United States and its possessions, the invention,
included in WIRELESS, then any and all of DOE's payment
obligations under this Agreement shall be reduced by
one-half.

11. <u>Exchange of Information</u>. While this Agreement is in
effect, DOE shall communicate to INVENTOR and INVENTOR shall
communicate to DOE promptly fully-detailed information
regarding any know-how, technical data, methods and other
information, regarding the manufacture, use and sale of
WIRELESS. Such information shall be treated as confidential
to the extent that and so long as such information shall not
be information generally available to the public; and, with
the exception just stated, each of the parties hereto agrees
that they shall not, without the consent of the other party
hereto, transmit to any third party any such information.
INVENTOR shall, at DOE's expense, take steps to apply for
patent on WIRELESS or on any part thereof, if deemed
desirable by DOE.

12. <u>Obligations of Employees and Assignments</u>. DOE and
INVENTOR shall use or cause to be used in connection with any
and all research and manufacturing operations in
connection with this Agreement only employees or other
personnel who are obligated by contract not to disclose to
others confidential information, as defined in this
agreement, and to assign directly or indirectly to DOE or
INVENTOR all inventions made by them in the course of their
employment.

13. <u>Patent</u> <u>Protection</u>. DOE shall cooperate with INVENTOR and INVENTOR shall cooperate with DOE on request thereto by the other party hereto, in seeking patent protection on WIRELESS in countries designated by INVENTOR or DOE, if INVENTOR or DOE shall be entitled to seek such patent protection. The expense of obtaining patent protection, requested by DOE, shall be DOE's.

14. <u>Legal</u> <u>Action</u> <u>against</u> <u>DOE</u> <u>by</u> <u>Others</u>. In case DOE shall be threatened with suit or be sued by a third party alleging that DOE's performance under this Agreement includes acts or things constituting infringement of any patent held by such adverse party, and such alleged infringement is caused, directly or indirectly, by INVENTOR, DOE shall within 30 days thereafter notify INVENTOR thereof; and in case any suit is brought against DOE, INVENTOR shall defend the same at its expense and save DOE harmless from any judgement or other expense arising out of the same; pending the final outcome of any such suit, DOE may withhold any payments due under this Agreement and, to the extent available, pay any reasonable expenses incurred by DOE or judgment suffered by DOE in connection with such suit out of such amount so withheld; any amount so withheld and not so paid, shall be paid over to INVENTOR promptly after the final outcome of any such suit, provided that DOE may take such lawful part therein as it may elect.

15. <u>Legal</u> <u>Action</u> <u>against</u> <u>INVENTOR</u> <u>by</u> <u>Others</u>. In case INVENTOR shall be threatened with suit or be sued by a third party, alleging that any conduct of INVENTOR, including performance under this Agreement, includes acts or things constituting infringement of any patents held by such adverse party and such alleged infringement is caused, directly or indirectly, by INVENTOR, INVENTOR shall within 30 days thereafter notify DOE thereof; and in case any suit is brought against INVENTOR, INVENTOR shall defend the same at its expense and save DOE harmless from any judgment or other expense arising out of the same; pending the final outcome of any such suit, DOE may, if made a party to such suit, withhold any payments due under this Agreement and, to the extent available, pay any reasonable expenses incurred by DOE or judgments suffered by DOE in connection with such suit out of such amounts so withheld; any amounts so withheld and not so paid shall be paid over to INVENTOR promptly after the final outcome of any such suit; provided that DOE may take such lawful part therein as it may elect.

16. <u>Legal</u> <u>Action</u> <u>against</u> <u>Others</u>. In case DOE or INVENTOR shall become aware of any acts by others constituting infringement of any patent in respect to which rights are granted hereunder, DOE or INVENTOR shall within 60 days

thereafter notify the other party hereto and, at the same
time, supply full information regarding identity and
location of the infringer, and the acts or things considered
by it to be in violation of said rights and harmful to DOE or
INVENTOR. Within 30 days after request by either party
hereto, DOE, INVENTOR and/or any other appropriate parties
shall bring suit against such infringer under the rights
herein granted to stop such infringement and to recover all
damages and profits arising therefrom and accruing
subsequent to the issuance of the patent or patents inolved.
All negotiations, if any, regarding such infringement, shall
be conducted jointly by DOE and INVENTOR. DOE and INVENTOR
shall bear equally the expenses of such suit and share
equally any damages recovered therein.

17. <u>Termination</u>. This Agreement shall terminate as follows:

17.1 At DOE's option, upon ten days, notice to INVENTOR,
if there is a breach in INVENTOR's obligations under
this Agreement.

17.2 Automatically, when Section 10.3 applies, at the
end of the five years next succeeding the date as of
which reasonable time to obtain a United States patent has
elapsed.

17.3 At INVENTOR's option, upon 30 days' notice to DOE,
in the event of DOE's default with respect to any
obligation hereunder, which shall not be remedied by
DOE to INVENTOR's satisfaction within ten days after
notice to DOE of such alleged default, and <u>vice versa</u>.

17.4 At INVENTOR's option, upon 30 days' notice to DOE,
in the event that DOE does not begin to sell, rent or
sublicense a product, which includes WIRELESS, on a
commercial basis, with respect to which DOE has payment
obligations, within the five years next succeeding the
date of this Agreement.

17.5 At INVENTOR's option, upon 30 days' notice to DOE,
in the event that DOE shall become insolvent, or commit an
act of bankruptcy.

18. <u>Rights and Duties on Termination</u>. In the event of any
termination of this Agreement, as provided under Section 17,
DOE shall be the owner of all facilities and equipment;
provided, however, that all completed laboratory models of
WIRELESS shall become the property of INVENTOR. DOE's
obligation to make any payment to INVENTOR arising out of
events which occurred prior to such termination shall
survive such termination.

19. <u>Notice</u>. Any notice, request, approval, consent or
other communication from one party hereto to the other shall
be in writing and shall be determined to be duly given when
sent by one party hereto by registered mail to the other party
hereto at its last known address; until other notice is
given, the addresses of the parties hereto for the purposes
of this Agreement are as follows: With respect to DOE:

> Doe Electronics Corporation
> 580 W. 57th Street
> New York, N.Y.

With respect to INVENTOR

> Inventor Corporation
> 50 Anywhere
> Lakeland, N.J.

20. <u>Amendments</u>. This Agreement embodies the entire
understanding of the parties hereto. This Agreement may not
be amended or modified, except by a written instrument
signed by both parties hereto.

21. <u>Partial Invalidity</u>. The invalidity or unenforceability
of any provision of this Agreement shall of itself have no
effect upon the validity or enforceability of any other
provision of this Agreement.

22. <u>Governing Law</u>. This Agreement shall be determined to
have been made in the state of New York and shall be
construed according to the laws of that state.

23. <u>Arbitration</u>. Any question which shall arise as to the
obligations of any party under this Agreement or the
interpretation of any provision thereof, as to which the
parties cannot agree, shall be settled by arbitration
pursuant to the laws of the state of New York.

24. <u>Assignment</u>. This Agreement shall inure to the benefit of
and be binding upon the parties hereto and their respective
successors and assigns.

IN WITNESS WHEREOF, the parties hereto have caused this
Agreement to be duly executed as of the day and year first
above written.

ATTEST: INVENTOR CORPORATION

_____ by _____
John Jones   William H. Shames
Vice President   President

```
        ATTEST:                          DOE ELECTRONICS CORP.

————————————————————————  by  ————————————————————
        John Smith                       John Doe
        Vice President                   President
```

Inventor as Employee or Consultant

Related to the licensing agreement as a method of compensation for the inventor-innovator, particularly where the licensee prefers not to make a down payment or pay a minimum royalty, is for the inventor to sell his services to the company as consultant or full time or part-time employee. The actual nature of the services rendered, will, of course, derive from the nature and state of development of the inventor's idea or invention. For example, if further refining of the product is required, the inventor may work in the company's shop or laboratory, along lines suggested by the licensee.

An ancillary agreement relating to the employees of the inventor company during the research and development period is shown in the following section.

```
                ANCILLARY AGREEMENT TO AGREEMENT FOR
                   DOE ELECTRONICS CORP. LICENSE

    AGREEMENT, dated ————————— between INVENTOR CORPORATION. a
Delaware corporation (hereinafter called INVENTOR), WILLIAM
H. SHAMES, JOHN JONES and DOE ELECTRONICS CORP., a New York
corporation (hereinafter called DOE).

    WHEREAS, INVENTOR, William H. Shames and John Jones are
entering into this Agreement in order to induce DOE to enter
into the Agreement with INVENTOR, dated —————————;

    NOW, THEREFORE, it is agreed among the parties hereto as
follows:

    1. During the entire research and development period, as
defined in the Agreement, DOE shall have available to it
periodically the services of Mr. Jones, as a technical
consultant, and Mr. Shames, as a sales consultant, on such
matters as DOE shall determine.

    2. While rendering such services, Mr. Jones and Mr.
Shames shall become parties to any arrangements, by contract
or otherwise, which DOE may have to protect its rights in any
```

invention developed or improved while such services are
rendered and to insure the confidential character of all
information obtained while such services are rendered.

3. The rights granted herein to DOE may be enjoyed by it
without any obligation to pay any consideration therefore in
addition to DOE's payment obligations to INVENTOR in the
Agreement.

4. The provisions in the Agreement concerning notice,
amendments, partial invalidity, governing law and
arbitration, shall operate with respect to this Agreement.

INVENTOR CORPORATION

ATTEST: by _____

                                      William H. Shames
                                      President

_____   _____
John Jones   William H. Shames, in his
Vice President   individual capacity

_____   _____
William H. Shames   John Jones, in his
President   individual capacity

ATTEST: DOE ELECTRONICS CORP.

_____ by   _____
John Smith   John Doe
Vice President   President

The Technology Transfer Industry

The independent inventor, often unable to commercialize his invention by
himself, is turning to a new industry; technology transfer. The inventor's
problem is a lack of ability to appropriately communicate the opportunity he
believes he has. What must be communicated includes a description of an
invention, its advantages as compared to the state of the art, a listing of the
markets available, and the nature and terms of the contract the inventor is
prepared to conclude. The professional handling of these facets of a new
product is the business of the technology transfer industry.

Sources of new productsfor technology transfer are not limited to the independent inventor. Increasingly, established companies, which spend millions each year on research and new-product development, are seeking to

"spin off" ventures that do not fit their needs. Sometimes products or whole divisions are sold because they do not meet the requirements of a large company, but are an interesting opportunity for a smaller organization.

General Electric Co. is a pioneer in exploiting its own developments, which were once rejected as being too small or outside its own business. GE's Business Opportunities Service, less than ten years old, is a source of income, and in the process provides a forum for others to communicate.

General Electric Business Opportunities Service

GE is offering business opportunities for which it usually has "no present need" to other companies with an "ability to utilize." Occasionally, products being manufactured and sold by GE are also offered for license. Through its publication, *Business Opportunities*, it is providing a clearing-house between other sellers and buyers. In "General Information," "Leveraging New Product Opportunities," and a description of a typical product, the "Intravenous Flow Regulator," GE tells the story:[1]

GENERAL INFORMATION

Business Opportunities Service provides a unique means for efficiently evaluating selected technology available for licensing. We carefully and systematically review the wide-ranging activity of General Electric's Research and Development Center, the other corporate laboratories and the operating components to identify opportunities that have potential for use by others. Some of the features of Business Opportunities Service are described below—all designed to provide vital information for the effective appraisal of technology and its profitable use.

"Business Opportunities," a bi-monthly publication in which the opportunities are presented.

Members selected technologies can be published in "Business Opportunities." Members can use our established procedure to submit their opportunities. Submittal forms are available on request.

Summary Reports—Comprehensive studies are available for many of the General Electric opportunities, providing detailed information for indepth evaluation. These can be obtained for a nominal charge by completing the enclosed order form.

Consultation—Prompt, professional assistance is offered at any time during your business evaluation of any General Electric opportunity.

1. All three items reprinted from *Business Opportunities* with permission of Business Opportunities Service, General Electric Company, Schenectady, N.Y.

General Electric Reports—Chosen from a broad range of technical and business disciplines, these reports are offered as an additional feature of membership in Business Opportunities Service.

News of Industry-wide Reports and Publications—Members will be advised of significant published information relating to management of technology and business planning.

The described General Electric Opportunities usually involve one or more related issued patents, patent applications and/or as yet unfiled inventions.

The licensing terms proposed for each General Electric opportunity are *proposed* terms only, and are subject to negotiation. Any negotiated terms must reflect a mutual understanding of the potential for the particular technology.

For some opportunities there may be a limit to the number of licenses available.

It is understood and agreed that the indication of any business opportunity or patent as available for licensing under or in connection with Business Opportunities Service shall not be binding upon any party in any way.

Your comments and recommendations can play an important role as we grow Business Opportunities Service and increase its value to you. Contact us at any time.

Business Opportunities Service
General Electric Company
P.O. Box 43
Schenectady, New York 12301
Phone (518) 374-2211, Ext. 5-2128.

LEVERAGING NEW PRODUCT OPPORTUNITIES

When one achieves business goals through the use of leverage it's like throwing and completing a long forward pass instead of "grinding it out on the ground." The use of leverage is not new. People have been using leverage in the financial field longer than anyone can remember. However, the current use of leverage in the field of licensing warrants a closer look at its advantages.

What is leverage in this context? It's a technique for using a small amount of money to acquire desired products, patents, tooling or other income generators actually worth much more.

The technique's effectiveness depends upon the needs and expectations of the companies at both ends of the lever. As the sketch below indicates, a company with a combination of ability and a little cash can often have a good bargaining advantage for another company's product package.

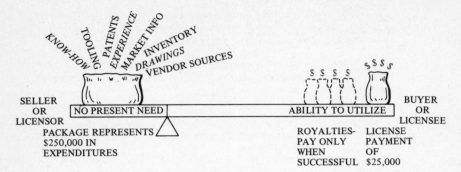

The sketch depicts an actual business recently offered by Business Opportunities Service (Nov./Dec. 1970, page 8). In this case the initial leverage is 10 to 1 not considering future royalty payments from sales.

The major benefits of this type of leveraging is a reduction in overall risk and investment. You are investing less initially, making available more funds for market and product development and the other areas that reduce the likelihood of new product failure. Most, if not all, of the commercialization of the development may have been accomplished at the licensor's expense. The price you pay for the reduced risk is only a portion of future profits that would not have been available to you without the licensing program.

Other benefits that may be realized by initiating a new program through licensing leverage include having faster positive cash flow, better overhead write-off, better use of labor and facilities resources, a stronger company image projected to the financial community and the security that results from not having all your eggs in one basket.

This all sounds pretty good, but the perceptive businessman knows that there are no free lunches. If a company's licensing package is so good, why would they want to part with it? This question is timely and appropriate. The reasons for a licensing package's non-use by the licensor must be considered and these reasons applied to your own proposed program to exploit fully the leverage opportunity. Many reasons are obvious. The licensor may:

Lack the facilities to produce

Lack the specialized personnel

Foresee an insufficient ratio of sales potential to company size

Serve a primary market not related to the new development.

It really comes down to a matter of priorities. Rather than pursue and develop the missing links for product x, y, or z, a company will have to place its investments and manpower in areas more compatible with its present strengths. The decision to "divest" one's interest provides the real leverage opportunity for another company that has the skill, talent and desire to move the product forward.

General Electric has been a leading proponent of this concept and has established Business Opportunities Service, and this publication, to act as the fulcrum for licensing leverage.

I hope that each of you upon reviewing these opportunities will take note of your special abilities and be willing to use Business Opportunities Service for leveraging new profit dollars through licensing.

Manager, Business Development Services

INTRAVENOUS FLOW REGULATOR

The intravenous (IV) flow regulator is a device that provides two very real benefits to hospitals, nursing homes, biological laboratories, etc. First, it offers a means for adjusting and regulating the rate of flow in intravenous feeding much more easily and precisely than the manual control now in common use. Second, it saves time for the always overburdened nursing staff. With a working prototype already developed and with a large and growing market available, the IV flow regulator offers a unique business opportunity.

Description

The IV flow regulator is a compact unit (approximately 4" x 5" x 5") weighing about 2 pounds. It consists of a drop sensing unit electrically connected to a regulating unit. (See illustration—lower right.) The regulator is designed to be used with standard commercially available administration kits. It is capable of handling flow rates ranging from 10 to 990 cc per hour in 10 cc increments. Changes in the flow rate are easily and quickly made by a simple dial setting. The flow rate is controlled to within ± 10% of the dial setting.

Advantages

Some advantages of GE's IV flow regulator in addition to those already cited are:

Automatic compensation for changing conditions such as patient movement, tube creep, change in bottle height, etc.

Automatic sensing of empty bottle condition and shutoff of flow with simultaneous visual and/or audible warning given.

A significant degree of portability.

Adaptability to any of the IV kits presently available, to battery operation, to feeding all solutions normally used, to mixing of two or more solutions, to use with centrally located controls.

Market Potential

The number of hospitals and nursing homes is steadily growing, and existing hospitals are constantly increasing in capacity and services rendered.

Thus, the IV flow regulator has a large existing market and great growth potential. Animal hospitals and pharmaceutical laboratories also do intravenous feeding, and so offer an even wider market.

Proposed Licensing Terms

General Electric would provide a licensee the following:

Engineering sketches

Electrical schematics of circuitry

Specifications and sources of purchased items

Loan of a demonstration unit (to be negotiated)

24 man-hours of technical consultation.

Compensation to General Electric would include:

An initial payment of $8,000

Royalty payments of 5½ percent of the net selling price of units sold

Minimum annual royalties of $1,000 for the first year with increases each year of $1,000 until annual rate is $5,000.

Other Large Technology Transfer Companies

The *Wall Street Journal*[2] has described companies, in addition to GE, engaged in spinning off previously hidden assets:

Philips Petroleum Company, owner of more than 5,900 active United States patents, has so thoroughly exploited licensing opportunities that its royalties paid for almost all the company's research and development. National Cash Register and American Standard also have set up special departments to locate forgotten or sidetracked developments and offer them to other concerns. "We call them latent assets," says T. R. Stansfield, NCR's manager of patent and technology marketing. "They just need a little more effort to cross the threshold, but they don't fit into our present organization." NCR emphasizes that it supplies know-how, not just patents, to help licensees get off to a good start. Last year, this business-machines maker launched a quarterly called *New & Now* which reaches about 1,000 subscribers. A recent issue offered such items as an anticorrosion material, an electrical connector to be attached by an adhesive, an electrical motor, and a magnetic printing or coding process.

2. "Mining Latent Assets: Large Firms License Small Concerns to Use Rejected Ideas from Research Departments," *Wall Street Journal*, Sept. 25, 1970, p. 28.

The first issue of American Standard's quarterly, *Products & Patents,* went out earlier this month to about 1,000 companies that pay $100 a year for the service. It draws on a wide variety of American Standard product categories; including plumbing fixtures, transportation, construction, electronics, and graphic arts. "There's a tremendous reservoir of untapped technology at hand and we want to bring it to market," says B. H. Friedman, general manager of the company's advanced technical products department.

The Rationale of Client Companies

The *Wall Street Journal* article also discusses the rationale of some of the smaller concerns for doing business with GE:

> [GE's] technology marketers trussed up the tester and offered it around. The bite came from Emcee Electronics, Inc., a small manufacturer in New Castle, Delaware, with about $500,000 a year in sales.
>
> For rights to the product, it agreed to pay GE an initial license fee of $5,000, plus a slice of all future tester sales. Then it set about to modify the unit to test a broader range of electronic circuits. Before long, Emcee will be marketing the testers for $95 each for use in servicing computers and other electronic gear.
>
> "We think we can reasonably expect an increase in total sales volume of 20 per cent over the next couple of years from this product alone," says Max Corzilius, Emcee's president. . . .
>
> "Small companies have an awful problem coming up with new ideas," he says. "We spend 7 per cent or 8 per cent of our gross sales on R&D and we think that's a substantial amount. But it's only $30,000 or $40,000, and you can't develop too much for that."
>
> The tester still required a considerable investment for Emcee. Mr. Corzilius estimates the company spent more than $30,000 to get it to market. "But that's a lot less than it would have cost us to develop the product ourselves," he says.[3]

Taking the Plunge

An operating company contemplating entry or reentry into a new-product area must develop a new set of sensitivities and reflexes. In a way, the company president is in the position of a man who has been married several times and is contemplating taking on a new bride. Although he has done it all before, in one sense, in another, he has not done it at all. Some of his experience will apply. Some will not. Times have changed. He has changed. The

3. Ibid. Reprinted with permission of the *Wall Street Journal.*

demands and expectations of the new product or industry may have changed radically. These demands will take on their own logic and evaluation pattern.

Many companies contemplate new products with a mixture of feelings, many misconceptions, and some self-defeating assumptions. For example, one sees instance after instance in which companies seem to prefer to fail by internal developments or with a large consulting firm, rather than the business gamble of dealing with a small company. This protective attitude is readily understandable. A top executive can go before his board of directors and explain away a loss with, "We bought the best guidance we could."

And unlike the view in which companies are represented as rushing eagerly to the end of the rainbow to find the pot of gold, many companies treat new-product development as a necessary evil. Few of them hire business managers to run the new-product organization, considering it a technical function. The technical people in product development are mostly interested in the actual product that they are working on. Their relationship to the company for whom they are working is like that of the American Cancer Society to the general public. They get "grants," depending on the mechanics of the budgeting situation, with which to develop their toy. They have little concern with whether anybody has the problem that they are trying to answer. Often they answer questions that nobody is asking. They reinvent the wheel.

When a company seeking to diversify goes to the outside, it is almost always for an "expert." An expert, in this sense, may be defined as a person who offers broad credentials and claims he will solve the problem. The fact is, there are no experts in this area of the business world, only some people who are better informed than others. It is a truism that the better informed a person is about a particular subject, the less creative he is. He knows everything that cannot be done. A good rule of thumb for new-product development is not knowing too much about why it cannot be done. You risk being naïve, but you have the opportunity to be genuinely creative.

There are specific benefits an outside product development or technology transfer company offer to prospective clients:

RESULT ORIENTATION   Unlike performance standards that are somewhat obscured by the proximity and personal involvements of inside departments, the outside consultant can be judged by what he has turned up for the client company "lately."

ELIMINATING THE NEED FOR DECISIONS   In a company of any size, the decision-making process tends to impede the development process. Many of the subgoals involved in the new-product development become major hurdles in an operating organization. However, in the consulting firm, particularly the one-man or small firm, pressing for results, the decision making takes on an operating quality, as opposed to a policy quality, and accordingly it can be done in matter-of-fact fashion.

SHORTENED COMMUNICATION LINES　In a larger organization the need for two-way communication in the overall organization tends to complicate communication lines and slow both the understanding of problems and the development of solutions and decisions. The consulting company usually avoids these organizational disadvantages.

These factors are benefits for the client company *in general.* But the extent to which these advantages accrue to the client depends in part on the qualities of a given consulting firm. As a question, the proposition becomes: "How can I evaluate the claims of representatives of new-product consultants that come knocking at my door?"

In new-product consulting, as in any kind of consulting service, there can be no hard-and-fast rules. For one thing, the factors that make for a successful consultant-client relationship include many that are subtle and elusive. For another, even the highest-qualified consultant and the most intelligent client may join forces and fail because of factors of timing and developments beyond their control.

Choosing a New-Product Consultant

The size and reputation of a new-product consultant are crucial considerations for many companies, but there is more to be said about the basis for making an evaluation. A company will probably engage a consultant if a profitable relationship seems likely, but the average businessman knows that consulting is a mixed bag. Talk to a dozen executives in companies that have used consultants, and for all those who indicate that the consultant "did them a world of good" you will find an opposite number who assert, "They nearly ruined us." More companies than not are dissatisfied with the results of their relationships with new-product consultants.

For the company being courted by a consulting firm, and with good internal reasons for considering a favorable decision, the problem of distinguishing a "good" consultant from a "bad" one must be answered somehow. In many cases it is done in the way an individual chooses a doctor or a TV repairman, on the basis of a "feeling," an intuitive decision based pretty much on the interaction between the parties in the selling and buying exchange.

Other factors that influence the decision should include:
1. People
    a. Those you deal with directly—their sincerity, intelligence, and alertness

   b. "Supporting staff"—everyone from receptionist to the head of
      the firm
   c. Professionalism—status, appropriateness to your areas of interest
2. Reputation, record of success
3. Physical facilities
   a. Appearance of offices (rate a "working shop" atmosphere higher
      than a slick, flashy one)
   b. Appearance and extent of work areas, labs, etc.
4. Length of time in business
5. Understanding of your business
6. Fairness (not lowness) of fees

Perhaps most important in coming to a decision on a technology transfer
consultant is that of his commitment—in other words, his willingness to bet
on what he is selling you. "How much of his own time and money will he
spend?" "How much will he spend to make me a proposal?" "Will he accept
payment from me that is partially or totally dependent on success?" "Will he
contribute his time, if I pay direct expenses?"

As in other decisions of the players in new ventures, each participant
should ask the others these questions. In this instance, the established company is qualifying and deciding on a new-product consultant. But the inventor, on the other side of the transaction, should size up the technology transfer firm in a similar manner. The patent attorney, before choosing partial
ownership of the invention instead of cash, should assess the inventor's
commitment. And so forth.

The Types of Technology Transfer Firms

There are probably some 500 firms whose primary business is bridging the
gap between the sources of new products and the sale of new products to
companies looking to diversify. The large companies discussed in the previous section are in a class by themselves, and the rules of thumb for other
technology transfer companies do not apply. For example, the large
company's name provides instant credibility to the new venture being offered, and the only question the potential buyer has to ask is, "Is this product for my company?" The average firm touting a new product, on the other
hand, spends half its selling time, or more, in proving its credibility.

Furthermore, an established company has built up an inventory of
products and processes, at no cost to the technology transfer arm of the company. Whatever the company can get in addition is gravy, as compared with
keeping it on the shelf. Finally, the established company has hundreds or

thousands of specialists, available to the technology transfer group, as close as the telephone or down the hall. They are available at little or no cost and have to be paid for only when used.

Mergers and acquisitions are another activity of the company looking to diversify. Here, too, the guidelines are different from the considerations of most technology transfer firms. The buyer and seller in the case of a merger or acquisition are capable of dealing in very concrete terms, including a track record that can be measured tangibly. The new product and its seller, however, are judged entirely on estimates and prognostications. An acquisition is a one-shot investment, and it is considerably higher in cost than a new product.

There are many other types of firms which engage in technology transfer as a peripheral part of their business: investment bankers and stock brokerage houses; venture capital managers; independent and corporate patent attorneys; trade publications; commercial banks; factoring and leasing companies; and the friends and relatives of the seller. For the most part these firms' activities are *ad hoc*.

Most of the several hundred companies primarily engaged in technology transfer are just a few years old. As in any new industry, many are still experimenting with the types of services to offer. The industry was born because of a series of events: The increase in the availability of venture capital; the technology explosion which has increased the demand for new products and other new ventures by established companies looking to diversify; the decrease in available companies for merger and acquisition as more and more companies are seeking to diversify; the influence of the television industry, which has popularized and glamorized technology as being modern; the variations in employment of engineers and other technologists, which have forced entrepreneurship on many of these technically oriented people during bad times. And perhaps the most important influence has been the American attitude of equating newness with satisfaction.

Most technology transfer companies are entirely oriented to the marketing of new products. Typically, they are paid *only* by either the inventor or the company seeking diversification, in order to preserve their integrity. Their inventory consists of the patents or new product ideas of their inventor clients and/or the product areas in which their client companies seek to enter. Increasingly, they advertise the use of a computer to do a more accurate and speedy job of wedding the buyer and seller. They may or may not request the power of attorney from the inventor in negotiating agreements.

Other new-product services offered to established companies seek to train the company's own personnel to be more creative. Usually, away from the everyday working atmosphere and offices of the company seeking new products, the consultants use one of a number of techniques to decrease the inhibitions of the trainee. A variation of this service is a joint "brainstorming session." There are a number of firms primarily engaged in editing publications that bring together the buyer and seller of new products. These publications are similar in structure to the GE format, but usually include less information about each opportunity offering. A subscription may run anywhere from a few dollars to a few hundred dollars, depending on the other activities of the publisher.

Sweden, Russia, Japan, France, and several other countries have companies, sponsored and paid for either by government or private capital, that are seeking to bring existing products and new products and processes to the Unites States and vice versa. Several United States companies specialize in marketing products overseas. Others specialize in making market surveys for new products. It is safe to say that there is at least one technology transfer company in every metropolitan area, offering all services associated with the invention and innovation process.

The cost of getting into the industry, if the technology transfer company does not bet on any new products, can be as small as a few thousand dollars. All that is required is a marketer, a telephone, a letterhead, a brochure, and a mailing list. The entrepreneur need only ensure that most of his time is paid for by someone else. The risk is that he will have enough credibility to get in the door of the inventor or buyer, but not enough to make the sale to either.

Credibility and other selling problems face the inventor or company selling new products. Let us follow the sale of a new product, step by step.

Suspect and Prospect Companies

Generally a sale is made when the buyer decides that the cost of the merchandise is less than the cost of the problem he has. A sales situation ends *abruptly* when the buyer says "no." Making the sale of a new product is a *continuum* of "yeses," requiring patience of the seller, for it almost always takes place over a period of months. The sale is the last step in the qualifying three-stage cycle by which (1) suspect companies become (2) prospect companies and finally (3) customers.

Before discussing suspects, prospects, and customers, let's review the outlines of the selling situation. The sale of a new product or a new-product service is an intangible sale, like selling insurance. The potential customer is rarely excited by his purchase, because at the time he signs the contract he still has many doubts. Salesmen selling major appliances or automobiles are selling a tangible. In a tangible sale the salesman is accustomed to gauging the situation by bringing the customer to an increasing amount of excitement and measuring the effectiveness of his presentation, accordingly. But in the course of the sale of an intangible, the measuring of a decrease in wariness, rather than mounting excitement, is the way to judge your progress.

The buying company is insecure if it is dealing with the seller in order to diversify. The company's need to diversify is likely to have evolved as a necessary evil, rather than primarily as a new opportunity. "We want to diversify" is probably an intellectualization that will take a while to be internalized. The seller's lack of overwhelming testimony of the patentability, producibility, marketability, and profitability of the new product will feed on the prospect's insecurity. Negative details will be magnified.

It is in this connection that the seller has to ensure that little or nothing occurs by chance, that every particular has been considered in advance, and that an appropriate response, or other evidence, is available to minimize each worry. Furthermore, it is important that items that will be construed negatively by the potential customer be brought to his attention by the seller—and that they not be left to be discovered by the buyer. Finally, the seller must ensure that he tells the truth about each item under consideration. All credibility will be lost otherwise, because twenty or thirty other items of truth will be colored by a single misstatement.

Finding suspects is a combination of research, insight, and luck. This form of research can be divided into several categories:

1. Personal contact and mailing lists from trade associations. The Licensing Executives Society[4] includes "any person who in his business activities has significant responsibility for the licensing of industrial or intellectual property rights..." and has several hundred members, mostly from large companies. Most industries have trade associations with membership lists and, in some cases, active diversification efforts for their members (e.g., the Association of Home Appliance Manufacturers, Chicago, publishes a directory).

2. There are numerous specialized books and publications that can provide suspects. *How and Where To Look It Up*[5] provides thousands of sources of information. The Macmillan Company, McGraw-Hill, Prentice-Hall, the *Thomas Register*, Standard and Poor's, Dunn and Bradstreet, and Dow-Jones & Co. provide numerous books and services that are helpful in finding suspect companies.

3. *The Wall Street Journal, Barron's, Forbes's, Fortune, Business Week,* and other business magazines provide suspects in their stories on the new-product programs and on the mergers and acquisitions programs of companies, changes in personnel, and so forth.

4. *Licensing Executives Society By-laws*, Oct. 23, 1969, p. 10.
5. Robert W. Murphy, *How and Where To Look It Up* (New York: McGraw-Hill), 1958.

4. Many companies provide standard mailing lists, categorized in many manners (e.g., one can buy a mailing list of all manufacturing companies in the United States with sales of $10 million or more, printed on gummed labels ready to be placed on envelopes).

Finding suspects is often a shotgun operation. However, unlike a soap company, a technology transfer company does not have to mass merchandise. Letters should be personalized, not mass produced. "Canned" paragraphs and letters can be used, but the suspect should always have the feeling that the writer is catering to his individual needs. The suspect has little or no other evidence of the seller's credibility, and will judge him on erasures or smudges on a letter, or from the literature and the other bits of information he does have available.

I sent the letter shown below to eleven manufacturers of electrical connectors. Six did not respond. Three responded in the negative. Two wanted more information, which was given in telephone conversations and eliminated one of the companies. The eleventh company, a manufacturer of electrical connectors, signed a licensing agreement with the invention company six months later.

```
Mr. John Rowe, President
Rowe Connectors, Inc.
682 E. 57th St.
New York, N.Y. 10016

Subject: Electrical Connector with 200 Connections Per Square
         Inch

Dear Mr. Rowe:

  It is not often that the term "ingenious" can be honestly
applied to a new product. Our company has made a major
breakthrough in the field of high density miniature
electrical connectors. We feel you too will concur after you
have heard our story.

  Briefly, here are the features: up to 200 connection
points per square inch, without pins to bend; hermaphroditic,
making the male and female ends the same; snaps and holds
together without external clamping; may be manufactured from
plastic or any metal and to meet all military specifications.

  This connector is in the patent pending stage and the
principles applied for lend themselves to virtually all
electrical component applications. Included are: tube and
canned component bases and sockets and larger electrical
connectors. A patent and literature search reveals nothing
close to our principles.
```

    Our immediate desire is to meet with the appropriate people
    in your company to discuss this matter in more detail.
    Ultimately, we should like to sell, lease, or license the
    rights to your company.

    The information contained in this letter is of a
    nonconfidential nature and has not been solicited by your
    company.

                        Very truly yours,

                        INVENTOR COMPANY

                        _____

                        William H. Shames
                        President

The letter, as in all advertising campaigns, should have as close to a *single purpose* as possible. In the case presently under consideration, my goal was to talk on the telephone to each of the companies and get a good listening. The purpose of the telephone conservations was to determine whether there was sufficient interest to invest the time of a personal meeting.

Mailing lists continually updated are a major part of a sales program. Even suspects who do not become prospects at the time of the initial contact should be added to the list if they seem to be the kind of company you might want to deal with in the future. The product you are selling now may not be appropriate, but such companies may become prospects in the future. Regular mailings may increase your credibility as suspects see your company continuing to survive.

Good Prospects

What kinds of companies are good prospects? And what suggests that a company may be a poor prospect?

In the course of their consulting, experienced new-product firms develop a sense of a company's readiness to make use of outsiders. Obviously, if an organization has undertaken its own program and is satisfied with its progress, outside help is not likely to be sought. But significant distinctions can be made among companies not satisfied with their own progress.

Companies that have not made any effort to investigate or develop the new-product field are generally poor prospects. A typical reaction to the approach of a consultant is a response along these lines: "We're satisfied with our company situation. We make a superior product in our field. We've been

operating profitably for the past twenty years and feel we've got another ten
or fifteen years ahead of us before we have to worry."

Another revealing response by key executives is that they may decide that
their ability to take advantage of new products is minimal. For example, one
company dealt with a major manufacturer of dolls' eyes which operates
profitably because the manufacturing process and the marketing practices
are both highly efficient. Since the manufacturer felt that his product is a
staple for which there is no likely substitute, and since the combination of
manufacturing and marketing efficiency made it unlikely that a serious competitor would come into the field, his assurance about the future stability of
the company was final. If a prospect company believes in its existing products this strongly, it is not worth the sales time to try to change the belief.

To convince a key executive in the organization that he should risk the un-
certainties of a new-product development is also often presumptuous. Frequently, a company is persuaded by the consultant's sales talk or convinces
itself of the desirability of product diversification, but then the conclusion
may be, "Thanks for the idea. However, we've decided to go ahead with our
own people." Or the prospect may decide to hire his own full-time employee, and the consulting firm must write off the entire expenditure of time
and energy as a loss.

Another type of prospect that experienced consultants tend to rule out is
the service-oriented company. The obstacle here is that in the large majority
of cases, service companies are not patent-oriented. Nor does a new service
ordinarily lend itself to patent protection. Therefore, a logical reaction would
be, "Why should we pay for the development of a service that a competitor
could duplicate at almost no expense and in short order?" Also, service-
oriented companies are seldom interested in entering the manufacturing
field. They might consider doing so through merger or acquisition, but certainly not as the result of undertaking an expensive new-product development program on their own.

Large companies are better prospects than small ones because generally
they can afford to pay the costs involved or to wait a longer period of time for
investments of this kind to pay off. On the other hand, medium-sized companies may be better prospects than big companies *if* they can be ap-
proached at a higher executive echelon. In the same way, corporate offices
are usually more responsive than division offices, almost regardless of how
high the echelon contacted in the affiliate or subsidiary might be.

The age of the executive contacted is also a factor. As one observer puts it,
"Young people in a company are more reponsive than people who have been
there a long time. The younger man tends to be more prone to take risks and
to be more forward-looking, and he tends to feel he has an empire to build.
The older man is more likely to think in terms of retaining the status quo—at
least until his retirement."

There is also a considerable difference in the reception of new-product proposals among various professional groups. For example, engineers tend to be more receptive than lawyers or accountants. Engineers are more open-minded in their listening and more imaginative in translating the information they receive into answers to the basic questions: What can this do for my company?

However, even though engineers seem to "get with it" more quickly, they also tend to be jealous of their professional standing, and as a result tend to feel threatened by the competitive aspect of the outside product or service. As a result, the outside consultant sometimes finds it difficult to win acceptance from an executive who, one way or another, sees himself as a competitor. And, of course, it is the same executive who consciously or unconsciously puts obstacles in the way of the acceptance of ideas submitted by the outside consultant.

High-echelon sales and marketing people seem to be very impressionable. They listen in sympathetic appreciation to the benefits described by a consultant. The conversation moves ahead very rapidly. It is often easy to get a sales person to become enthusiastic about a proposal, and the seller may think he will make a sale. When he tries to get a signature on a contract, however, it may not be forthcoming. If he calls a few days later, many times the prospect seems to have forgotten who the caller is.

IS and NIH—Two Opposing Forces

In the mutual exploration and evaluation that takes place between the consulting firm and prospect company, two opposing forces are often operating. One is the "internal salesman" and the other is the "not invented here" syndrome.

IS—THE "INTERNAL SALESMAN" Among the executives of the prospect company, the behavior of one type of individual is noteworthy. He is the man who, for personal or corporate reasons, decides that it is a good idea to champion the outside consultant within the company. He clears away the red tape that often interferes with getting approval for the retaining of the consultant or the licensing of a product. Usually a person of status within the company, he takes it on himself to exert his personal influence on behalf of the outside company to answer questions about the benefits or to get answers from the consultant and use them in his espousal of the deal.

The internal salesman may have for his motivation the belief that a consulting firm offers services that are desirable to his organization and are not available inside. Another possible explanation is that his advocacy may be meant to stimulate, by example or competition, services already existing in the company which will be paralleled by the consulting service. And company politics being what they are, in some situations the internal salesman because of dissatisfaction with the progress, the administration, or the personnel of the company's ongoing new-product efforts, may see in the outside firm a chance to "back a winner," with eventual career and political advantages to himself.

NIH—"NOT INVENTED HERE"   This factor works in the opposite direction from the internal salesman. The NIH attitude is strongly negative. It is a major cause of turndowns. On the other hand, it is often used as an excuse for poor salesmanship. The NIH attitude can be explained by a number of situations inside the company ranging from a simple antipathy to an unimpressive idea to a bad experience with previous outside inventors or companies.

In its most simple form, the NIH attitude is that no one outside the organization can possibly know as much about the problems, and therefore the solutions, of new-product needs as the inside people. Many companies have had poor results from consulting services. There is an understandable logic in the question: Why should we pay outside people retainers for teaching them our business? And there's also logic in the feeling that outside people may be unable, in a comparatively short period of time, to become knowledgeable enough about the industry and the company to lead the way to successful product development.

However, underlying the NIH reaction is the tendency of many internal new-product people to be cautious and ineffectual. The last thing they want is an outsider to come along with a new yardstick that would show their failings. It seems clear that the NIH syndrome exists both among those executives who have something to fear from an outside organization's success and among those who fear its failure.

Next Step

Assuming that the company that is looking to diversify has become a prospect for the purchase of a new product or a new-product service, the technology transfer company now faces a series of steps that may be described as negotiations. The new-product licensing negotiations bring out the latent paranoid tendencies of both the seller and the buyer of new products. Therefore, companies that regularly deal with outside companies have well-established legal practices to protect both ends of the potential transaction.

More casual entrants into the field play it by ear and are usually much more flexible.

If one is selling a consulting service instead of a new product, the legalistic considerations relate to the future, when there will be one or more proprietary products. In many ways, this is an advantage because the negotiations do not concern a product. Both sides will tend to be more flexible.

In selling a new product the first serious step in the negotiations is concerned with the *disclosure* of the product, the patent, and the know-how to the buyer.

Disclosure Agreements

Disclosure agreements are used by independent inventors or technology transfer firms and companies seeking to diversify for their mutual protection. Essentially they are contracts that define the responsibilities and obligations of each party to the other.

Such formal agreements tend to inject awkward restrictions on the parties and usually more so on the inventor. The average company, perhaps overly conscious of its susceptibility to damage suits, sees the agreement as a device to limit the inventor's freedom of action. For example, much of the burden of proof is placed on the inventor in the following agreement, which is representative of the terms of most large companies' *standard* agreements:

```
Large Company A

Gentlemen:

I hereby submit to you certain suggestions and ideas
relating to
_____.
I make this submission with full notice and acceptance
of your policy that you cannot receive such
suggestions or ideas in confidence and that you
therefore consent to receive and consider my said
suggestions and ideas only on the following terms and
conditions:

1.  You shall obtain no rights under this agreement in
    any of my said suggestions or idea or under any of my
    patents or patent applications relating thereto.
```

2. Your acceptance of any of my disclosures shall not prevent you from using any suggestions or ideas under consideration by you or by any of your representatives or employees prior to my making such disclosures or from using any suggestions or ideas in the public domain.

3. Neither you nor your subsidiaries or associated companies shall incur any obligation of any kind by reason of the matters to which this agreement relates, except insofar as such obligations shall be expressed in a separate formal written contract between us.

4. My rights and remedies arising out of the disclosures hereunder or the use thereof by you or any of your representatives or subsidiaries or associated companies shall be limited to such rights and remedies as may be accorded to me from the date of issue of a valid letters patent by the United States Patent Office; and you shall be as free at all times to contest the validity of any such patent or any alleged infringement thereof as if you had received no disclosure from me.

5. Your acceptance and consideration of the disclosures hereunder as an exception to your general policy are an adequate consideration for this agreement.

I agree to all of the foregoing terms and conditions and request that you consider under them the ideas and suggestions submitted herewith as well as such additional ideas and suggestions as I may hereafter submit to you from time to time.

Witnessed _____

Date _____

Signed _____

Address _____

_____

Representing _____

Companies which recognize the possibility of undefinable constriction in the arrangements have instructed their legal staff to be more flexible in this area. One approach is to receive from the inventor, in the early stages of discussions, only information that is entirely nonconfidential. The company will become more seriously interested only if its representatives are satisfied that a disclosure by the inventor is in their best interest. They assume that the product is valid. An example of this arrangement from another large company is an "information exchange agreement":

> In consideration of providing a basis for unrestricted communication pertaining to certain manufacturing and technical information of [inventor] relating to [product], Large Company B and inventor agree that neither party will assert against the other or its vendees or lessees, any claim for use or transmission of oral or documented information acquired by either party from the other in the course of discussions or communications concerning such product, on [date].
>
> Nothing herein, however, shall operate to prejudice the rights of either party under the patent laws of the United States or any foreign country.

Inventor
_____

Large Company B
_____

Other companies actively seeking to create a freer exchange of information between the inventor and themselves have changed their disclosure policy. Several of these companies have cooperated with me to evolve an agreement which over the years has been signed by hundreds of large and medium-sized companies. The inventor wants to provide a company certain information and the receiving company believes it has a vested interest in receiving the information. In some instances, the inventor or technology transfer company may charge a disclosure fee to the company when it is believed that the technology to be disclosed is particularly significant and when the inventor's investment in disclosing it is high enough that the company seeking information should have its interest severely qualified. The agreement that has evolved follows:

DISCLOSURE AGREEMENT

AGREEMENT dated _____, between INVENTOR CORPORATION, a Delaware corporation ("Inventor"), and
_____, a _____ corporation ("Company").

WHEREAS, Inventor and/or its subsidiaries has invented or developed _____
_____,
such products and the data and concepts associated therewith, being hereinafter collectively called the Information; and

WHEREAS, Inventor is willing to disclose certain of the Information in confidence to the Company for the purpose of enabling it to decide whether to enter into a business relationship with Inventor or its subsidiaries in respect of the exploitation of all, or any part of the Information under terms and conditions mutually agreeable to the parties, and the Company is agreeable to receiving such of the Information in confidence from Inventor for such purpose, all on the terms and conditions hereinafter set forth;

NOW, THEREFORE, Inventor and the Company agree as follows:

1.   Inventor agrees to disclose to the Company such part of the Information as it deems necessary or appropriate for the purpose of enabling the Company to determine whether to enter into a business relationship with Inventor on mutually agreeable terms.

2.   The Company agrees, on behalf of itself, its officers, directors, agents and employees, that it and they will keep the Information disclosed to it by Inventor and its subsidiaries confidential and shall refrain from disclosing same to others without express written permission of Inventor.

3.   Inventor and the Company agree that the Company's obligation to retain the Information disclosed to it in confidence shall not apply to any part thereof (a) which is already in the possession of the Company, provided it makes prompt disclosure in writing thereof to Inventor, or (b) which the Company may lawfully obtain from sources independent of Inventor and/or any confidants of Inventor or (c) which is now or hereafter becomes generally available to the public, from and after such public availability.

4.   The Company's obligation to retain the Information disclosed to it in confidence shall in any event terminate three years after disclosure thereof to it by Inventor, except to the extent that any requirement of confidentiality may be imposed by a subsequent agreement between the parties.

5.   If no agreement or business relationship is mutually agreed between the parties on or before_____

months from the date hereof, the Company shall return to
Inventor all descriptive matter, documents, drawings,
sketches, models or prototypes, photographs, and the
like, and all copies thereof, as may have been disclosed or
submitted by Inventor and/or its subsidiaries to the
Company.

EXECUTED as of the day and year first above written.

INVENTOR CORPORATION

By _____

_____

By _____

As in all legal agreements, the inventor will usually be able to make a fair disclosure agreement, even with the largest companies, in proportion to the company's basic interest in the invention.

Negotiation between Inventor and Company

Inventors who know what they want or know how to negotiate with a company are rare; this is one of the reasons for the growth of the technology transfer industry. In many cases, the inventor is unrealistic in his lack of preparation for a presentation or "sale" to a possible purchasing organization.

It helps both the inventor and a prospective purchaser for the inventor to preplan his presentation. Briefings with his patent attorney and other trustworthy counselors can eliminate some of the negotiating obstacles. Drawings, models, test results, correspondence, studies, and so on that bear on the invention can be helpful adjuncts to a verbal presentation.

The sale of an invention, on whatever basis, is seldom a one-meeting operation. The inventor must be prepared to negotiate with one or more executives, possibly going through one or more echelons in the organization. Most companies, particularly those with experience in this type of negotiation, have a fairly set idea of the kind of deal they want to make, assuming that they want to make one at all. As a matter of fact, the inventor would be well advised to ask during the first meeting whether the company has previously dealt with an outside inventor or developer. If the answer is "no," the less revelation there is of crucial facts about the invention, the better. Although it is important to establish an honest communication level, the inventor should learn early how serious the company's interest is. It makes for better communication when an inventor states frankly what aspects or areas of his invention he will not reveal. Any attempts to be evasive are usually damaging. A forthright assertion—"I would rather not talk about that aspect of the device at this time"—makes for better rapport. The inventor should tell the company *what* instead of *how,* early in the discussions.

No licensing agreement or sale will take place unless a prospect has a very strong interest in the invention. Diagrams, models, and patent applications (which are all indications of reduction to practice) make for a clear and specific presentation.

Also, the more the inventor knows about the business aspects of his creation, the better. Ready answers to questions like these make a favorable impression:

- What is presently being done in the field?
- What are the competition problems the product might face?
- What about the production problems of the invention?
- What special marketing problems or opportunities exist?
- Why should the prospect be especially interested in the product?

To answer the last question the inventor should learn as much as he can about the company with which he is dealing—everything from its other products to its financial situation, as represented by its annual report.

Judging the caliber of the company representative can be helpful. Is he a lightweight or a heavyweight? Is he a "put-off" man, or is he really able to commit the company, partially or wholly, to a sale?

When the Negotiation Gets Nowhere

Failure with a particular prospect may come in many guises. If the inventor is fortunate, he will be spared a trip down the garden path: He will get a quick turndown from a responsible executive who says his company has no interest in the proposal.

Less fortunate is the inventor who, for one reason or another, and often without any malice on the part of the company, despite appearances to the contrary, becomes the victim of endless conversations that never lead to a "yes" or "no." The deal simply dies of old age without ever actually being born.

It is easy for the inventor to be misled either through his own wishful thinking or through the "interest" of an executive who knows he can be as enthusiastic as he likes without committing his company to anything. Usually this executive is substituting talk for real action, and the deal eventually collapses. And yet, an inventor can legitimately ruefully describe the eventual turndown as a deal that was "practically in the bag."

A deal is never made until the contract is signed. It even happens that an inventor leaves a final negotiation with the promise that a contract will be in the mail, and the contract never arrives. The negotiating executive may have had good intentions, but a colleague or superior, faced by the need to affix his signature to a document, to finally commit the company's resources or energies, at the last minute decides against doing so. His reasoning may be that most new products will not be a commercial success, and that it is easier to turn the opportunity down than to risk the consequences of signing the contract.

The inventor, like the salesman, must be prepared for failure. In the average case, multiple presentations must be made before a successful outcome. Many products, even some that have been successfully marketed, have been rejected many times for a variety of reasons.

There is a much-told anecdote to the effect that executives at IBM twice turned down offers to acquire the Xerox process in its early stages. IBM executives have not taken the trouble to deny the seeming misjudgment. What they do say is quite revealing. In the 1950s, when the opportunity was presented, IBM could not have done as single-minded and successful a job of developing and exploiting the computer market if it had permitted itself to get involved with the pioneering of Xerography as well. Their point is that it may be a wise judgment on the part of the prospect to turn down a proposal because of the company's own particular situation and needs, even if the proposal is essentially sound.

Fine Points of Negotiation

The following considerations can help minimize the complexity and duration of negotiations:

1. Before disclosing a product to a company have one or more business meetings so that before you determine whether they will say "yes," you have defined what "yes" will mean.
2. In discussing what is referred to as a "ball park deal," all *vital* interests should be brought up. They are almost impossible to credibly bring up later. You may drop one of them later, at the same time the company agrees to drop one of their vital interests and make it a trade-off.
3. At the time of a detailed negotiation, the businessmen should agree on all aspects of the deal before the lawyers are brought into the deal. Negotiation of terms between the inventor's lawyer and the company's lawyer has to be seen to be believed. Almost all com-

panies will indicate their agreement with this practice so that normally it is not a problem to avoid the lawyers until serious negotiating has been completed.

4. After the terms have been negotiated, suggest that your lawyer do the first draft. This means that it will be done in a week. Waiting for the company lawyer to do the first draft sometimes takes months.

New-Product Agreements

Usually, the most desirable form of agreement between an inventor and a company is a licensing agreement. This can take various forms with variations and limitations depending on both the inventor's and the licensee's interests and desires. Licensing agreements can be thought of as having two parts: *boiler plate* and *numbers*.

"Boiler plate" refers to the bulk of a licensing agreement. It covers the ownership of the invention and defines words and phrases. Usually included are specifications on the length of time covered by the agreement, circumstances under which termination may be achieved, and obligations and responsibilities of the company and inventor to each other both during the agreement and after it ceases. The agreement should also cover such specifics as the manner in which the inventor and company will communicate with each other (*i.e.*, reporting responsibilities and accessibility of information); the appropriate state or national law to be applied to interpretation of the contract; responsibilities in the event of company bankruptcy; a partial invalidity clause; an arbitration clause; and definitions of special and peculiar circumstances.

"Numbers" refers to the consideration to be made by the company for the benefit of the inventor. Normally, the negotiation involves the payment of front money at the time of the signing of the agreement; the amount of royalty, either as a flat dollar amount per product sold or as a percentage of net sales; and the minimum royalty to be paid regardless of the actual sales of the licensee.

FRONT MONEY   The inventor takes the position that he has spent a considerable number of dollars and is entitled to front money. The company takes the position that it has to make a considerable additional investment before anyone will realize any income and therefore the inventor is entitled to compensation contingent upon the performance of the product. Often the compromise is that the inventor receives a nominal down payment. The negotiators may compromise by agreeing to either front money or minimum royalty, instead of both.

ROYALTY   Royalties vary depending on the nature of the market into which the new product will go, the practice of the industry, the gross profit and net profit expectations of the licensee, and the strength of the desire of each of the participants to buy and sell. Tradition also has a role in the determination of the amount of royalty. A fair amount is obviously that which the buyer is willing to pay and the seller is willing to accept. The range of royalty payments seems to be from ½ percent to 10 percent, with 2½ percent to 5 percent being more or less average.

MINIMUM ROYALTY   Minimum royalties tend to be one of the means used by an inventor to ensure company diligence in its exploitation of the product. It is assumed that if the company has to pay anyway, it is more likely to move forward. There is no absolute way to solve this major problem in all licensing agreements. While there is no logic in a company's signing a licensing agreement and then shelving the product, the fact is that company people changes and other alterations may shift company objectives.

The problem of minimum royalties is usually solved by their size being relatively nominal. This allows the inventor to rationalize that he is getting something, while the company has limited its payments. Another frequent compromise is to have the minimum royalty begin after the time period it will take the company to start up the exploitation of the new product.

Independent inventors also can protect themselves from the vicissitudes of company operation by a clause stating that the rights to the product revert to the inventor if, within a specified time, the company is not manufacturing at least a certain volume of the product, selling a certain volume, expending a stated sum of money for marketing and promotion, and so on.

The difficulties in wording a licensing agreement become clear when one considers the problem of defining a concept such as "manufacturing a product." Can a company be said to be "manufacturing" when one machine turns out ten items a day? Or must a minimum quantity be indicated to ensure the inventor that the company is satisfactorily fulfilling its obligation?

A sample of a licensing agreement was shown earlier in this chapter. Other forms of agreements that are appropriate in the technology transfer industry will be discussed in the next chapter. They include agreements to invent and develop products for a company on a continuing basis, plans for joint ventures, and development contracts relating to the stage-by-stage development of a particular product.

Getting Started as Consultant

With the terms specified and the agreement signed, the parties are ready to start the cooperative effort. If the agreement is a licensing agreement, the inventor may or may not have an active role. The new-product consultant must learn as much as possible about the nature and operation of his client. This "getting-to-know-you" period may vary in length of time from a few days of intensive meetings and conversations to a few weeks. Both organizations continue to learn about each other as long as the relationship exists.

The consultant must quickly form a useful model of his client—the company's size, its pattern of operation, the nature of its products and its method of production, its markets, its methods of marketing, and so on. A form, like the one shown below, for writing down the salient information about a client can be useful.

Most of the questions usually have been answered before the prospect has been transformed into a client. It is the kind of information a consultant must have before his representatives can make an intelligent sales call on a prospect. But after the relationship has been firmed up, these questions can be answered more authoritatively, and more completely, than may have been possible in preliminary sales contacts:

COMPANY BACKGROUND QUESTIONNAIRE

Interview Date_____

persons interviewed:

_____

_____

I. GENERAL

1. Company Name _____
   Address _____
   Phone No. _____

2. Name and Title of person in charge of new products _____
   _____

3. Do you have a new product committee? ☐ Yes ☐ No
   If yes, please list titles of comittee members
   _____
   _____
   _____

4. Company's Industry–Product Classifications (e.g.
   automotive, electronic, construction equipment)
                                                        %
   _____   _____
   _____   _____
   _____   _____

5. Is the end use of your products:

%

Industrial   ☐   _____

Consumer   ☐   _____

6. Are you essentially a producer of ☐ a complete product or ☐ components?

II. MARKETING FACILITY

1. Annual Sales _____

2. Are Sales ☐ International ☐ National ☐ Regional? If only regional, specify territory.

_____

_____

_____

3. What % of your sales are private brand?   _____

4. Marketing function is performed

%

☐ Direct to End User   _____

☐ Through Distributors   _____

☐ Directly to Retailer   _____

5. Do you use manufacturer's representatives? ☐ Yes ☐ No

6. Major Product Lines   Approximate % of Total Sales

Major Product Lines	Approximate % of Total Sales
_____	_____
_____	_____
_____	_____

7. Rank in industry by major product line and share of market.

Product	Rank	Market Share
_____	_____	_____
_____	_____	_____
_____	_____	_____
_____	_____	_____
_____	_____	_____

8. What is company's most successful individual product or component?

_____

9. Do you want to diversify from present product lines? ☐ Yes ☐ No If yes, in what categories _____

_____

_____

10. Do you employ formal market surveys on your present product lines? ☐ Yes ☐ No

    Do you conduct such surveys of proposed new product or lines? ☐ Yes ☐ No
    If yes, please describe _____
    _____
    _____

11. Do you test market a product before marketing? ☐ Yes ☐ No

12. Please list five new product areas of prime company interest.
    A. _____
    B. _____
    C. _____
    D. _____
    E. _____

III. RESEARCH AND DEVELOPMENT FACILITY

1. Do you employ personnel whose engineering activities are primarily the following:

   Consultant   In—House
   ☐   ☐   Requirement Surveys
   ☐   ☐   Basic Research
   ☐   ☐   Drafting
   ☐   ☐   Product Engineering
   ☐   ☐   Design Engineering

2. How many new products (excluding design, package and quality—price product changes) have you developed during the past 24 months? _____

3. How many of these have been marketed? _____

4. How many of these are presently marketed? _____

5. How is new product development responsibility organized?
   ☐ By Division ☐ Company Wide ☐ Both

IV. MANUFACTURING FACILITY

1. Do you primarily

                        %
   ☐ Manufacture   _____
   ☐ Assemble   _____
   ☐ Contract   _____

2. To what extent do you subcontract or purchase products from the outside?

_____

_____

3. What % of present manufacturing and/or assembly capacity is occupied? _____

4. Plant   Location   Size
   A._____   _____   _____
   B._____   _____   _____
   C._____   _____   _____

V. OUTSIDE CONSULTANTS

Are you or have you ever used any of the following type consultants?

Past	Present	
☐	☐	Management
☐	☐	Advertising Agency
☐	☐	Public Relations Agency
☐	☐	Hard Goods Engineering
☐	☐	Human Engineering

VI. PATENTS AND LICENSES

1. Do you have a patent attorney? ☐ Yes ☐ No
2. Do you now have any proprietary products? ☐ Yes ☐ No
3. Do you own any patents? ☐ Yes ☐ No
4. Were the patents developed inside your organization? ☐ Yes ☐ No
5. Have you ever licensed a product from the outside? ☐ Yes ☐ No
6. Are you now manufacturing or selling a product under a license? ☐ Yes ☐ No

It is usually preferable for one man in the outside firm to be assigned the responsibility for all activities related to the client company. If possible, it is also practical to have a single-person contact within the company.

The how-to methodology of technology transfer is increasingly available as more companies enter the field.

The struggle of the inventor and the technology transfer company is always to find more profitable and more salable products and services. The correct answer is specific to the needs and talents of those betting time and money on the inventor or the technology transfer company. Sibany's evolution from an inventions company into a company whose business is primarily starting companies, built around an invention, is a bridge into the venture management business.

Good communication between an inventor and a company seeking new products is a rarity. The next chapter will show what happens when entrepreneurs and inventors, or entrepreneurs-in-training and inventors-in-training, are put under the same roof.

Chapter 3

Sibany: A Venture Management Company

Starting a company is a very personal thing. Later it becomes less personal, but there is always the sense that it is an extension of yourself. To start a business without much money or backing, you must make up for that initial financial lack by greater commitment, which is made up of equal parts of stubbornness, wisdom, naïveté, faith, and hard work and patience.

Picture it as follows: Having been a vice president and corporate officer of CCI Corporation, Tulsa, Oklahoma, I resign in the spring of 1961 because it has become increasingly difficult to roll out of bed every morning to go to work. I have made some money in the stockmarket, and my family and I agree that I will try to find something I really want to do.

I rent a house in Westport, Connecticut (which is country, quaint, and near the beach). Other than talking to some people whom I know, the only specific new career ideas I have are to finish my master's degree in political science, go on for a Ph.D., and then teach at a university; or to start a business of some kind with an old friend, Marvin Miller, he handling the inventing and engineering and I the business and sales.

The idea of changing the world by teaching eager and open-minded college students is very appealing. But, while walking around the campus, thinking of my own days as a student, and talking to some of the political science faculty, my dream confronts reality, and as a reality it is not for me.

Among these academic grown-ups—committed playfully to discussing, instead of seriously doing—I felt all right at age twenty, but now feel somehow menial and sad at thirty. I reject an academic career.

Having rejected the university life, the possibility of doing something with Marvin becomes more interesting. The idea of creating new products is so appealing that I avoid serious discussions for a few months to lengthen the time I can relish it without suffering disappointment. My Depression upbringing dampens my belief that one can go into a business and make a living at it, still less enjoy it. Probably I am also victimized by the prevailing attitude, a hand-me-down from the Puritans, that business and pleasure do not mix. The more I think about it, the more the business with Marvin seems just such a mixture of business and pleasure, delicious to contemplate.

You can't go around talking to people and thinking about a new career full time, but I do, three or four dozen hours a week. I use a loose-leaf book with a section for each business idea or scheme. Anything pertaining to a potential business is noted in its section until a few items blend into a larger thought, which I then elaborate in more detail, and so on.

Into this notebook—later misplaced—go all the businesses I did *not* go into: a chain of order-by-computer stores in shopping centers (dropped because I am ignorant of all aspects of this business, although obviously it will come some day); a brokerage office, with or without seats on the exchanges (dropped because I do not have enough money or the know-how to find people with enough money); a partnership with a friend, who had found that Trans World Airlines 6½ percent bonds with warrants attached are selling for $87 so that an investment of $15,000 at 20 or 25 percent margin, could perhaps be levered into $50,000 to $75,000 within three years because the warrants would soon have come due (but this too is dropped).

More ideas go into the notebook. Deciding that homeowners would pay a yearly fixed fee for being able to secure the services of a carpenter, electrician, plumber, exterminator, and so forth, by calling one central office (and also getting billed from just one source), I consider starting such a business. I also think of at least half a dozen businesses centered around the name "Games O'Shames," and seriously give consideration to trademarking it.

The bull market of 1961, after John Kennedy's election, suggests to me that I can make an excellent living as a professional investor, watching the stock tape and investing by hunch. A few losses, even before the fiasco of the spring and summer of 1962, convince me otherwise.

All people conveniently pigeonhole things in order to better understand them, or perhaps to remember them better, or in some other fashion to come to grips with them. In going around and talking to people, I am pegged as an administrator type, probably because I have been a vice president of a listed company.

At the time, the stockbrokerage office in Westport is Williston & Beane and I become a regular customer and get to know the registered representatives personally. One of the fellows who works there gets the idea that Williston & Beane and I are made for each other and sets up an appointment with Alf Beane (of Merrill Lynch, Pierce, Fenner and Beane—now Smith —fame), the senior partner.

Mr. Beane always has been a hero to me. At the University of Oklahoma Business School, one of the courses I took included two lectures by the partner in charge of the Oklahoma City office of Merrill Lynch. I remember that at that time (in 1950) there were eighty-three partners, and they handled 10 percent of the volume on the New York Stock Exchange. And "He" had his name in "Their" name.

Those are my thoughts as I shake hands with Mr. Beane, who is strong and gracious. The meeting lasts about an hour and a half, and I meet some of his other partners and associates. His office overlooks the East River and New York Harbor, and I think, "What a view . . . what a man . . . and he's so nice, even with all those millions." His manner is very disarming because he talks neither up nor down to me, but straight at me, and with enough detail to indicate sincerity. Essentially, he tells me that Williston & Beane is growing rapidly and the administration of the organization is not keeping pace. He is looking for an administrator type to put things in order. He prefers someone from the outside, someone without a lot of previous assumptions about the brokerage business. I will train, first, in the Westport office for three months, because it is convenient; then for three months in the main office; and then get some sort of executive-administrator status.

At the end of the interview he offers me the in-training job; and I ask for a few days to think it over. I turn it down the next day, because the aura and trappings of the job and the man are really an end in themselves.

I rarely have misgivings about the past, but when Williston & Beane is later forced to close, at the time of the salad oil scandal, I think longingly of whether it may have been different had I taken the job.

In September of 1961, in my living room in Westport, Marvin Miller and I decide to start a company called Sibany to manufacture and market a bowling game.

At CCI there had been a company-sponsored bowling league—bowling leagues having been very fashionable in 1960 and 1961—and I had participated as a player on one of the eight teams. At first it had been enjoyable, and regular bowling raised my average to about 160. But as the season progressed, it became boring to bowl every Monday night, and in the last half of the season I began to think of it as work, an obligation of my executive status to be one of the boys.

So in my notebook I started making a list of the various appeals that bowling has for the people on the CCI bowling teams and the people I meet socially who are also on bowling teams, and by September 1961 I have accumulated eighty-three reasons why bowling is attractive to various kinds of people. They are categorized into physical reasons, health reasons, competitive reasons, and financial reasons.

In the years that Marvin and I were growing up, he would invent a product, we would do nothing about it, and subsequently we often would see the product on the market from some large company. The cartridge pen is an example. With such memories and armed with my list of reasons for the success of bowling, he invents a new game for bowling alleys.

We get together on a Sunday afternoon with the feeling that we are going to start a business. Marvin invents the game, which we feel can increase enjoyment and competition for the bowler—and increase revenue for the bowling alley operator.

It sounds great to us. We both are sure it will make us a million dollars. As I reflect on it now, it was a rather naïve basis on which to end my seven-month quest for a business opportunity. Nevertheless, the decision to start Sibany is made, enthusiastically, that Sunday afternoon.

The product never made it to the market, as the reader may have noticed from recent visits to the bowling alleys, and the remote telephone became our first product.

In October 1961 we are sitting around Marvin's kitchen table with his brother Bob. Somebody says, "I think you can answer the telephone when you're not at the telephone." I say, "I think that's a great idea if it can be done." At the end of the discussion, we agree it can and should be done and that Bob Miller will do it because he is an electrical engineer and the electrical and electronic aspects of the problem are the most crucial.

Bob is at this time living with his parents in New York, working full time on a regular job during the week and on the remote telephone at night and on weekends. By February 1962, encouraged by Marvin and me, Bob manages to prove that the remote telephone (as we are beginning to refer to it) is a better product than the bowling game, and that the approach decided on around Marvin's kitchen table will not work but that a new approach will.

Through this period Marvin continues with his regular job and I remain unpaid, running around talking to everyone I know about Sibany and trying to determine how each of them can profitably participate by investing.

In March 1962 we have a demonstration prototype that actually answers the telephone from distances up to one-half mile away from the stationary telephone unit.

The expense of making the telephone, forming the corporation (November 1961), and other miscellaneous expenses are paid for by Marvin and me. With a working prototype of the remote telephone, for the first time we feel we're in business.

Throughout March we conduct meetings for potential investors and begin to get serious investor interest.

Our immediate goal is to get a little money into the company, so that Marvin can justify quitting his job to work for Sibany full time and so that I can start getting paid. That justification occurs in a meeting in White Plains, New York, on a very cold, snowy afternoon.

The five gentlemen attending the meeting can afford the luxury of spicing their lives by investing relatively small amounts of money (by their standards) that will reward them by having something interesting to talk about in the short run and potentially large returns in the long run. They are brought together at the home of one of the potential investors.

The format for the meeting has by then become a routine. Marvin and I stand to the left and right of an artist's easel on which there are twenty or so four-color presentation cards. The artist's drawings and the text serve as a focal point for the attention of our audience and as a reminder of the proper sequence of presentation to Marvin and me. He handles the inventing and engineering part of the presentation, and I handle the business and sales parts.

After the presentation and before the question-and-answer period, we walk with one potential investor to a place several blocks away from the telephone carrying with us the portable remote telephone. The potential investor has previously called his wife and told her to call the telephone number of the telephone attached to the Sibany product. When she calls the telephone number, we hear it ringing several blocks from the regular telephone, and answer the phone by pressing the transmitter of the hand-held unit. Marvin and I talk to the woman to ensure that the volume setting is appropriate and that everything is working okay and then hand it to the potential investor, who then talks to his wife. It is an impressive demonstration.

After the demonstration we answer questions about Sibany and the remote telephone and ask for an indication of interest.

The very last part of this particular meeting is conducted over coffee and cake with the seven of us sitting around the table. One of the gentlemen indicates that he will invest $5,000, and not to be outdone, the other four indicate they will invest similar amounts. A few days later, Marvin gives notice and he and I become paid, full-time employees of Sibany on April 1, 1962. Subsequently, one of the investors actually invests, a second puts us off for over a year, and finally does not invest, and the other three do not invest. Typical, we have since learned.

But many potential investors are impressed after similar demonstrations, and between April 1962 and the following January, Marvin and I have found a dozen other investors to join us in investing about $60,000 in Sibany.

Marvin makes modifications of the prototype at a laboratory we rent in Fair Lawn, New Jersey. Every week we meet twice, once in Westport and once 63 miles away at the Sibany laboratory.

We then invent a "nonradio paging system" for a company which will include it in a bid of a larger system to the New York Stock Exchange. It may enable up to 1,500 people on the floor of the Exchange to get six different messages. It is nonradio to avoid mutual interference. But the company we deal with decides not to bid and nothing has been done with this product to this day.

We next invent what we call a "selective stock ticker," but we do not have the time or the money to do anything about it. In 1968, completely independent of any of the conceptualizing we have done, a similar product is introduced by another company as a personal stock display.

We invent a "remote meter reader" which enables an electric or gas utility company to drive up and down the street, recording a radio signal from each home indicating how much electricity or gas has been consumed since the previous check. Before we have an opportunity to do anything, we find a continuing series of patents issuing regularly to independent inventors using the same approach we have in mind.

In July, through our corporate counsel, we are introduced to a law firm which specializes in new public issues of stock and has "good contacts." They tell us that Sibany would make an excellent public offering if we can make a deal with American Telephone & Telegraph. A truism. The senior partner of the law firm happens to be a good friend of Frederick Koppel, then chairman of AT&T. Through Mr. Koppel we are introduced to the appropriate people at Ma Bell, and after polite conversation are told that we will hear when a decision has been made. Several months go by and in November we are told that a second meeting is in order, including a demonstration.

By this time we have met the chairman of Chromalloy-American Corporation, and have had several meetings under the direction of the president of Chromalloy. We sense that we may be getting close to a licensing agreement with Chromalloy. Because an agreement with Chromalloy is so imporant, we are afraid to believe that it will really happen despite their continuing interest.

There is a second meeting with AT&T. We think we know how the meeting will go, but we are wrong. They make a firm offer of a relatively small amount of money, but at least a commitment. We now have our first independent verification from a source with a huge vested interest that the product may have real value.

First Report to Shareholders

The following excerpts from the first Sibany report to shareholders, dated August 31, 1962, describe concurrent activities of Sibany and spotlight the kind of clutching at straws that venture managers do:

The short—term goals of the company continue to be two—fold. First, to develop and market Sibany's own products. Second, to provide enough working capital to properly develop and exploit the Remote Telephone, and the other products on the project list. The following summarizes activities for the past several months:

· Several relatives and close friends of Miller and Shames have been added to the list of stockholders.

· The firm of Pennie, Edmonds, Morton, Barrows, and Taylor has been retained as patent attorneys. They are the largest and most respected firm in New York.

· Martin N. Leaf has been retained as corporate counsel.

· The firm of Bernard Cooper Advertising, Inc., has been retained.

· Two patent searches on the Remote Telephone have been positive and a patent application has been filed.

· An article in the 1962 Proceedings of the Institute of Radio Engineers, ("Future Developments in Vehicular Communications," Austin Bailey, Fellow, IRE, pp. 1415–1420) discusses the need for portable telephone equipment, and concludes, "It seems quite reasonable to expect that before 1980 all of the functions then required for a two—way mobile telephone can be provided in a unit no larger than one of the paging system receivers." The paging receiver referred to is the "Pagemaster" distributed by the Bogen Presto Division of the Siegler Corp., and apparently also licensed to the telephone company, and they offer it under the name of "Bell—Boy." It is approximately six inches high.

· An article in Look Magazine, 'World's Biggest Business' (Look Magazine, August 28, 1962, pp. 22–40) discusses AT&T at many levels. One point made, important to us, "AT&T officials . . . [say] . . . at some futuristic day, telephones will be freed from cords and fixed locations, and every customer will be able to call any other from a telephone in his pocket."

Soliciting Outside Inventors

In addition to the remote telephone, and the several other product ideas, Sibany solicited outside inventions through advertisements in the classified sections of several local newspapers:

<pre>
Classified Department   June 4, 1962
Paterson "Eagle"
15 Lee Place
Paterson, New Jersey

Gentlemen:

Please insert the following classified advertisement in your
newspaper for the next three weekly Sunday issues:

  PATENTS AND INVENTIONS: The Sibany Corporation bridges the
  gap between the inventor and the user. Holders of patents
  or applications are invited to contact us. Our clients have
  product needs in all fields. P.O. Box 727, Westport, Conn.

Thank you for your consideration.
</pre>

The several dozen responses concerned products of no interest to us, or the inventors were unrealistic in the arrangements they sought. Over the years, this has continued to be the pattern.

The Remote Telephone

By now, the die was cast. Sibany was an inventions company, and at least for the plannable future, not capable of spending its own time or money to make and sell one of its products as an operating company.

This decision was finalized when a licensing agreement of the remote telephone was signed with Chromalloy-American Corporation. Sibany's continuation, at least for a while, was assured.

A story in the *Wall Street Journal* brings into focus the remote telephone as a business, instead of merely as a product development, in the eyes of Chromalloy's management:

Chromalloy Introduces 'Pocketfone', a Phone Extension Minus Cords

Tiny Portable Unit Gets Calls From Regular Phone Receiver Over an FM Radio Frequency

———

By a WALL STREET JOURNAL Staff Reporter NEW YORK—A new cordless pocket phone that permits you to receive and place calls even though you are not near your regular home or office telephone was introduced by Chromalloy Corp.

The tiny "Pocketfone" is in effect a portable extension of the regular telephone. The Pocketfone—smaller than a pack of cigarets—receives an incoming call from the regular telephone receiver over an FM radio frequency. A buzzing sound from the Pocketfone indicates an incoming call. You then press a button on the Pocketfone to receive the call.

By pressing the button, you are automatically lifting a lever off the two contact buttons on the regular telephone, thereby permitting the call to come through. The lever is connected to a Chromalloy-built cradle on which the regular AT&T receiver rests. The lever is lifted automatically by an electronic induction method.

Press Button to Talk

To talk to the other party, you press a button on the Pocketfone. To listen, you release the button. When the call is over, the lever will drop on the contact buttons of the regular telephone.

A call may be originated with the Pocketfone through a private switchboard.

In this case you turn the Pocketfone on, alerting the switchboard operator. Speaking into the Pocketfone, you tell her the number you want dialed. You then receive the call through the cordless Pocketfone unit.

Chromalloy said the range of the unit is up to 25 (sic) miles, but that most users won't require such distances.

The company said the device might be used in offices and factories to replace loudspeaker and pocket-paging devices used to alert persons to incoming calls. In these other devices the person must go to a fixed phone extension to answer the call.

Testing Within Six Months

Joseph Friedman, chairman of Chromalloy, said a production model will be test-marketed within six months. The company may both sell and lease the device. The monthly leasing rate would be "well within the price range of other telephone accessories now offered to subscribers," Mr. Friedman said.

American Telephone and Telegraph Co. said it was shown the Chromalloy equipment about a year ago. AT&T said it had no other comment to make at this time.

Chromalloy makes high temperature metallurgical products for the turbine engine and other industries.[1]

The article also points up another problem of the inventor, licensing a product to a large company. Nowhere is Sibany given credit as the inventor. By this time, the vital importance of credibility to a new-product develop-

1 Reprinted with permission of the *Wall Street Journal* from its publication of Oct. 4, 1963.

ment company has become ingrained in all our activities. We had other products we wanted to license, and from time to time we required new investors, a few thousand dollars at a time.

The Fur-Matching Machine

Another Sibany development in 1963 shows the hand-to-mouth nature of an inventions company. This project was undertaken as a favor for a stockholder who offered to pay all development and production costs. We turned out a fur-matching machine capable of electronically pairing identical pelts of precisely the same color and quality for mink and sable coats, stoles, and other garments. There is virtually no demand for the device in an industry where "expert matchers," many of them owner-operators, will never accept a machine as the equal of their own eyes.

First Institutional Brochure

The inventor and the entrepreneur, Miller and Shames, the only employees of Sibany, were learning to work together, although often there were loud compromises. A hazy idea of how to pursue the inventions business was becoming somewhat clearer. Early in 1964, several new investors for a total of $20,000 were found, the first Sibany institutional brochure was completed, and an engineer and a secretary were added.

The institutional brochure, somewhat näive and certainly presumptuous, was enclosed with direct mail letters, and used as a confirmation to potential customers who were contacted by telephone or in person:

THE SIBANY CORPORATION AND NEW DEVELOPMENTS

THE SIBANY CORPORATION

Most companies acknowledge that they cannot afford to keep on their staff all of the technical people that may be required for their operations. Therefore, the gap between business and specialized technical knowledge grows every day.

The Sibany Corporation (SC) takes its place in this gap between business and the sources of new technical developments. We make available to business concerns the experience and training of highly capable engineers and scientists. We provide a link between the creators and the users.

SOMETHING TO THINK ABOUT!

More than half of the products now being marketed were not in existence 25 years ago. And this trend toward change is accelerating at an increasing rate as every frontier of knowledge is pushed back as never before.

Where does your company stand in developing new products? What diversifications will your company have made ten years from now? To have *any,* you will have to start earlier. Why not now?

NEW PRODUCT POLICY + PEOPLE + MONEY = SUCCESSFUL NEW PRODUCT POLICY!

According to some popular songs all that is necessary for success is wishing. For one thing, the high mortality rate among new products indicates otherwise.

Most companies find that new product development programs combine a well-thought-out policy, the time of qualified people, and money. While the relative importance of these factors may vary, none of them can be avoided.

The SC can advise you in developing your new product policy. We can provide you with patents and ideas for new products, or answers to technical questions from our team of scientists and engineers.

NEW PRODUCT DEVELOPMENT

Useful products and ideas can come from a number of sources, inside or outside your company. But the policy decisions and the responsibility for success in a diversification program must be borne by the management of your company. These decisions are the creation of the people who are intimately aware of the qualifications that make each company unique.

As consultants, we can guide and assist you. We can enable your technical staff to more capably handle a technical situation. Our staff can completely develop a new product when you tell us what is required by your manufacturing and marketing. We can make available new products and ideas from sources of new developments outside of your company.

WHAT ARE THESE OUTSIDE SOURCES OF NEW DEVELOPMENTS?

1. Our highly specialized personnel with the experience and training to handle almost any technical problem that your company may encounter.

2. Our engineers and scientists capable of developing new products for the industry in which your company operates.

3. Products and patents SC develops by our own inspiration.

4. Independent inventors with patents or ideas requiring more time and money.

5. Patents owned by other companies that are available on a cross-licensing or other basis.

6. Patents owned by or developed for the United States government.

7. Research and development by independent and university-sponsored laboratories and other facilities.

WHAT SERVICE CAN THE SC PERFORM FOR YOU?

SC brings together business concerns, the users of new developments and ideas, and the scientists, engineers, and inventors who are the creators of new developments and ideas.

Your company's specific needs dictate the characteristics of the services. Typically, certain forms of assistance have evolved:

For a business concern

Make available the training and experience of highly capable technical people that a company may not be able to afford or whose technical specialties are outside of the normal activities of the company.

Create new products in the field designated by our client.

Provide patents and new products created by independent sources.

For the inventor

Find a commercial market for his patent or product

Provide technical assistance, facilities and money to complete a patent or product.

WHAT IS THE BUSINESS RELATIONSHIP WITH OUR CLIENTS?

A business concern retains us on an annual fee basis. This retainer covers the cost of answering all technical questions and handling routine technical problems. In addition, we provide information to each of our business clients on the patents that independent inventors have given us the right to market. This makes available to you, without any additional expense, a selection of prime patents.

Our company's staff is also available to develop new products for your company and to handle research and development of a more time consuming and complicated nature than routine problems or questions. This fee is based on the scope of work to be performed, or occasionally in developing new products, on a contingent fee basis.

For inventors the Sibany Corporation acts as an agent in marketing their patents. If a pending patent or idea has merit we will work with the inventor in completing the patent process or developing the idea into a workable product.

In licensing or selling a new product or patent we operate on a contingent fee basis. No charge is made for consultations and examinations.

CONCLUSION

The Sibany Corporation seeks profits for its independent inventors, clients, and for itself. These profits are created by establishing a marketplace for the designers and the users of new ideas.

To anyone concerned with new ideas we say that we are ready to serve you. If there is any possibility that we may assist you, we will be pleased to meet with you to discuss your situation.

Direct Mail

Various formats for direct mail have been experimented with. The following letter is an example:

```
Mr. John Doe
Vice President, Corporate Development
Medium or Large Size Company
100 Main Street
U.S.A.

   Subject: Innovate or Die: Innovate and Lose Your Shirt

Dear Mr. Doe:

   Innovate or die: innovate and lose your shirt; a paramount
dilemma of most companies' management. Sibany's New
Business Opportunity program, is designed to help marketing
and manufacturing organizations to resolve this dilemma.

   In our society there are many unarticulated needs. These
needs can best be satisfied by companies whose foresight
enables them to make and sell solutions to these needs.

   Sibany is a management consultant with a different focus.
As an organization that invents and develops new products,
perhaps we can assist you in your efforts to diversify.
```

    If you are interested in learning more about this program,
please contact us for additional information.

Publicity

Reprints of the publicity attendant to Chromalloy's early marketing efforts
were effectively used to increase our credibility with potential clients. Several consulting agreements were signed. Chromalloy's public relations man
agreed to work in exchange for Sibany common stock and out-of-pocket expenses in cash.

By exploiting our accomplishments to the limit, we started producing professionally written literature for what was now beginning to be called the
technology transfer industry. The introduction to the "1964 Annual Report
to Shareholders" was typical:

The Sibany Formula

Sibany set out to deliberately invent and market items not available elsewhere that would have universal and profitable appeal. The first question it
faced: What would people buy, if they could? Next: Why wasn't it available?
Then: Can Sibany make it? From a long list of suggested products (Sibany
has a research file of items already proved technically feasible that would
take at least five years to develop), we have chosen those with the greatest
immediate marketing potential. Some items have been suggested by clients.
Others by our own research section. Our consultant service to industry produces numerous queries: "Can you invent for us . . . ?"

As products have been developed, Sibany has found major manufacturers
eager to license them for continued development and marketing. Presently lacking the substantial funds required to engage in national marketing
itself, Sibany has found this a profitable route. In the future, on selected
items, Sibany shall weigh the possibilities of its own marketing programs. If
you have ever wondered, "Why don't they invent . . . ?" here are some of the
possible reasons:

Large companies frequently do come up with new product ideas for which
they believe there may not be a market sufficiently attractive to justify the investment in continued development. The ideas die aborning. Researchers,
working in committee, often hesitate to offer "breakthrough" suggestions for
fear of being considered "eccentric." The continuous refinement of "last
year's developments" is a more certain, more safe road to advancement.

Inventiveness—creativity—is a rare commodity. Sibany Corporation was
formed in 1961 to wed genuine creativity to the tough management problems of developing new products, creating a market for them, and seeing
them sold profitably.

First Public Offering

With the remote telephone about to go into production, and another product licensed, Sibany's major preoccupation became a "shoe-box size" air conditioner, the early development of which was successful. With several important compromises, a showable prototype was quickly assembled. A license was granted to Grant Pulley and Hardware Corp., West Nyack, New York, for rights to make, use, and sell the product for the cooling of electronic cabinets.

The product, in typical patent language, was described in patent No. 3,397,739, issued to Marvin Miller on August 20, 1968:

Heat exchange apparatus utilizing an expandable heat exchange fluid which apparatus comprises:

(1) a rotatable shaft having a main conduit and a constriction intermediate its ends defining an orifice within said conduit;

(2) means for rotating said shaft;

(3) heat exchangers mounted upon each end of said rotatable shaft;

(4) a flexible conduit mounted upon said shaft;

(5) each said heat exchanger further having a plurality of ring-shaped heat exchange tubes defining circular heat exchange passageways disposed in planes arranged transversely to the axis of rotation of said shaft and in communication at their one end with the interior of said main conduit, and in communication at their other end with said flexible conduit for carrying the fluid in centrifugal forces acting against the flow of fluid in either direction substantially unchanged in value; and

(6) pressure contact means in pressure contact with said flexible conduit for forcing said heat exchange fluid in a continuous path through said flexible conduit upon rotation of said rotatable shaft then through one of said heat exchangers, through said main conduit and the orifice therein, through the other of said heat exchangers and back into said flexible conduit.

It was decided to push the air conditioner by means of an operating company. Sibany Manufacturing Corporation, a subsidiary owned by the parent company, was formed. The air conditioner and several other products were assigned. In order to sell shares to a broader market of investors, a Regulation A public offering was completed and about $160,000 raised for the new company in the summer of 1965. An announcement of the public offering appeared in the *Commercial and Financial Chronicle:*

ISSUES FILED WITH SEC THIS WEEK

Sibany Manufacturing Corp.
June 7, 1965 ("Reg. A") 200,000 common. Price—$1.25. *Business*—Research, development and manufacture of air conditioning units. *Proceeds*—For purchase of equipment, and working capital. *Office*—115 Plaza Road, Fair Lawn, N.J. *Underwriter*—None.

By the end of 1965, development of the air conditioner had slowed considerably. It was apparent that in order to make the compressor function commercially a new breakthrough was required. Making and selling air conditioners would have to wait.

The new public investors had bet on an air-conditioning company. They were still given a run for their money. The new company was continued as an inventions company, the personal identification system (now Identimation Corp.) was assigned to it, and later, Sibany Corporation, still a private company, was merged into the present corporation.

First National Publicity

To this point Sibany had spent about $150,000 of venture capital gambled by several hundred investors. Expenditures were $8,000 per month and income about one third of that. The licensed products required no further investment and were equities for potential future income. Most important, within the company there was a greater confidence in our ability to manage and exploit Sibany inventions, and outside the company, the financial climate for technology companies was getting better. As explained in the next chapter, Sibany had been formed at the tail end of the first major peak in the venture capital industry and was about to participate in the beginning of the second major peak.

Sibany now began to expand. A larger Sibany laboratory was established in Greenwich, Connecticut, with five additional engineers and technicians, and a sales program which resulted in reaching a cash-flow break-even in the final months of 1966.

Instrumental in the kickoff of the sales program was a well-researched article by Steven Shepard in the trade publication *Product Engineering*. The article brought in a flood of inquiries, several of which resulted in licensing and consulting agreements.

New-Product Program

Basic to the expanded sales program was the "new-product program." The terms of a representative agreement (which follows) provide additional insights into the problems and opportunities of both the company interested in new industries and the technology transfer company.

AGREEMENT FOR THE DEVELOPMENT
OF NEW PRODUCTS BY
SIBANY CORPORATION

AGREEMENT, dated this ____ day of ____, 1964, between SIBANY CORPORATION, a Delaware corporation, hereinafter called "SC", having a principal place of business at 6 Neil Lane, Riverside, Connecticut, and _____ a _____ corporation, hereinafter called CLIENT, having its principal place of business at _____.

W I T N E S S E T H:

WHEREAS, SC is a new product development company with research and development facilities, and;

WHEREAS, CLIENT desires to engage SC for new product development and may desire to engage SC in research and development;

IN consideration of the promises, mutual covenants, and agreements hereinafter set forth, the parties covenant and agree as follows:

1. CLIENT agrees to engage SC for a trial period of three months and CLIENT agrees to pay SC at the rate of ____ per month.

If not cancelled at the end of the third month following the execution thereof, this agreement shall be automatically renewed at the same monthly fee and shall continue until sixty (60) days after notice of the intention to terminate is given by one party hereto, by certified mail, to the other party hereto at his last known address. Until other notice is given, the addresses of the parties hereto for the purpose of this agreement are as follows:

    (a) SIBANY CORPORATION
        6 Neil Lane
        Riverside, Connecticut

    (b) CLIENT

2. SC agrees to provide CLIENT with such technical and other recommendations and advise on CLIENT's present line of product(s) as CLIENT may, from time to time, reasonably request.

3. CLIENT recognizes the necessity for disclosing and discussing all information concerning CLIENT's business which is essential to SC's fulfilling the terms of this agreement.

4. During the term of this agreement all new products invented by SC related to the existing business of CLIENT in the following product area _____, shall be disclosed by SC to CLIENT. SC warrants that it shall not knowingly contract with any other companies for new products in the product area described. SC shall determine in its sole discretion whether any such new product developed by SC is to be classified as within the definition and intent of this contract. If this agreement is cancelled by SC, then for a period of 12 months from the date of cancellation of this agreement, CLIENT shall continue to have those rights to products in the product area(s) which are set forth herein.

5. Prior to any licensing agreement, the CLIENT shall at all times have the right to reject any product and to discontinue any research and development program by written notification to SC.

6. (a) Upon the disclosure of a new product development by SC, SC shall immediately furnish all details pertaining thereto to CLIENT. CLIENT shall have a reasonable period of time, but not more than 60 days from said disclosure to accept the product. For the purpose of this agreement, acceptance is defined as a written research and development contract and/or licensing agreement.

(b) Research and development shall be jointly agreed upon based upon the respective abilities of CLIENT and SC, with all costs of research and development borne by CLIENT, whether such work is done at SC's facilities, the CLIENT's facilities, or at the facilities of a third party.

Furthermore, if the research and development on said new product is to be performed by a third party, a licensing agreement shall be executed within 60 days following the acceptance of the new product by CLIENT.

(c) The terms of any licensing agreement shall be mutually agreed upon, except that the parties hereto agree that:

Pertaining to any licensing agreements concluded between SC and CLIENT:

(1) CLIENT shall have the exclusive domestic rights on all proprietary products, to make, use, and sell the product;

(2) CLIENT shall obtain the exclusive foreign rights to make, use, and sell the new product or improvement in any foreign country in which CLIENT pays for patent applications and processing;

(3) On all non-proprietary products CLIENT shall receive the exclusive international rights to said product;

(4) SC shall receive a royalty not to exceed (5%) five percent of the total net sales on products;

(5) SC shall receive a royalty not to exceed (3%) three percent of the total net sales on non-patentable products.

7. On any product which CLIENT rejects, discontinues, or abandons, during the period covered by a written research and development contract, SC shall have the right to negotiate in good faith, an agreement with any third party relating to said new product. If SC is successful in arriving at terms of a licensing agreement or other business arrangement with a third party, CLIENT shall have the right to enter into an agreement with SC containing equivalent terms as with said third party. If CLIENT does not enter into an agreement within fifteen (15) days after notification, all rights, title and interest in and to said new product shall revert to SC and SC shall have the right to enter into any agreement with any third party relating to said new product.

8. Except as otherwise provided herein, the parties agree that neither will at any time during the term of this agreement or afterwards disclose, divulge or reveal either directly or indirectly to any person, firm or corporation any confidential information relating to the business of either party, its methods, processes, techniques and equipment that may have heretofore or hereafter been revealed to either party or as acquired by reason of this agreement. The parties agree and covenant that upon the termination of this agreement and except as herein provided to the contrary, neither will directly or indirectly, either on its own account or as an employee or consultant for any other person, firm or corporation, practice or make use of any of the confidential processes, techniques, trade secrets, confidential information or other secret matter or documents of either party.

9. SC and CLIENT shall use or cause to be used in connection with any and all activities in connection with this agreement only employees or other personnel who are obligated by contract not to disclose to others confidential information, as defined in Section 8, and to assign directly or indirectly to SC or CLIENT all inventions made by them in the course of their employment.

10. This agreement embodies the entire understanding between the parties and may not be changed or terminated orally and no change, termination or attempted waiver of any of the provisions shall be binding unless in writing and signed by the party against whom the same is sought to be enforced.

11. This agreement shall be governed by the laws of the state of New York and shall be deemed to have been made and executed therein.

12. It is agreed by and between the parties hereto in the event that any controversy arises between the parties with respect to the duties or obligations of any of the parties hereto or with respect to the making of this agreement or any provision thereof, said controversy shall be submitted to the Supreme Court of the state of New York, county of New York, for determination pursuant to the New York Simplified Procedure for Court Determination of Disputes, as provided for by CPLR 3031 et. seq.

IN WITNESS WHEREOF, the parties hereto have signed their hands and seals the day and year first above written.

SIBANY CORPORATION

Attest:

by: _____

Attest:

_____

by: _____

_____

Analysis of an Inventions Company

By 1967, Sibany had proved that it could develop products to form the basis of a new venture by Sibany's clients. Important agreements and product development contracts had been concluded with major United States companies. The organization was known to a handful of important companies and over 500 shareholders.

But there were important problems. High-technology product developments moved forward at a snail's pace. After they were licensed to companies seeking to diversify, the rate of progress did not increase. Income from licensing agreements were still meager. Expenditures, even at the rate of $250,000 per year were not nearly enough to either move enough products out of inventory or for Sibany to exploit them.

An excerpt from a story in *Business Week* presents a balanced picture of neither success nor failure, but rather the experience of so many technology-oriented companies: *survival*.

NEW PRODUCTS
Inventions for hire,
but not for sale

Tiny Sibany Mfg. Corp. dreams up a product, starts developing it, and then licenses it to someone else to manufacture and sell. The goal: a continuing income

Stock sale. Sibany has managed to survive in the risky, competitive world of new products—despite its low income and profits—mainly on its licensing and development fees and stock sales, including a recently ended sale of 53,500 shares of common stock at $3.25 per share. Moreover, the company has demonstrated a knack for getting others to pay for developing its ideas. In its short life, Sibany has spent only $300,000 of its own money, while encouraging others to spend more than $2-million on products invented by Sibany—money that doesn't show on Sibany's balance sheet.

What Sibany does is to start evolving a product, and somewhere along the development road license it to another company for manufacture. It thus keeps ownership of the product, deriving continuing income from it; this continuing royalty approach is what distinguishes Sibany from other new product consultants.

First to finish. Right now, the company expects its method to pay off on seven or eight products that will be reaching the market in one to five years. The first of the Sibany inventions to complete the long trek from laboratory to marketplace—and the one that launched the company in 1961—is about to go into full-scale production at Chromalloy-American Corp. It's a cordless telephone accessory, trademarked Pocket Fone, that enables a person to talk and listen over his desk phone, though he may be as much as a half mile away from it.

Chromalloy licensed Pocket Fone in 1963, and has been test marketing it about a year. Sibany will collect a royalty on each unit leased.

Another customer. Sibany has also licensed two products to Fairchild Hiller Corp. One, an air conditioner, now being developed by Fairchild's Stratos Div., is smaller than conventional units and can be packaged in various shapes. A possible application: automobile air conditioning.

The other product is an electronic airport sign to display arriving and departing flights. Sibany has licensed it to Fairchild's Electronic Div. The sign, which has no moving parts and thus should be relatively free of maintenance problems, was suggested by Rodney King, director of marketing equipment research and development for American Airlines. As a potential customer, American has been paying for part of Sibany's development of the sign.

American Airlines recently gave Sibany purchase orders for research studies on five other new products, including automatic baggage sorters and weighing scales. Says King: "Sibany is the finest inventive group I've bumped into in a long time."

'**Not just kooks.**' That inventing group was started in 1961 by William Shames, formerly sales vice-president for CCI Corp., an Oklahoma construction equipment company, and Marvin Miller, who had been a development engineer for Reaction Motors. Their goal was a business-oriented inventing company that would ferret out a commercial need and try to meet it. Miller would be the idea man, Shames the salesman. "We wanted products that would establish us as sound businessmen, not just some kooky inventors," says Shames.

The Pocket Fone, invented by Miller, met this criterion. It was easy to demonstrate and had a mass market potential. Shames and Miller raised money from friends and relatives, and built a working model in a few months. Prototype in hand, they marched right to American Telephone & Telegraph Co.

"At first it didn't work," Shames recalls, "but Marvin tinkered with it and fixed a loose connection." Finally, AT&T was impressed enough to invite them back, and then offered $3,000 to $5,000 for a year's study. Shames and Miller rejected that deal.

In rapid succession, Pocket Fone was turned down by General Telephone, ITT, IBM, and Motorola. At last, Shames and Miller signed a development contract with Chromalloy—rescuing not only Pocket Fone but also the embryonic Sibany.

Finding clients

With Pocket Fone on its way, Sibany turned its attention to other products and other companies. Progress was slow, partly because money was tight and because companies were reluctant to deal with a small, unknown outfit. "We kept running into the 'NIH syndrome'—not invented here," says Shames. "Companies didn't even want to listen to our ideas, fearing that they might be in areas they were working themselves. We had to establish our credibility—and credibility is still our most important product."

Today, Sibany is still very dependent on the efforts of Miller and Shames, both of whom are 36. Miller's younger brother, Robert, recently (sic) joined the company as an inventor-engineer, and a handful of technicians have been brought in to test the ideas as fast as the Millers grind them out.

Shotgun approach. Sibany began searching for clients by what Miller calls the "shotgun approach. We sent letters to 300 companies, and when we got a 10% response we knew we were in business."

One of the replies provided plenty of grist for the Millers. It came from IRC, Inc., a $49-million maker of electronic components, and is a good example of how Sibany's new product client program works. As Shames tells it:

"We made a company profile on IRC. What did they want to get into? What was their manufacturing capability? How much did they want to spend on new products? Then we proposed nine new product areas. IRC was interested in four, and asked for a proposal on one—an information retrieval system that can randomly pick out voice-stored data. IRC then issued a purchase order for one feasibility prototype."

How the scene looked from IRC's side of the fence is told by Felix Troilo, manager of product planning: "We were looking for new products, but found it hard to identify what people needed without their coming to ask for it. We thought Sibany could provide that service. After all, the cost wasn't so great; it was worth a try."

When Sibany completes the prototype, IRC will decide whether to complete the pre-production development itself, let Sibany do it, or, of course, drop the whole thing.

Synthesis. Troilo characterizes Sibany's collective inventiveness as a "flair for ideas based on existing technology. They don't invent new technologies." Chromalloy's Robert Coe feels the same way: "Marvin Miller is good at putting together existing technologies from various areas. He doesn't make break-throughs in the state of the art."

Once an idea has been found worthy and a patent applied for, Sibany clamps down the security lid. Because of the lag of roughly three years between the initial application for a patent and the final issuing, Sibany can protect its ideas without revealing how they work. The company has even installed a buzzer to alert lab technicians when a stranger enters the office.

Not all of Sibany's ideas have worked, of course, let alone paid off. Thus the air conditioner licensed to Fairchild has run into serious design problems. "The basic idea is good," says Fairchild's R.C. Iwans, "but we need efficient components to realize its potential."

Feeling secure. After 5½ years, Shames feels that Sibany is safely out of the woods. "One mistake won't kill us," he says, "as it might have a couple of years ago." Shames and Miller have poured back all of Sibany's meager earnings into the company; neither they nor the other 390 stockholders have realized a return. Shames thinks this year will mark the turning point.

If it does, Sibany hopes to move on to another goal this year: having its stock traded publicly. "Our ultimate goal," says Shames, "is to have a fixed number of companies to serve—sort of inventing on order."[2]

Even before the *Business Week* story, it became clear that like many other companies, we had not known what our business was. Yes, we were an inventions company, but what was our goal? What would we be doing in five

2. Excerpted from "Inventions for Hire, But Not for Sale," *Business Week*, March 25, 1967. Reprinted by special permission of the copyright holder, McGraw-Hill, Inc.

years? What was the rationale of the company? How could we get beyond the narrowness of technology orientation and attract managers and marketers?

For five years we had been on a treadmill. Without analyzing what a product meant to us, or could mean, we spent money to develop it, and sought to license it to a diversifying company. Most critically, our time and talents were directed not by corporate goals, but instead by the chance and circumstance of the companies that chose us.

At the end of 1967, Sibany went into the venture management business. Each product development became a new business venture. Management and marketing voids in Sibany could better be identified because there was now a more complete picture and missing pieces were more obvious.

Two basic corporate goals were identified:

1. Inventing to provide current income.
2. Creating new business ventures in the form of equities that, hopefully, would increase in value for Sibany shareholders.

The real assets of the company became clear for the first time; the inventory of product developments in various stages of development; budgeted amounts of cash, assigned to the exploitation of certain assets; a business format that would be attractive to potential employees and venture capitalists; five years of success and failure, resulting in know-how and—in a high-mortality industry—credibility; a publicly owned, and after the *Business Week* article, publicly traded, stock that could be used to raise money or acquire assets.

In 1968 and 1969, five companies were started, financed by a public offering of $300,000 and a private offering of $2.5 million. Two of them are today operating companies, Identimation Corporation and Metrodyne Corporation. In addition, minority investments were made in two other companies.

In 1968, Sibany acquired for common stock the patents and rights to certain air-flow inventions. Any income received from the commercialization of this technology is to be divided: 70 percent to Sibany and 30 percent to the seller.

The terms and conditions of a second joint effort with a large consumer products company are explained in a letter agreement between Sibany and the company whom we shall call Consumer Products, Inc.:

```
Sibany Manufacturing Corporation
6 Neil Lane
Riverside, Conn. 96878

Gentlemen:

  We are pleased to confirm the details of the Agreement
between SIBANY and CONSUMER PRODUCTS, INC., under which you
```

will cooperate and consult with this division in the fields
of consumer communications devices, toys and games, and
personal appliances, looking towards the commercialization
of these products worldwide. All consumer products, ideas,
concepts and developments in the fields of these products will
be exclusively developed by the parties to this Agreement
according to the terms set forth below. For convenience sake,
we are numbering the following paragraphs. Consumer
Products will be referred to as CPI and the above enumerated
fields will be collectively referred to as PRODUCTS.

(1) It is understood that you will from time to time meet
with representatives of CPI to discuss your various
existing inventions in PRODUCTS, to discuss possible
changes and modifications of these PRODUCTS on the basis of
current marketing needs, and to discuss your
developments of new inventions in PRODUCTS which may fill
existing needs in the market place. Out of these
meetings may come research and development programs which
you may undertake on behalf of CPI and for which you
will quote to CPI a fee to conduct such research and
development on a time and material basis, and for which
CPI will pay you one half of such amount. It is
understood that CPI shall not be obligated to pay any
research and development and related expenses unless such
expenses are approved in writing by CPI in advance.
Provided however, should you have PRODUCTS already in
varying stages of development at the time of the signing
of this agreement and CPI decides to utilize the same, CPI
shall pay you one half of the development costs of said
PRODUCTS already incurred by you.

(2) It is understood that if any PRODUCTS developed
by you pursuant to this agreement are or become protected
by a patent or patents issued in your name or owned by you,
you shall assign all right, title, and interest in and to
said patent or patents, and patent applications, to CPI.
All preliminary searching, to determine whether any
PRODUCTS developed by you are patentable or infringe any
existing patent or patents, shall be conducted by¯CPI at
its expense and the results of such searches shall be
made available to SIBANY at its request. In the event that
it is determined that the PRODUCTS are or may be
patentable, CPI shall, after consulting with you, select
outside Patent Counsel to prosecute the same, the costs
thereof to be borne equally between us.

(3) Notwithstanding the foregoing, if after a period
of eighteen (18) months from the completion of the
prototype(s), as hereinafter defined, or any such
PRODUCTS which are protected by a patent or patents as
set forth in Paragraph 2, neither CPI nor any of the

divisions or subsidiaries of CPI, introduces said
PRODUCTS to the market or informs you in writing that it
intends to do the same, said patent or patents, or patent
applications shall be re-assigned to you.

(4) In the event that your research and development
activities result in the development of PRODUCTS which CPI
in its sole discretion, feels has a market potential,
CPI shall proceed to manufacture or to have manufactured
a prototype(s), the cost of which shall be borne equally
between us. If your company has facilities to
manufacture PRODUCTS and you desire to manufacture the
prototype(s) thereof, CPI agrees that you will have the
right to quote on the manufacture of said prototype(s)
and CPI will give consideration to your quotations along
with those of other manufacturers, but CPI shall have
the sole right to decide whether to have such items
manufactured by you or by a third party, based on sound
commercial principles. The term prototype(s) as used in
this agreement shall be construed to mean a feasibility
and demonstration prototype(s); that is, one that is
suitable for testing and for determining costs of
building the final design model.

(5) In the event CPI eventually markets said PRODUCTS,
it shall be free to choose any marketing method it deems
feasible based on sound commercial practices. The
following are the basic methods envisioned by CPI for
marketing PRODUCTS, and your payment shall be according
to the following formulas, which are based upon these
presently envisioned marketing methods:

(a) CPI may license third parties to make, use, and
sell products and in that event you and CPI shall share
equally in any royalties received.

(b) CPI may license other divisions or subsidiaries
of CPI to make, use and sell PRODUCTS and in that event
CPI shall pay you a royalty of $2\frac{1}{2}$ percent on the net
sales price of such PRODUCTS.

(c) CPI may market products by a general offer to
the public and in that event CPI shall pay you a royalty of
$2\frac{1}{2}$ percent on its net sales price of said PRODUCTS.

(d) CPI may contract with a third party to market
PRODUCTS for the account of CPI on a commission basis, or
CPI may assign all right, title and interest in and to
said PRODUCTS, and trademark rights and patents covering
PRODUCTS to a third party for a lump sum payment, but in
either such event you and CPI shall share equally in the
net proceeds received.

(e) Payment to you based upon any method of marketing not specifically enumerated above shall be made after good faith negotiations between us, and on substantially the same terms and conditions as the foregoing.

Provided, however, that payment for PRODUCTS protected by, or which may become protected by a patent or patents shall cease upon the expiration of said patent or patents. Payment for unpatented PRODUCTS shall cease fifteen years after the date of introduction to the market.

(6) Net sales price, as used in the foregoing paragraph, shall be the CPI (or other CPI subsidiaries and divisions as the case may be) invoice price for such PRODUCTS, less promotional allowances, cash discounts, taxes, and credits on returned goods.

(7) In the event that payment for PRODUCTS is to be made from countries outside the United States and its possessions, said payments shall, if possible, be made to you in the currency of the United States of America. However, if remission is possible and conversion not, we will pay foreign payments to you in the United States but in the currency of the countries in which the sales of the PRODUCTS shall have taken place. If both remission and conversion are restricted, we will deposit such payments in the currency of the foreign countries in a bank account in said countries in your name. Any income, transfer, remittance, stamp or similar tax due or payable on or in connection with payments to you hereunder and paid or withheld by us together with any fees or expenses incurred in connection with such payments or the remission thereof shall be for your account. In the event that we shall convert the currency of any country into United States currency in computing and making payment hereunder, the exchange rate shall be the commercial rate of exchange prevailing in New York City, New York, at the close of business on the last day of the period in which the sales of PRODUCTS upon which said payments are based were made.

(8) It is understood that you may develop certain ideas, inventions, designs, products, and patents which do not arise out of your cooperation with CPI under this agreement and which are not in the field of PRODUCTS. With respect to these ideas, inventions, designs, products, and patents, you may offer them to CPI or third parties as you deem desirable and subject to negotiation. Nothing herein is intended to keep you from exploiting such items to third parties. It is only the specific PRODUCTS on

which you quote and perform research and development
for the account of CPI which are intended to be covered by
this agreement.

(9) It is understood that your company has or may
eventually have facilities to manufacture PRODUCTS and
it may be your desire to manufacture and supply said
PRODUCTS for sale by CPI or other divisions and
subsidiaries of CPI. In that event, CPI agrees to
consider your quote therefore on the same terms and
conditions as provided in paragraph 4 hereof concerning
the manufacture of prototype(s).

(10) The initial term of this agreement shall be for
six months from the date hereof, but shall be terminable
by either party at any time during this initial term by
notice in writing given at least thirty days prior to the
date upon which termination is sought. In the absence of
termination during the first year, this agreement shall
continue from year to year, but shall be terminable by
either party at any time by notice in writing given at
least thirty days prior to the date upon which termination
is sought.

(11) Termination of this agreement shall not affect
PRODUCTS introduced to the market prior to termination
and you shall continue to receive payment therefor as
provided in Paragraph 5. However, in the event of
termination, CPI shall have the right, but not the
obligation, to continue or have you continue the work on
PRODUCTS underway prior to termination, including
research and development activities, prototypes and final
design work, and PRODUCTS marketing, all on the same
terms and conditions as provided in this agreement. In
the event that CPI chooses not to continue with any
particular PRODUCTS activity after termination, we
shall pay you, pro rata, our contributory share of the
expenses incurred by you for such work as of the date of
notice of termination.

(12) We both agree that during the term of this
agreement we will not voluntarily reveal to any person,
firm or corporation any confidential information
disclosed by each of us to the other, except by mutual
agreement or unless and until such confidential
information shall become a matter of public information
through the act of SIBANY, CPI, or any third party, as
the case may be. We both further agree that we will not
voluntarily, without each other's prior written consent,
reveal to any person, firm or corporation the knowledge

that we have entered into this agreement, or reveal the nature or contents hereof, or use this relationship for advertising or promotional activity.

(13) This agreement shall not be assignable by either of us without the prior written consent of the other.

(14) All notices shall be in writing and shall be deemed to have been given after delivery or mailed, first-class postage pre-paid to, as the case may be:

       (a) Consumer Products, Inc., 600 E. 57th Street, New York, New York 10022

       (b) Sibany Manufacturing Corporation, 6 Neil Lane, Riverside, Connecticut 06878

(15) This agreement shall be construed and the rights and duties of the parties determined in accordance with the laws of the State of New York.

(16) This agreement shall not be modified except by a written instrument signed by both parties or their duly authorized agents.

If the above complies with your understanding of our agreement, would you kindly so indicate by signing and returning the enclosed copy of this letter. The date of your acceptance shall be deemed the date of this agreement.

                     Very truly yours,

                     CONSUMER PRODUCTS, INC.

            By   *|s| John Doe* _____

                     John Doe
                     President

AGREED TO THIS_____
DAY OF

SIBANY MANUFACTURING CORPORATION

By _____
William H. Shames
President

Inventions for Current Income

A successful Sibany would generate enough cash income from inventions to at least cover all cash expenditures in a particular year and concurrently create a number of new venture equities whose value, as they matured, would be Sibany's net profit.

In terms of cash income, Sibany, as an inventions company, came closest to this definition of success in 1966, realizing about $2 for every $3 spent and breaking even in the fourth quarter.

New Business Venture Equities

In the 5½ years ending in 1967, Sibany invested an average of $100,000 per year in product developments. In the next three years, an average of $1 million per year was invested in creating new business ventures. Subsequently, Identimation and Metrodyne sought their own corporate financing. Only the future will determine whether ten times more value was added by the higher investments.

During those three years, from 1968 through 1970, Sibany evolved into the business of managing and investing in new business ventures. Several dozen inventors, entrepreneurs (as well as inventors and entrepreneurs in training), and other employees of Sibany and Sibany companies and their respective families have taken the risk of betting on Sibany. They have been joined by several dozen customers and suppliers, and almost 2,000 shareholders.

The largest group, almost 2,000 individuals and institutions, have risked their venture capital. A few have made hundreds of thousands—and many more have made tens of thousands—of dollars in profits that have been taken. Others have lost some, or the overwhelming portion of their investment. Until new ventures are managed better, such variations in success and failure are in the nature of the venture management industry, as will be discussed in the next chapter.

Chapter 4

Venture Capital: Investment in New Companies

"It's easy enough to find out whether a new machine will work," says a partner in a Wall Street brokerage firm. The tough part is judging whether a business can be made of it. Many venture capital people believe that if you have a great product like Xerography, anybody can make it a success. That hasn't been my firm's experience. And I suspect that investors often judge the product or technology instead of the people because it lends itself to objective analysis and is therefore easier to do."

This partner is a member of the institutional part of the financial community which invests in new companies or existing companies that want to expand. People like him are also known as "sophisticated investors." They function in a new industry dealing with "ventury capital" which is attempting to learn how to finance the accelerating technology explosion of the 20th century. They invest their own money and they manage the investment of other people's money.

The venture capital industry reached its first important peak during the years 1958 to 1962. For the first time investments that increased in value many times were available to more than a handful of people. American Research and Development Corp. became a well-known company in the financial community. Open-end and closed-end mutual funds were started, devoted to investment in private companies and to buying "private stock"[1]

1. Securities acquired in a transaction not involving a public offering.

in companies already owned by the public. Many eloquent and business-oriented engineers, chemists, or physicists could raise enough venture capital to start a business without too much difficulty. The predominant types of new companies invested in were technology-oriented and were run by only one manager. The setting was quite unlike that where the 19th-century individual was both entrepreneur and inventor.

This cycle of venture capital investing ended abruptly with the bear market of the first half of 1962. Although New York Stock Exchange company stocks were starting a new bull market in the second half of 1962, the venture capital industry continued to be wary of start-up companies through 1966. This is apparently a classical pattern in that the stock exchanges lead the type of stocks bet on by investors, both up and down.

The second peak of the venture capital business was the period from 1966 through 1968. The pattern of investment in technology-oriented companies continued. Thousands of entrepreneur-oriented and inventor-oriented companies were able to raise hundreds of thousands or millions of dollars to start a new company or to expand an existing company.

This second peak of venture capital investment showed an important difference from its predecessor. Having been burnt often by the entrepreneur-inventor as a single individual, venture capitalists were now betting to a greater extent on "teams." A degree from the Harvard Business School was now as important as a degree from M.I.T. or C.I.T. Having a degree in both fields was even better.

To many venture capital groups, the business plan (see Chapter 5) was as important as the résumé. And the group *seeking* venture capital had to be as erudite on the topic of gross profit as on Newton's laws of motion. Having seen physicists or engineers who had clever new products but who could not "put it all together" into a profitable company, the venture capital people were more sophisticated in the judgments they made. Losing large sums in the high percentage of new-company mortality, the venture capitalists had developed more sophisticated means of picking winners and making more educated gambles. Adequate appraisals, the heart of the venture capital business, became the focus of venture capital organizations.

Many venture capitalists began to realize their own lack of understanding of the business and human dynamics of the technical and nontechnical innovation process in a business. A major factor in this lack of understanding is the perversion of the role of the specialist in our society. We erroneously take it for granted that only the specialist can understand how the machine being offered will accept white paint and pour out red paint, and that only the specialist can improve a telephone or argue a point of law. On the other hand, *everyone* is considered an expert on marriage, interpersonal relationships, and raising children. Similarly, some people assume that *everyone* can run a company and supervise people because all of us have had experience in dealing with people. Not so! A good top manager is worth several worth-while services or markets.

However, there was greater recognition of the specialty nature of organization and management during the second peak than during the first peak of venture capital investment. And it seems to have positively effected the results. Venture capitalists that went through both periods seem to believe that their investments did better in this second round of venture capital financing. On the other hand, the second round of financing brought so many new venture capital people into the field—including many large companies—that the overall success ratio, dollar for dollar, measured as return on investment, may not have been very different after all. At a guess, several times more venture capital was available from 1966 to 1968 than earlier in the decade.

There will be a third major peak of venture capital investment. Before discussing its likelihood and the changes that may be expected, let us first briefly look at the components of a venture capital transaction and the sources of venture capital.

The Components of a Venture Capital Transaction

Stripped to its bare essentials, a new venture consists of people, *plus* a product or service, *plus* money and time. The "people" in a new company are usually a combination of entrepreneurs and inventors. They create the new product or service, plan the new company (Chapter 5), concretize the plan (Chapter 6), and shake down the new company as required (Chapter 7).

The entrepreneur invents business ideas, and the inventor invents technical ideas. The inventor conceives of an idea and the entrepreneur translates the idea into the economy by innovating. Both are idealists concerned with *what can be* instead of *what is*. You don't have to give them much, except the possibility of future tangible and intangible rewards, and they are motivated.

The hundred years before the Second World War was the age of the inventor-entrepreneur. In most cases, one man had to be *both* during that period. He had to know how to convert his invention into a business. If he failed to manage well, he lost his company. Thomas Edison, despite his tremendous desire to be an entrepreneur and run his own company, had to settle for being the most prolific inventor of all time.

Since the Second World War, and to some extent because of it, there has been a great increase in the rate of technological advancement. No single individual, group, company, or even government can stay on top of the rapid changes. These changes have created the need for and the existence of a new type of entrepreneur: the organizer and manager of large numbers of people and things. To a great extent, the inventor is now allowed to specialize. Today's Horatio Alger is the venturesome manager who takes over millions of dollars of assets and turns them around into a profitable, growing company, saving the old company from a loss—or the entrepreneur or inventor who is smart enough to start a Xerox Corporation.

The investor and manager of venture capital is consciously taking a great deal of risk in the expectation of a much-higher-than-average return on the investment. Two "almost maxims" of the venture capital industry are almost universally accepted. The first is that the higher the technology of a successful start-up company, the higher the return on investment. The second is that the earlier the investment is made, in a new company, the greater the risk and, accordingly, the greater the return on investment should be. Thus, it may be deduced that the risk investment of the first investors in a high-technology company is the highest and their return on investment will be very high if the company succeeds.

One complication: How do you judge success along the way? While I was president of Sibany Manufacturing Corporation, I saw the problem of judging illustrated in an interesting and dramatical manner. According to an article on Sibany in the *London Sunday Times* of June 30, 1968:

> An infant "inventions company" has among its products a supposedly foolproof "personal identification system." With the stock recently selling at $26, the company's market value is more than $20 million. 1967 results were: sales about $100,000; net loss $26,000. The story is this could be the super technology stock of the future.

Before that item appeared, small individual investors in Sibany (as a private company) had paid 33 cents a share in 1962 and 67 cents a share in 1963 and 1964. In 1965, at a public offering price of $1.25 per share, and in 1966 at $3.25 per share, hundreds of individual investors made the decision to invest between a few hundred dollars and $10,000. Until the spring of 1967, and after the *Business Week* story, there was no "over-the-counter market" for the trading of Sibany stock, because there was little or no demand to buy or sell. From spring of 1967 to spring of 1968, the bid price of Sibany stock fluctuated greatly, in a gradual upward trend, so that Sibany's third public offering in January 1968, was at a price of $9.75 per share.

After the story appeared in the *London Times*, the bid price of Sibany stock reached a peak on November 22, 1968, at a price of $48.50. During this 1968 run-up, "sophisticated investors" made the decision to invest in Sibany for the first time. At a time when the bid price of Sibany stock was around

$30, seven institutional investors invested $2.5 million in the company at a discounted price of approximately one third, or $20 per share, because they were buying "private or letter stock." However, many small and relatively unsophisticated investors, as well as a few institutional investors, all watched the price of Sibany stock fall to a price of $1 per share in 1973.

Hundreds of individual investment decisions were made after late 1968, by both small and large investors, and there did not seem to be a pattern (except to sell). Some sold out all their investment in Sibany, and others did not sell a single share. Others sold a small or large portion of their shares of Sibany but remained investors.

In retrospect, more people should have made the investment decision to sell, and should have made it earlier; but if more people had sold earlier, there would have been an entirely different pattern of prices of Sibany's stock. On what basis did people make the decision to hold, sell, or partially sell? The price of Sibany, like the prices of so many other stocks traded in the over-the-counter market, tended to be more extreme on both the up and down side than the Dow Jones Average.

How does one judge the inherent value of a venture management company? Solely on the basis of sales and earnings, Sibany has performed poorly. On the other hand, those deciding to invest in the company were betting on the potential and the concept of the company. It seems fair to say that, at least in technology companies, the general investment climate was more of a consideration than the objective facts that were available.

Increasingly, these investment decisions are not made by the owner of the money to be invested, but rather by a "money manager." He calls himself by many names, depending on the nature of his business; but when *he* can decide whether or not to invest in the start-up or small company, *he* is the manager of venture capital.

He is *almost always* bright, intuitive, relatively young, an absentee manager of someone else's money, willing to bet on his judgment, experienced, eloquent, and very up to date on the theory and implementation of the latest techniques of the best business schools.

He is *almost always not* experienced in how an operating company works, a detail man, experienced in managing more than a few people, and consistent, from day to day, in explaining what will be required to make a deal with him. He will always want to see a business plan before the first or second meeting.

It is only in the last few decades that money management has become a profession. Commercial banks always have put up money only when there is safe collateral. Investment banking was invented to meet the needs of new companies which could not provide collateral when they needed capital. Investment banking is so new that the children and grandchildren of the founders and innovaters of the industry are presently managing the investment banking firms.[2] The management of venture capital is a riskier version of investment banking.

It is the business of the venture capital manager to invest funds in speculative companies in the expectation of a much-better-than-average return on an investment. He is in no way doing a company a favor when he decides to invest in it.

So here is the prizefight ring of venture capital: In one corner, the entrepreneur-inventor, and in the other, the manager of venture capital. The referee is the process used by the venture capitalist in judging whom to bet on and whom not to bet on. Venture capital continues to struggle to find a scientific way of judging which deal is most likely to succeed despite the thousands of investments that have already been made. As this chapter has indicated, the manager of venture capital is getting better in making these investment judgments, but in the final analysis, he makes an intuitive and *ad hoc* judgment.

There are many considerations for the venture capital manager when making a venture capital judgment. The entrepreneur and the inventor, struggling to prove that they, among many others, are winners, have to cope with each of these considerations. Most are obvious. However', a few less generally known deserve attention.

What Is Your Business?

Maybe such an obvious question deserves an obvious answer. "My business is carrying people from one place to another for the cost of a ticket." "My business is building carriages, to be pulled by a horse, to carry people from one place to another." "My business is making steel." "My business is making automobiles." In most cases the answer is not so obvious. If the answer were really obvious, Studebaker would not, alone of 3,000 manufacturers of carriages and buggies, have gone into the automobile business. The New York Central would own Eastern Airlines. Polaroid would be a division of Eastman Kodak. IBM would be a division of RCA, General Electric, or Westinghouse.

The business of a company is making a maximum rate of return on investment for its shareholders, including appropriate risk taking and changing with the times. American Research and Development Corp., a leading and the first publicly held venture capital firm, says its business is, "To help out-

2. For a readable and informal history of the invention and early growth of investment banking, see Stephen Birmingham, *Our Crowd* (New York: Harper & Row, Publishers, 1967).

standing individuals build companies of stature and to create capital appreciation for the owners of these businesses and for the ARD stockholders."

Falling in Love with Your Product

You have struggled in your garage to make the damn thing work. You have hocked your life insurance policies and sold your soul to get your cousins and neighbors to invest a few thousand dollars. At last you get the damn thing to work and you are demonstrating it to a venture capital firm. Regardless of your feelings, your product is only a means to an end in what is totally a business transaction. Your baby is of no consequence unless it becomes a successful operating company. The manager of venture capital must be coldly calculating and must pay no attention to his possible personal admiration of you in making his judgment on whether or not to bet on you.

The High Cost of Reaching the Market

The total time and cost of getting the product to the marketplace are staggering, as compared with the time and cost spent on invention and engineering. In most cases, to the new entrepreneur (and sometimes to the manager of venture capital), the time and cost involved seem almost unbelievable. The cost may even be unfair, when you consider the entrepreneur's difficulty in gaining even the few dollars it took to get him to the point of facing the venture capital firm.

Figure 4-1 depicts the typical use of proceeds by the entrepreneur and the inventor when he is successful in raising venture capital and later in creating a new business.

How Much of the Company?

All new ventures and expanding companies get into serious trouble. As salesmen in a different context used to say, "It goes with the territory." On those days, or during those weeks and months when the sky in every direction looks either black or dark gray, the entrepreneur often wonders if he will have the strength to continue. Will he panic and leave, or will he panic

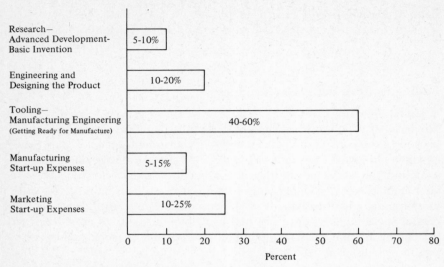

Figure 4-1   Typical Distribution of Costs in Successful Product Innovations.

SOURCE: "Technological Innovation: Its Environment and Management," U.S. Department of Commerce, January, 1967, p. 9.

and stay? Will the venture capital firm be there to help or will they have forgotten his name?

The entrepreneur and inventor are unrealistically high in their estimation of what their new company is worth. The manager of venture capital is unrealistic about what his money is worth. In a successful venture capital investment, both sides end up a little unhappy because of having to give up more than they expected. Most venture capital firms will back away from an investment where they get either too much or too little. If they get too little, it is not worth their while to make a risky investment. If they get too much, they believe that the entrepreneur and inventor do not believe in their company enough and are therefore less likely to succeed, or they are demotivated, with too small a stake. Most venture capital firms are sophisticated enough to leave the principals of the new company with an incentive large enough to motivate them to work harder. Often the supplier of capital will want to structure the investment in such a manner that he can step in and have an effective voice when the business is going badly. All entrepreneurs who believe in their new company resist this possible encroachment. A happy medium is usually reached on a good-faith basis rather than in the structuring of the investment.

Lack of Knowledge

As the new venture capital industry ages and grows, there is an increasing trend toward educating the person and group seeking venture capital. Since institutional investors are more identifiable and better organized, they have taken the lead in this educational process. An outline of the seminar given by AMR International, Inc., in the spring of 1970, is a good example of this work:

"AMR presents an in-depth two-day seminar designed to help new and growing companies understand the opportunities, advantages, and intricacies involved in raising 'start-up' or expansion capital."

The seminar outline is an excellent example of the areas of concern for the entrepreneur and the ones in which the manager of venture capital has already become experienced:

I.   Critical Considerations for Companies Securing Venture Capital
   A. Why and when to secure venture capital
   B. Raising the proper amount of capital
   C. What do venture capitalists expect with respect to return on their investment
   D. Alternative methods of securing start-up capital
   E. Pitfalls in going the venture capital route

II. Going Private vs. Going Public—Which Route Is Better?
   A. The public offering as a possible alternative
   B. When you raise money publicly
   C. Private money as an interim step
   D. Dilution going private vs. dilution going public
   E. Cost of a private placement as second step financing if private vs. if public
   F. Requirements to going public as a "start-up"
   G. What you can and cannot do with letter stock

III. Sources of Venture Capital
   A. Venture capitalists—corporations and individuals
   B. Financial institutions—insurance companies, mutual funds, investment trusts
   C. Investment bankers
   D. Small business investment corporations
   E. Private syndicates

IV. How Venture Capitalists Seek Investments
   A. What industries they like
   B. What industries they avoid
   C. What they are looking for with respect to management experience
   D. How they explore opportunities

Early in the game, the entrepreneur and the inventor learn that little will happen to their dream without money. What are the sources of venture capital? While there are numerous ways to catalog this information, let us divide these sources into four categories: the individual investor, the small business investment company, the large operating company, and the institutional investor.

The Individual Investor

Scratch the average man and you'll find a would-be investor, dreaming of making a major killing with a small investment. Clearly, the odds against such an outcome are enormous. On the other side of the equation are experiences, repeated so that they loom large, that tell the dreamer what he wants to hear. For example, American Research and Development Corp. started with an original investment of $3.5 million and in twenty-five years appreciated that sum to $400 million. Can a small individual investor do likewise, starting, of course, with a smaller base? A few have! But the vast majority have failed.

The small investor, possessor of discretionary funds, (i.e., cash not needed for living essentials) is often a would-be investor. His greatest risk and opportunity is to invest in an embryonic concern that later can go public.

The small investor normally buys a part of these companies by buying stock in the company in a new issue. A "new issue" is a first public offering of stock registered with the Securities and Exchange Commission, by a company that was previously privately owned. The company "goes public" in order to obtain a new source of capital: investment by a portion of the 30 million shareholders of public companies. Raising capital by public means,

3. Quoted with the permission of AMR International, 1370 Avenue of the Americas, New York, New York 10019.

for an embryonic company, is normally only possible when the stock market is in a bullish trend.

The most dangerous time to invest, but also the best for potential gains, is the first private or public offering of a firm's stock. To learn of these offerings, the investor should arrange to receive from registered representatives, or other involved parties, the so-called red herrings, or prospectuses of companies that are seeking venture capital. Careful reading (and somewhat discouraging reading, since optimistic assumptions are not permitted by the SEC) may lead to a choice of one or more of these fledglings. investment of nominal amounts of discretionary income, perhaps 100 shares each time, and making at least ten, or more advantageously twenty, such investments, might provide the small investor-speculator with any of the three following results:

1. Wiped out: Each and every investment turns to ashes, and no cash is available from sales of wallpaper stock.
2. Typical losses and gains, but an overall effect somewhere around zero with a few large gainers offsetting large losers and small gainers offsetting small losers. The probability is that the total investment will still be worth less than the original investment.
3. Rare but possible: One or more of the investments turns out to be successful and the price appreciation in the successful stock more than offsets the losses in the other stocks.

The investor, besides having discretionary funds of which he may lose 100 percent, also must have patience. Since investing in this type of company for a short term usually will result in a greater quantity of losses, the speculative investor should make the decision only if he is willing to wait several years to see his decisions vindicated.

Such stock should be sold only when selling half of it can result in the recovery of the initial investment (including all investments made at the same time), or when the inflated price of the stock seems to be the result of hysteria, or when one suspects the company will not succeed in its endeavors. As soon as the stock has increased in price by several times over the original offering, the investor should be looking for reasons to sell. One of the best mechanical ways (if it is allowed) to sell a "hot stock" is to use stop-loss orders, placing a stop-loss at a price 10 percent under the price at which he feels he should sell, but doesn't want to because he fears the price will continue increasing. One should never lower the stop-loss order when the price of the stock begins to fall. The only time a stop-loss order should be changed is when the price of the stock moves up and so far away from the stop-loss order that it should be increased to protect the additional gain.

Of course, with this practice, you will not be the one small investor that invested early in IBM, held on to his small investment through thick and thin, and is now worth umpty-ump thousands of dollars. You might, however, become a successful speculator who has lots of fun investing in interesting opportunities, who learns to judge prospectuses with a professional eye, and whose investments when viewed on a total basis are successful.

After the investment has been made, you should establish immediate contact with the company and ask to be placed on its mailing list. You should ask questions when you want to by telephone or letter, because in this way an informed investor obtains a sense of the progress of the company and whether or not he should hold on to his stock. A small struggling company is happy when its investors are interested enough to want a personal view of what is going on. For the most part you will receive considerate and courteous attention; your questions will be answered, and you will have an opportunity to get to know about your investments more intimately. In what often seems a cold, impersonal world, you will probably have a warm and personal relationship with the people in your favorite small company.

As there are more than 100,000 individuals in the United States with a net worth of $1 million or more, such individual investors are a prime source of income in venture capital. And almost all of us have been asked at one time or another to invest a few thousand dollars in a new grocery store or to back a neighbor's invention.

Many of the larger investors have systematized the choices for their investment portfolio by using their own professional organization to learn and judge investment opportunities.

Small Business Investment Companies

In the United States since the Second World War, a rapidly expanding source of funds for companies has been federally financed loans. Starting in 1958, when Congress passed the Small Business Investment Act, and continuing into the early 1960s, this trend reached a peak carried along by two basic factors: the increased power of the federal government in general, and the recognition of the leverage of venture capital for new ventures, in creating jobs.

The leverage of venture capital is not confined to return on investment in a successful company. It also creates jobs. One estimate is that an investment of about $20,000 can create a job in the average company. According to a survey by the Sloan School of the Massachusetts Institute of Technology (Table 4-1), about $1,525 of venture capital creates a new job. The difference is accounted for by the more rapid growth of the embryonic companies in a shorter period of time.

TABLE 4-1   **Venture Capital Dollars per Job: An Illustration**

Number of companies	21
Average time period	4.2 years
Increase in sales—average	$3,567,000
Increase in sales—total	$76,806,000
Increase in employment—average	147
Increase in employment—total	3,096
Initial venture capital—average	$225,000
Initial venture capital—total	$4,720,000
Initial venture capital requirement	$1,525 per job

NOTE: This table does not take into account the additional, derivative employment resulting from these primary jobs.

SOURCE: *Technological Innovation: Its Environment and Management*, U.S. Department of Commerce, January 1967, p. 44; and Sloan School, Massachusetts Institute of Technology, Cambridge.

Small business investment companies (SBICs) are licensed by the Small Business Administration and are privately organized and managed. Investment decisions are entirely at their own discretion.

In general, for a company to qualify for an SBIC loan, it must have fewer than 500 employees and less than $250,000 of net earnings for each of the previous two years.

SBICs were very popular in the early 1960s, but more recently they have become a much less significant factor in venture capital financing. These companies borrow money, generally $5 for each $1 of cash they have available for loans to other companies, from the Small Business Administration of the United States Government. The smaller SBICs have essentially aimed to make a return on their investment by the interest charged on the loans to new companies. Larger SBICs have been heavily involved in the venture capital business. With a handful of exceptions, they have done very poorly. The SBICs, as a class, have notably been reluctant to invest in technologically oriented businesses because of the extra difficulties of analyzing them. Less than 10 percent of the $1 billion invested by all SBICs have been put in this area.

Large Companies

Some large companies have established new venture management groups, separate from their operating businesses, in order to get a view of technologies that they are not already involved with,[4] and to create a portfolio.

4. General Electric is an interesting exception. The company indicates that its purposes are to create new vendors and potential acquisitions—not to build a portfolio.

They are also interested in creating an environment in which the entrepreneur and creative individual is less stifled and more encouraged to use his natural talents.

Three formats for venture management are used by large companies, and there is a tendency for them to start with the least formal organization and, by reason of less-than-expected results, evolve to the more formal organization. *The task force*, being the least formal, is the one that usually is first tried because it is the easiest. Gaining limited success, the large company then either drops the venture management program altogether or evolves to the *venture management department* which has its own budget and operates on a continuing basis. Again, depending on success or lack of success, the venture management department is then either dropped or turned into a separate *venture management company* which, experience has shown, has to be separately managed (with distinctly separate decision-making) from the basic operation of the large company.

According to a survey of thirty-six large United States industrial companies, by Towers, Perrin, Forster & Crosby, the steps involved in the venture process are generally the same for almost all of the companies. They are: idea search, idea screening, idea investigation, venture development, venture commercialization, and disposition of the venture.

An increasing number of large companies have set up new venture and venture management groups. General Electric, Alcoa, Boise Cascade, Coca-Cola, General Mills, International Paper, Mobil Oil, Travelers Insurance, Singer, U.S. Steel, Dow Chemical, 3M Company, and Exxon all have been very active.

A corporate development executive at General Foods quips, "A business of less than $25 million a year gets rounded out of our financial figures at the end of the year." DuPont has made a number of investments in industries which they do not expect to enter within the next ten years.

As a source of venture capital funds, the large company is increasingly a more vigorous factor. An article in the *Wall Street Journal* tells the story:

Venturing Out
Corporate Giants Now
Providing Some Capital
For Risky New Business

———

GE, Others Seek Technology
Rather Than a Fast Buck;
Rejections by the Hundreds

———

Where's a Xerox of Future?

———

By Richard Martin
Staff Reporter of The Wall Street Journal

NEW YORK—In his tiny office tucked high in a corner of the aging General Electric Co. building, T. Walton Storm spends a lot of time listening to the hopes and dreams of complete strangers.

He gets about 10 phone calls a day from people he has never heard of asking for half a million dollars or so to get themselves started on the road to riches. "I try to talk to them all," says the grandfatherly GE executive. "I almost always turn them down, but I'd hate to think I missed the next Xerox just because I didn't pick up a phone."

Mr. Storm is GE's resident venture capitalist. He bankrolls enterprising young scientists and engineers who are trying to start brand new businesses of their own. It's a new specialty for GE—and for dozens of other big industrial companies, including Standard Oil of New Jersey, Dow Chemical, Singer, American Can, Cabot Corp., Hercules and Emerson Electric.

Most traditional venture capitalists—mostly wealthy individuals, brokerage firms, insurance companies and investment bankers—are in the risky business of providing entrepreneurial seed money because they hope to at least quadruple their money about every five years. But the opportunity for big investment gains isn't what is bringing the corporate newcomers into the field.

On the Ground Floor

"In most cases the big corporations getting into this cannot possibly make enough money on their ventures to make any impact on their corporate earnings," points out Stanley M. Rubel, whose Chicago firm publishes a newsletter on the industry and directories of venture capital sources. "They're doing it as external research and development work, to get in on the ground floor of new technoligies."

General Electric's wholly owned subsidiary, Business Development Services Inc., set up at the end of 1968, is probably the biggest and most active of all the new corporate venture groups. BDSI has 25% to 45% interest in each of a dozen little companies and, since 1969, has invested about $7 million of the $25 million GE has set aside to carry it through 1973.

"We're looking for growth areas related to GE's business, and this encompasses a very large spectrum," says Mr. Storm, who is BDSI's president. So far, the spectrum includes artificial kidneys and other human organs, reactors for manufacturing integrated circuits and semiconductors, plastic extrusions and coatings, analytical instrumentation systems, three-dimensional electronic drafting devices and a speech synthesizer that would enable computers to talk.

"We hope to help develop some of these small companies to a point where they'll become desirable acquisitions for GE," says Mr. Storm. "If we can get about three new department-sized businesses out of every 10 ventures it will be very helpful to GE's long term growth. Those that don't fit, we expect to sell off and make money on."

Many Examined, Few Chosen

It's a tough, time-consuming selection process. BDSI has looked at more than 500 possibilities in the past three years to find its dozen ventures. Four men pick the ones to invest in. Mr. Storm, a 60-year-old computer expert, ex-banker and ex-Wall Street venture capitalist, has been at GE 15 years and formerly managed the company's $2 billion pension-fund portfolio. His two vice presidents, Ralph T. Linsalata, 33, and Robert T. Foley, 35, were formerly with private venture capital firms; both are electrical engineers with MBA degrees and operating experience in both marketing and finance. BDSI's treasurer, Stuart A. Fisher, 29, is on loan from GE's own corporate finance staff.

The selection process usually starts with a letter or phone call to one of them from an entrepreneur, a venture-capital finder or a GE man who knows somebody with a bright idea but no money to bring it into the market place.

The first step is to get a written proposal from the entrepreneur detailing his plans, financial data and backgrounds of his key men in 20 pages or so. "We eliminate most of the proposals because we don't like the technology or the market, or because the guys lack operating experience," says Mr. Foley.

When one looks good, the entrepreneur is invited to bring in a five-year plan, and at least two BDSI men spend anywhere from two hours to all day grilling him about it. "We're looking for the long-term potential fit with GE, something that can grow into a $100 million business in 10 years," says Mr. Linsalata. "But mostly we're looking at the guy himself. When a venture deal goes sour, it's almost always because of the people running it rather than the product."

Calling In the Experts

Only about one out of 10 proposals gets beyond that first grilling. Most of those that do are weeded out by an on-the-spot look at the fledgling company by BDSI men accompanied by GE technicians. "There's probably somebody in GE who has technical expertise in any area we might see," explains Mr. Foley. "Calling on them for expert assessments takes a lot of the risk out."

The BDSI and GE men look into everything from engineering drawings and manufacturing operations to bookkeeping entries for business lunches. They check competitors and talk to customers, if the little company has any. In a deal currently under consideration, one customer, a GE operating unit, provided a detailed evaluation of the company's product, comparing it to those of competitors.

The whole process usually takes two to four months. "We think it's unfair to keep a guy hanging eight months to a year as some firms like to do," says Mr. Foley. "But we do think it's fair to ask him to define certain near-term goals and then watch him closely over a period of two or three months to see how he accomplishes those goals."

Not all prospective ventures weeded out by BDSI fall by the wayside, however. "Our focus is at least five years down the road, but when we see something that might make a contribution to GE profits today or next year, we tell an operating department about it," says Mr. Storm. One GE unit sent BDSI a proposal from a scientist developing an automobile engine that BDSI says is "significantly different from anything in use." BDSI passed the proposal on to another GE unit that, unknown to the first group, was working on a similar project. The second group has since entered into a joint venture with the scientist.

Once a company is in BDSI's fold, there's practically no limit to the help it can get. "GE isn't about to give away any of the secrets locked up in its own research labs, of course, but they have a wealth of other information that's ours for the asking," says Michael McNeilly, president of Applied Materials Technology Inc., funded by BDSI in 1969. The Santa Clara, Calif., company "worked very closely with GE's lamp division to significantly improve our product," a reactor used in the manufacture of transistors and integrated circuits, he says. "As a result, we got a better product and they got a significant new customer," he adds, since the improved reactor uses GE's high-intensity infra-red lamps.

"GE has also given us very good recommendations on international financing and marketing," adds Mr. McNeilly. "By telling us certain procedures to follow and showing us pitfalls to avoid, they've saved us a lot of time and money overseas."

Mr. Foley of BDSI frequently attends talks to securities analysts by competitors of BDSI ventures, then sends his notes on to the venture's president. He similarly mines trade shows and Wall Street sources for information worth passing along. "We give them a lot of publicly available competitive data that wouldn't be easily available to them," he says.

He and Mr. Linsalata recently helped one growing venture recruit three key marketing, manufacturing and finance executives. They are asked for advice on everything from sales strategy to inventory levels, and when they don't have answers they can usually find a GE man who does.

Such help "is the prime reason entrepreneurs go to GE or some other big company for venture capital in the first place," says Fred Cook, a venture specialist at the New York consulting firm of Towers, Perrin, Forster & Crosby. "They can get things they couldn't get from Wall Street or the banks —management skills, marketing skills, financial controls and access to top scientists in some of the world's best research and development laboratories."

Great Industries of the Future

Mr. Cook believes corporate venture capital efforts "are bound to increase in the future. For a relatively modest investment, ventures can open some pretty important windows on new technologies."

"It's very difficult for anyone to predict what the great new industries of the future are going to be," says H. E. McBrayer, president of Standard Oil of New Jersey's venture subsidiary, Jersey Enterprises Inc. "But we do know that Jersey Standard wants to be in those new industries, whatever they are. So our mission is to get into new and different activities outside our normal oil and gas focus.

Jersey Enterprises got started early in 1970 and has made investments ranging from $250,000 to $500,000 in four startpup companies: one making computer memory systems, one working on a speech system for computers, one developing new types of rechargable batteries and one using a new process to manufacture fine wire.

American Can Co.'s ventures similarly aim at keeping the company "on the leading edge of change," says Herbert R. Brinberg, the vice president who heads a venture group formed in January 1971. American Can's ventures include fledgling companies in such varied fields as consumer research, specialty chemicals and information storage and retrieval systems.

Some companies venture only into enterprises tied closely to their own specialties. Emerson Electric, which set up its venture subsidiary in mid-1970, has a start-up company making integrated circuitry and semiconductors and another trying to produce low-cost modular concrete homes for which Emerson would provide complete electrical systems.

Removed From Mainstream

But most corporate venture capitalists are getting into areas further removed from the parent company's main business. Dow Chemical has ventures in medical X-ray and diagnostic equipment and an Alaskan housing venture. Singer's ventures include a fast-growing health-food company and a massive industrial real estate project on the Texas Gulf Coast. Hercules ventures do biomedical research, make weapons detectors for airlines and provide solid waste recycling and sewerage treatment systems. NL Industries (formerly National Lead) has a venture that turns squeezed citrus rinds into animal feed and pectin for jelly makers.

Industry observers count more than 20 companies that have set up special staffs to make venture deals and scores of others—including Eastman Kodak, Ford Motor and Monsanto—that handle occasional deals on a more informal basis. Ford, for instance, has put money into two ventures developing a steam engine and air bag restraints.

General Electric's Mr. Storm says over a dozen big companies have contacted him recently to ask how GE does venture deals. TRW Inc., the Cleveland-based conglomerate, "has been looking at the field for some time, but we're still formulating objectives and strategies," says a company spokesman. RCA Corp., McGraw-Edison and Nabisco are also looking into it.

Most companies are reticent about their venture activities—in part because most of them have been in the business less than three years and it typically takes five to seven years before they can be sure a venture will succeed.

"Some of the deals are bound to go belly up, and they naturally worry about what stockholders will think," says James Uffelman, president of Technimetrics Inc., a New York firm that publishes directories and does research on the venture capital field. "I've never seen a company's venture activities mentioned in an annual report," he adds. "Many times the corporate switchboard won't even know the guys doing the deals. They operate as special assistants to the chairman or president, or brew up a little subsidiary nobody's ever heard of."

"It's going to be 1975 before anyone can say for sure whether BDSI is an outstanding success or a failure," says GE's Mr. Storm, "even though it looks like it'll be the former, based on the success to date of a couple of ours."

But three of GE's ventures have gone wrong. One, in which GE had a $300,000 stake, is out of business. "We've got nothing to show for that one," says Mr. Storm. "We have a couple of others that have serious problems and may not make it; we've decided not to put any more money into one of those already. But they're all risky, and we can't be sure yet what's going to happen to any of them, so we haven't talked much about them."

One company that has already had second thoughts about ventures is Scott Paper, which has put about $1 million into three companies making burglar alarms, educational audio-visual products and modular housing. Scott's venture specialist is no longer with the company. "We're refocusing our attention on things that are less peripheral," says a spokesman. Some insurance companies are also eliminating their venture capital staffs and are putting money into pools managed by outsiders, notes Leroy Sinclair, a partner at Technimetrics.

Really a Lot of Work

"Venture deals are really a lot of work," explains Mr. Sinclair. "You've got to get in there and go to meetings and fire people. You have to provide lots of management assistance and watch things closely." He says one company hastily backed out of a venture deal when it learned the entrepreneur had used the company's initial check to make a down-payment on a business jet.

Some companies also worry about what they would do if they set up a venture group and their own employes came around asking for money to go into business for themselves. Soon after its formation, BDSI spurned one such group, reasoning that it didn't want to finance the exit of GE employes. Since then, however, GE has formed a special technical ventures group within its research and development department to help find outside venture capital for GE scientists who are determined to strike out on their own. GE's theory is that some of those who leave the fold will build successful businesses that they might someday want to merge into GE.

The problem of compensating the men running a corporate venture group is another reason some companies that would like to get into ventures are still hanging back. "It creates serious problems," says Albert J. Kelley, dean of the Boston College school of management, which runs seminars, makes studies and publishes directories on venture capital sources.

"You can't expect the guys who are helping these entrepreneurs become multimillionaires to stay happy on corporate salaries and fringe benefits," he says. "But if you give them a piece of the action so they have an opportunity to make millions, too, you create all kinds of unhappiness throughout the rest of the corporation's executive ranks."

Like GE, most of the companies doing venture deals currently prohibit employes from investing in them. But most of the companies are also considering changing their existing compensation plans for the venture groups—either by providing long-term incentive bonuses tied to the success of the ventures themselves, or by making their venture groups partly owned subsidiaries in which employes would own stock.

At least a couple of companies are also toying with the idea of letting top executives throughout the corporation put money into the venture group's pool of investment capital and share in its profits later, using a successful venture group to provide an added fillip to the company's executive compensation program.[5]

The Institutional Investor

By far the largest source of venture capital is the institutional investor: investment bankers and underwriters; closed-end and open-end investment companies; publicly owned venture capital companies; investment and hedge funds; and foundations and pension and other trusts.

The phenomenon of thousands of institutional investors is relatively new. For example, American Research and Development Corp. is the first publicly owned venture capital investment company in the United States, and this company is only twenty-five years old. It was the first company of its kind listed on the New York Stock Exchange.

The traditional source of venture capital is the investment banker or stock brokerage firm. He will raise capital for the new company by private or public offerings. Often he manages an investment for a group of institutional investors. He finds an investment opportunity, decides on the quality of the investment, and then invites several other institutional investors to bet on the new company with him. The risk is shared and he brings into the new company other sophisticated investors who may be able to help and profit from the embryonic company.

An advantage the investment banker has over other institutional investors is that often he can create a public market for the shares purchased by the investment banker's customers. Some investment bankers will support or actively assist the price of the new company's stock, making it higher than the public offering price so that the customers that they put into the stock have an opportunity to "bail out."

The Third Major Peak

It can be safely stated that there will be a third major peak of venture capital investments and that it will be significantly different from the crests of 1958–1962 and 1966–1968.

No doubt some of the older venture capitalists are gone for good, either because they were washed away or because they have left the water. Others

5. *Wall Street Journal*, Feb. 1, 1972, p. 1. Reprinted with permission.

have gradually come back. Some have been in the swim all along and will remain.

One long-time stalwart, Diebold Venture Capital Corporation, defined its role succinctly in one of its annual reports: "The essence of venture capital is to concentrate on fundamental factors that will have appreciation potential, and these fundamental factors simply do not disappear because of a period of economic turbulence." Diebold then went on to point out that in its opinion more attractive situations are available during down cycles of venture capitalism, when other sources are no longer available. The venture capitalist then is "in a position to pick and choose very much more selectively" and "can also obtain very much more advantageous terms for the investments" he makes.

These steadfast comments on continuity were asserted despite the fact that Diebold invested only $4.3 million in 1970, as compared with $9.2 million in 1969, in twelve new ventures as compared with thirty-two. Also, Diebold's net asset value per share decreased to $10.74 in 1970 from $17.60 in 1969.

Why are we convinced there will be a third crest of venture capital investment? Those that have participated in the search for new technologies, new products and services, those who have grown wealthy in the quest, and even those who have not, have known an exhilaration that is hard to match. It may be the closest a male human being can come to having a baby.

The environment for venture capitalism is propitious. Our economy is growing rapidly, and the need for new technologies is developing even faster. Between 1945 and 1965 successful companies, among them Polaroid, 3M, IBM, Xerox, and Texas Instruments, enjoyed an average annual sales growth increase of almost 17 percent, while the average annual growth of the gross national product was only 2.5 percent.

The growth of television, jet travel, and the digital computer, to mention only three industries that did not exist before the Second World War, have not only benefited our society, they affected the quality of our lives tremendously. The tangible and intangible rewards of the venture capitalist, entrepreneurs, and inventors who made it possible, have been commensurate.

Having been bitten by the technology-oriented venture capital bug, such areas of the United States as almost all of California, Route 128 in Massachusetts, Rochester, New York, Montgomery County, Maryland, and Fairfield County, Connecticut, are unlikely to be satisfied making only mundane investments for too long a period of time.

But as surely as a third venture wave is predictable, it is certain that it will be characterized by different standards and patterns of organization.

A partner in a large venture capital firm explains rather bitterly, "The next time I do a private deal I will keep control of the company. The investors in the deal, including my own firm, will in effect be betting on me, and I will be betting on individual companies with whom I will stay very close, demand tight budgetary controls, and hire and fire when necessary."

Adds the co-manager of a hedge fund:

> If I had not made 22 start-up investments, so that I was able to look at how 22 different groups of managements coped with the start-up of a new company, I would not have believed how long it takes for things to happen. This is the one aspect of my business that has been most difficult for me to learn to understand and incorporate into my judgment.

A manager of the venture capital segment of a large insurance company comments:

> All of our investments have gone bad in the sense that we have either lost a very high percentage of the value of the price we paid for the stock, or we have had to step in and reorganize the company ourselves. Our best investments, even though the stock price has gone down considerably since 1968, are in those few companies which were able to reorganize and redirect themselves.

Says the manager of venture capital in a large commercial bank:

> Most people underestimate the amount of time and money it will take to accomplish their goals. In making new deals I plan to stay close to the company and make sure they have available at least twice as much money as they think they need and as I think they need at the time I make the investment.

These professional managers of venture capital are thus critical of themselves. By not being close enough to company managements and not asking management to be responsible to them to the necessary extent, they and the companies have underestimated the time and money that would be required. Rather more realistically, they now expect that the managements they bet on will be able to get out of trouble, instead of expecting to avoid trouble. Money managers are likely to be more involved with their investments during the third wave.

The common denominator may well be the greater intimacy between the source and the user of venture capital. Large companies utilizing the technique of venture management to set up a completely separate organization with its own management reporting directly to the president are bound to become more significant in the next round. The high cost of their own product development adds to the attractiveness of venture capital investment for the large company. In addition, from profits as well as from their existing shareholders and new shareholders, these large companies have access to large amounts of money. They also have top managements that understand operating company problems. The only adjustment they have to make is in implementing the operating standards of the large companies in terms of the problems of the small enterprise. Companies such as 3M are already operating in this manner with increasing success; the new venture remains in its cocoon and does not become an operating division for five or ten years.

Small business investment companies and other venture capital seekers of funds from the government are less likely to be able to adjust to a greater intimacy. The attitudes and needs of persons choosing government service and the security of loan guarantees appear to be too far removed from those required in the venture capital business.

Investment bankers are capable of making the change but are not likely to. The problem seems to be that investment bankers do not attract employees that want to concentrate on the nitty-gritty details required to be intimately involved with a new start-up company. During bad times they intellectualize about the changes in attitudes that will be made. They are not likely to actually make the changes.

Because they start from the smallest base, in terms of venture capital availability, small operating companies devoted exclusively to venture capital management are likely to have the greatest growth during the third round. The success of ARD, Diebold, and others is an attractive magnet.

New approaches to attracting and keeping the top management of new companies will be theorized, shaken down, and perfected by these operating companies. American Science Associates, founded by Milton Schwartz, a successful starter of new companies and including in its management Carl W. Stursberg, Jr., formerly president of Beechnut, Inc., is another good example of this operating company philosophy.

American Science is managed by operating people who are paid a fee by individuals and other groups seeking new venture opportunities. The process of investigating the investment opportunity is handled by American Science, and any positive decisions to invest include an investment by American Science. The venture capital investors that the firm represents have the option of participating or not, per investment, except that they have to make a minimum amount of investment per year to continue participating.

A third operating approach is presently being organized by a prominent hedge fund. They have taken the position that venture capital groups have the problem of not wanting to be intimately involved in the operations of a company in which they have invested; the venture capitalist does not want to get tough. Their plan is to represent venture capital groups who will pay them a small annual fee to handle the job of staying involved with the embryonic company.

All these new approaches to venture capital financing have dual implications:

1. They require detailed planning of what the new company's management expects to do. Detailed reporting, month by month, is expected to show what actually has been done. Also looked for is comparison between the plan and the accomplishment, close to the time of the event.
2. They seek to ensure that the individuals in top management are experienced and have been tested as much as possible.

Appraisal of a Potential New Investment

Institutional investors are continuing to develop a high degree of sophistication in their appraisal technique. The classical (and perhaps, in venture capital, unattainable) definition of an investment is:

> Before anyone invests in anything, he should learn as much as he can about where his money is going and what he hopes to gain from it. He should always use facts, not just hunches, as his reasons for selecting a certain investment. He should study not only that particular investment, but also other investment opportunities for his money.[6]

That, of course, is the name of the game. We have stated that the final judgment of whom to bet on and whom to turn down is subjective and intuitive. But like other risky judgments, our economy allows the return on investment to compensate for the risk. Also, recognition of the tenuous nature of the judgments is the first step toward their betterment. Finally, better communication and more information—experience, as it is called—will lead to better intuitive and subjective judgments.

More effective entrepreneurs and inventors may yet change the world to make it a better place to live. Better venture capitalists may yet figure out on whom to bet. All three have to continue to learn how to work with each other and invest in each other. The next three chapters concern themselves with the planning, implementation, and shakedown of the new company—the common ground of the venture capitalist, inventor, and entrepreneur.

6. *World Book Encyclopedia*, vol. X (Chicago: Field Enterprise Education Corp.), 1965 ed.

Chapter 5

Business Plans: A New Venture on Paper

Paul Smith walks into the office of a partner in a Wall Street investment banking firm. He is seeking funds for his company. After three hours of conversation, he and the banker shake hands on an arrangement that within several weeks will provide $1 million of funding for Smith's company in return for a percentage of the common stock to go to the banker and a group of investors. During the conversation the banker asks Smith for a business plan, a description on paper that will communicate the past, present, and future of the company as Smith sees them. The deal is partly contingent on this description.

Increasingly the term "business plan" is being used to describe the background and to forecast the prospects of a projected new firm or a new suborganization of a larger corporate structure.

Business plans are developed in a number of standard situations to promote the investment of money by persons less familiar with the company or project than the promoters themselves. For example:

- The plant superintendent of the manufacturing division of a company submits a request for a budget approval to expand his facilities by 30 percent over the next twelve months. He attaches a promotional document which he may call a business plan, a business analysis, or background for the capital budget request.

- The vice-president of corporate development submits a report to the president suggesting the acquisition of a company he and the staff have been investigating. The staff consists of a financially oriented accountant, an economist, a long-range planner and an administrator.
- A three-year-old company puts together a brochure to help convince an underwriter to do a public offering.

Business plans have become as prevalent on the business scene as architects' sketches in the world of the prospective homeowner; and just as there are a dozen sketches drawn up for every home built, there are more business plans than executions.

Yet, there is good reason for the popularity of the business plan. Many conditions of our economy create a need for the business plan as a means of promoting, qualifying, and communicating: the rapid growth of mergers and acquisitions; the increase in specialization making communication between the specialist technologist and the generalist business manager more difficult; the vast growth and acceleration of technology, increasing the number of new ventures; the ease in starting a new company; the establishment of a new financial activity by which individuals, venture capital companies, operating companies with venture capital divisions, small business investment companies, and venture capital departments within investment banking firms all invest funds in a new enterprise; and finally, and perhaps most important, the mass media which have served almost as a public relations arm for each of these elements in emphasizing, mostly, the successful ventures such as that of H. Ross Perot of Texas, who has made a billion dollars in the electronics field. Such success is a message of hope to every garage inventor and entrepreneur.

Too Much of a Good Thing?

Despite the obvious needs filled by business plans, the fact is that they have been distributed on the work scene as freely and as unselectively as handbills passed out by a political candidate. And they have frequently become an end in themselves.

The fault is that both sides demand too much from the business plan. Many venture capital companies will not talk to the management of a new company without its first submitting a business plan for evaluation. Presumably, Thomas Edison and Alexander Graham Bell might have been turned down by such a firm before they had even had a first meeting. On the other hand, the head of an electronics company division estimated that he would have had to triple his staff just to read the business plans received from his own departments.

The president of one company, needing investors' money desperately, nevertheless started to walk out of a meeting because he was requested to submit a business plan. In this case, he felt that the value of the business plan had been distorted and he did not want it to be the pivotal factor in the investment decision.

Despite these exaggerations, the business plan, along with people-judging and outright guessing, has become a valuable aid in investment decision making. It forces the group putting together the plan to think through all the parts and considerations involved in their business, usually for the first time, and always for the first time in detail.

They have to create a company on paper. They have to make a myriad of decisions, at least tentatively, concerning the structure of relationships of the four fundamentals: people, functions, time and money. They have to force themselves to put on paper specifically what they have in mind.

As an experiment in such communication, get the cooperation of some other individial—a subordinate, friend, lawyer, or architect—and then after asking his opinion on a given subject (which he is likely to give you in the form of free-flowing ideas off the top of his head), ask him to confirm what he has told you in writing. He probably will either refuse or ask for a week or two to tell you in writing what he really thinks.

For the investor, the business plan provides a detailed explanation of the experience, attitudes, and intentions of the group inviting investment. In many ways, it also provides a measure of the group's ability to succeed in chosen objectives:

- Was the competition section sufficiently detailed and realistic?
- Did the organization chart indicate a proper understanding of span of control, line and staff functions, the proper balance between business and technically oriented people?
- And how about fine organizational points, such as an appreciation of the role of purchasing and inventory control for a product with low labor-cost content?

On seeing a market survey and business plan, holding several personal meetings, and researching the background of those involved and their new product, the experienced investor or money manager should be able to make an informed judgment concerning the likelihood of the success of a new venture.

As technology companies and venture capital analyses proliferate, the entrepreneur is finding better ways to advance his interest. Refinement of the business plan, of course, is a major tool in achieving such ends.

What Should Be Included?

Robert R. Kley, head of his own consulting firm in the venture-planning field in Ann Arbor, Michigan, assembled a twenty-four item checklist which provides an excellent framework for a business plan (used here by permission of the author):

1. Provide a one-page summary of the venture idea.
2. Describe the key problem areas (risk factors) and objectives.
3. Provide an in-depth market analysis.
4. List the names of six close competitor firms and briefly analyze their strengths and weaknesses.
5. List the anticipated selling price for each product and comparison prices.
6. Provide a list of potential customers who have expressed an interest.
7. Provide a one-page summary of the functional specifications of each product.
8. Show the physical forms of the products with photographic prototypes if possible or art renderings.
9. Provide a profile of key patents.
10. List and categorize the chief technologies and skills required to develop and manufacture the products.
11. Describe the alternative channels of distribution.
12. Describe the basis for determining if your products will be leased or sold.
13. Describe the type and geographical distribution of the anticipated field service organization.
14. Tell how you can modularize your product line with interchangeable subassemblies.
15. Show cost volume curves for each module with breakdown for material, labor and factory burden.
16. Describe the manufacturing process involved with block diagram illustrations.
17. Describe the types and quantities of capital equipment needed.
18. Present a flow-event-logic feedback chart, illustrating achievement milestones and showing step levels of when and how additional funds should go into the venture.
19. Project staff and plan space requirement over a five-year period.
20. Describe the rationale for choosing any single manufacturing plant location.
21. Present cash flow projections monthly for the first

```
          24 months and quarterly for the next three years.
    22.   Provide pro forma balance sheets for five years.
    23.   Provide pro forma profit and loss statements for
          five years.
    24.   Present your position on the degree of ownership
          control you seek and the extent to which these can be
          varied with time and profitability.
```

There are numerous one-line suggestions that may be made in connection with business plans. Here are only a few:

- A business plan should be professional but not slick.
- Financial projections should be accepted as gross orders of magnitude rather than precise expectations.
- Planning and knowing when to change the plan is an art instead of a science.
- The plan should be long enough to accurately communicate and project the company over a period of three to five years without adding to make it "thicker."
- The essentials of the plan should be businesslike and not necessarily written like a piece of literature.
- Clarity and precision are the two essentials of writing style.
- The words should reflect exactly what the entrepreneur-inventor has in mind.
- The plan should be considered as only part of the process of decision making, both by the entrepreneur on the one hand and by the venture capital group on the other.

Case in Point: Metrodyne

Lawrence Gerber, hired by Sibany to create and eventually take over the presidency of Metrodyne Corporation, a Sibany company that produces an electronic weighing device, had never heard of a business plan, still less done one. While the product was only a project, he wrestled so with the planning problems that he fell in love with his business plan and the prospects it created to a greater extent than oherwise might have been the case.

Faced with a new and unfamiliar technology, he first evaluated Sibany's preliminary plan, the direction of the product development, and the competence of the supervision of the project. He made changes, tightening communication between the technical people and himself. Satisfied, he then made a market survey of the weighing industry. Over a period of months he supplemented his market survey with additional information relating to costs, organization, availability of people, and so on.

Most important, he spent months internalizing a vast amount of information that was at first just words on paper, until it became more meaningful to him. Throughout this process he made tentative and then more clear-cut judgments, first about the key aspects of his business and then about lower-priority items. After seven months of collection of data, appraisal and reappraisal, biting, chewing, and spitting out, and then taking another bite, Gerber was ready to create his new company on paper. He asked himself basic questions: "Where are we?" "Where are we going?" "How will we get there?"

At this juncture Gerber could be described as the most worried man in the weighing industry—as well as the most informed man on new weighing technology and its marketability. He had by this time hired a chief engineer, and the product development project moved from the Sibany laboratory to its own facility, upgraded from a project to the Weighing Systems Division of Sibany. Later the division became Metrodyne Corporation.

With one eye on product development, Gerber lived closely with his market data, charts, and projections for three months. He was never seen without his plan close at hand. He added a new insight here, changed a word there, or changed the sequence of items for more logical presentation. He talked to everyone who gave him time to ask questions and had the time to answer them.

Finally, Gerber had his first draft of a business plan to guide his business operation for the next five years and possibly to induce venture capitalists to invest hundreds of thousands of dollars in his company.

The plan also developed unexpected applications. For example, Gerber used it in his personal life to inform people who were concerned about "what he was doing in his new job." He used it to convince major rubber companies to invest their research and development dollars in developing parts of his new product that they could supply. In December 1971 one of these companies, Uniroyal, Inc., signed a contract with Metrodyne to supply R&D relating to the weighing mat, which could eventually lead to the acquisition of up to 40 percent of the common stock of Metrodyne by Uniroyal.

He used his plan as an employee relations device with his subordinates. For the first time Gerber and his associates had the sense that they were dealing with a company instead of an abstraction.

Some key parts of Gerber's sixty-seven-page plan will suggest its nature. The Table of Contents and the Foreword of the plan devised by Gerber are shown below.

CONTENTS

FOREWORD

Metrodyne Corporation, a Delaware corporation, is a high technology operating company with a corporate goal to profitably exploit the metrological sciences.

The company's unique patented technlogy points toward the extension of an established industry, static weighing, and the potential creation of two new industries, automated inventory counting and control, and in-motion high-speed dynamic weighing. The company intends to pioneer in these new fields from an operating base. In the short term, the company will market 25 to 30 of its DYNE-A-MAT systems while at the same time utilizing its creative engineering ability to solve highly specialized commercial-industrial weighing and production automation problems on a contract basis. The company has delivered its first system to a major airline and has received additional orders for other DYNE-A-MAT applications.

Having adopted this format for corporate growth, the company can attain modest operating results in the existing scale industry, in the short term, and at the same time enable it to test and strengthen its organization, facilities, technology, and financial base on an orderly basis for later pioneering of high-speed weighing and automated inventory control.

The decision to first enter the scale industry was simple. The scale industry markets are firmly established and operating results and profits are realizable in a shorter period of time. Further, development of static weighing devices and scales is a logical and efficient milestone on the road toward development of systems for weighing of high-speed vehicles and automated inventory counting and control. Finally, the market development for the new industries will be slower and more expensive as they will have to be pioneered by Metrodyne.

The weighing of solids and liquids is a basic phenomenon of an industrial society. The continued commerciality of this very old science seems secure for centuries to come. Most of the present day systems use pre-1900 techniques and the surface has barely been scratched with new technology. The complexion of products will change but the requirements will always exist. The financial projections in this business plan include sales and revenue to be derived from the application of the DYNE-A-MAT as a static weighing system and from custom engineering contracts. Forecasts of sales from the potentially larger markets, automatic inventory control and in-motion weighing and foreign markets are not included.

The cash flow chart is intended to project Metrodyne's actual operating results and indicates that the company requires approximately $350,000 of investment, and is seeking $500,000, before attaining a positive cash flow position. However, the company's management may decide to accelerate product development and additional funds may be required before the company can sustain a positive cash flow. Metrodyne's intention is to satisfy these requirements through a private financing or through a public stock offering. [Metrodyne completed a public offering of its common stock in December, 1971.]

You should conclude from reading this business plan that:

Metrodyne Corporation justifies an investment of $500,000.

The financial projections are conservative because they do not include foreign sales and income and exploitation of automated inventory control product applications, the in-motion high-speed weighing markets, and other potential applications for Metrodyne's technology.

Being first on the market, Metrodyne may expect to capture up to 50 per cent of the market for new technology products.

The market for new technology weighing systems in the next ten years exceeds $600 million.

For Gerber and almost everyone else, the most difficult section of a business plan is what is usually called "financial projections." It is difficult because the investor is usually unclear about what he wants. He may say something like, "Give me pro forma balance sheets and profit and loss statements for five years and cash-flow projections by the month until you reach the black and then by the quarter for up to five years."

The entrepreneur is confused by the lack of specific direction by the venture capital group. He ponders, "Should I make the figures low enough so that I can beat them for sure? Or should I make them very high so that these guys will think my company is a great investment? How much financial detail should I provide?"

Financial Projections That Are Inflated

Sophisticated investors suggest how the writer of a business plan should handle financial projections:

"Be ultra-conservative so that you look like you are a capable and reasonable businessman."

"Use high figures because the reader is bound to cut your estimations in half, anyhow."

"Use three columns of projections, *High*, *Low*, and *Likely*, and let the reader make his own judgment."

Most experienced people suggest that financial projections be conservative because, first, you are more comfortable portraying what you believe is the truth; second, most people would rather bet on a conservative management with an interesting business opportunity than on an unrealistic projection; and third, the business plan will necessarily be distorted if it seeks to justify unrealistic financial projections. The cash-flow projection should be by the month, at least until you reach the black and are likely to stay there, and then by the quarter for three to five years.

Peter Drucker says about financial projections:

Forecasting attempts to find the most probable course of events, or at best, a range of probabilities. The entrepreneurial problem is a unique event that will change the possibilities, for the entrepreneurial universe is not a physical but a value universe. Indeed, the central entrepreneurial contribution, and the one which alone is rewarded with a profit, is to bring about the unique event; the innovation that changes the probabilities.[1]

Donald Woods, after discussing the pitfalls in making estimates of the future, points out:

Solutions are not easy because a complex set of socio-politico-economic interactions is involved. But when uncertainty is a vital factor in the final decision, positive steps can be taken to... make Uncertainty Visible....

For many decisions, top management has to assign a probability distribution to the uncertainty underlying the estimate sent up from below. But why place all the burden on the decision maker? Why not start at the beginning? Would it not make more sense to quantify the relevant judgments at various points in the organization as they are passed upward?[2]

Woods then goes on to suggest eliminating absolute estimates, utilizing one set of figures, in favor of "high, low, and probable," or "conservative, speculative, and probable."

Other literature in the field takes a harder line. Carl W. Stursberg, Jr., says, about cash-flow and earnings projection:

1. Peter F. Drucker, *Technology, Management and Society* (New York: Harper & Row, 1969), p. 130. Used by permission of the publisher.

2. Donald Woods, "Improving Estimates that Involve Uncertainty," *Harvard Business Review*, July-August 1966, vol. 44, no. 4, pp. 96–97. Used by permission of the publisher.

All sections of the brochure come to focus in the cash-flow statement. It reflects estimates and projections of the amount of financing needed; at what stages and generation of income as the company matures. Cash-flow and earnings' projections should be completed for at least three years, and for a longer period if the research and development phases of the enterprise are long term, and if the projections do not reflect at least one full year of market penetration. . . .

It is vital to prepare realistic estimates and projection of risks, growth of market, market penetration, manufacturing and development plans, costs, etc. Oversights and false optimism at this juncture result in undercapitalization and earlier-than-planned need for additional capital—one of the major causes of new venture failures.[3]

Detail Your Financial Projections

The outline that follows is a suggested financial section for a business plan.

FINANCIAL INFORMATION

NEW VENTURE COMPANY

I. Schedule of Machinery, Tools, and Dies
II. Schedule of Plant Modifications and Installed Systems
III. Schedule of Equipment
IV. Classification of Monthly Wages and Salaries
V. Profit and Loss Statement, Pro Forma, Years 1 to 3
VI. Balance Sheet, Pro Forma, at Organization, Year End Years 1 to 3
VII. Forecast of Gross Sales and Production, Years 1 to 3
VIII. Bill of Material
IX. Preliminary Specifications
X. Cost of Goods Sold
XI. General and Administrative Expense
XII. Schedule of Expenses Prior to Plant Occupancy
XIII. Schedule of General and Administrative Expense during Research and Development
XIV. Schedule of Indirect Labor Expense during Research and Development
XV. Schedule of Sales Expense, Years 1 to 3
XVI. Schedule of Financial Expense
XVII. Cash Projection Year 1
XVIII. Total Cost Per Unit
XIX. Schedule of Total Financial Requirements
XX. Schedule of Financing

3. Carl W. Stursberg, Jr., "A Guide to Venture Capital Financing" (New York: American Science Associates, 1970), p. 9. Used by permission of publisher and author.

Competition Section

Venture capitalists and others concerned with business plans feel that a detailed competition section is an indication of the professional management ability of the company seeking investment. It is one of the most difficult sections for an entrepreneur or inventor to develop. The assumption by an entrepreneur that a detailed competition section will frighten off investors is erroneous. A good case can be made that few new technologies exist, thrive, and grow without competition—a reality that should be recognized in writing.

Quite often a new company discusses its competition in the most general terms, affording the reader little real information. This is an incorrect procedure and will lose credibility for the start-up company. Competitors should be mentioned by name with the specific pricing, specifications, and features they are claiming for their product. A detailed analysis should be made comparing the new company's product point by point with those of the competitors. And concern that pricing is not the very lowest is unwarranted, as long as the prices bear a relationship to costs and to market acceptance.

Pioneering a New Technology

The group starting a new company with a product or technology that is relatively unknown faces special problems. Identimation Corporation, a Sibany company, is included in this category. The first questions that had to be considered were: What is personal identification? How is the problem of recognizing people presently being solved? How was it handled in the past?

Identimation decided to solve this problem in its business plan by making the foreword to the plan consist of a history of personal identification and an explanation of what commercial criteria would have to be satisfied by a personal identification device. In the competition section of its business plan, Identimation attempted to describe in a comprehensive outline all ways in which personal identification were presently being handled. The Foreword and Competition sections are shown below.

FOREWORD TO IDENTIMATION BUSINESS PLAN

"Your hand is a key." With that insight, several years ago, began the development of what is today the first commercial personal identification system based on the machine verification of human personal characteristics, the Identimat® products of Identimation Corporation. . . .

Since time immemorial man has sought practical methods of security. In the early days of civilization, physical security controls were depended upon to a greater extent than in our modern society. There was not only the problem of guarding material possessions and the lives of their families from human enemies, but they also had to protect themselves from wild beasts of prey as well. The early tribes took advantage of natural barriers for protection. Stone Age families took refuge in caves on cliffs and maintained their security by physically isolating themselves. During the Middle Ages, the well-known moat was employed to protect the castle, and cities were protected by high walls and barriers. Security guards and armies protected the entrance to the cave and the tribal areas. Locks were put on the earliest houses and strong boxes. Even the modern concept of psychological deterrents was utilized early when the first man threatened his enemy with the capacity for retribution. In the Old Testament there is a reference to "The key of the house of David. . . ."

Now, as then, the problem of security may be divided into three parts. First, is the problem of limiting physical access to only those who have a right to enter or open; second, is the problem of internal security; third, is the problem of the security of information, both internally and externally.

In physical access security today, as well as historically, most systems act mainly as a psychological deterrent. Faced with a series of external controls such as light, fences, and locks, the intruder is led to believe that the choice of another facility, where there are fewer or an absence of deterrents, is preferable. Today's missiles, hydrogen bombs, large armies, sophisticated bank vaults and passport systems are merely an extension of what has already been in the history of mankind.

The history of internal security is also the history of positive personal identification and is closely involved with man's development. Today, as from the beginning of time, sensory recognition is probably the most popular method of personal identification. We become familiar with the appearance and sounds of our family, friends, and fellow workers and personally identify in this manner. As our civilization has developed and more people have been involved, many of whom may not be personally known, we have depended upon uniforms, passwords, seals, banners, signatures, and letters of introduction to identify friend from foe. The work of the Central Intelligence Agency, the Federal Bureau of Investigation, the security guard at an Atomic Energy Commission facility, and the teller at a modern bank are modern extensions of history.

Historically, the security of information has been a relatively simple problem. Today, the problem is becoming increasingly more difficult and complicated as the information explosion affects, and in most cases leads, all factors of our society. Not only is the amount of information reaching staggering proportions, but the speed with which information must be processed has increased enormously. The growth rate of information is accelerating and should continue even more rapidly in the foreseeable future.

The development of the computer and all of its related products has given our civilization the ability to eventually store, catalog, process and retrieve all of the information as it is created. The data includes plans, strategies, personal information and other confidential information. Who will have access? Is he the right person? The right account?

Our society has effectively dispelled the old concern that automation leads to fewer jobs. In the information industry as well as others automation has actually led to an increase in the number of job requirements, mostly in software and related services. This, combined with a greater social realization of the needs of the mass of people, has led to a higher cost of labor. Security guards at a 24-hour gate cost $40,000 per year, plus overhead.

Wherever possible, machines will have to replace people in the task of physical security of tangible goods within boundaries, and the internal security within those boundaries, and the security of information.

Positive personal identification means automatic identification, which is based upon the physical characteristics of an individual. Whatever form it takes, a person is identified and verified based on physical characteristics which are sufficiently different from those of other people that the possibility of duplication is exceedingly small. Identimation has been active in research and development of positive personal identification systems for some time. Certain criteria must be satisfied:

1. Positive personal identification must be based upon a comparison of physical or special characteristics of the individual.

2. The comparison of these physical characteristics must be accomplished automatically, quickly and inexpensively.

3. The comparison and identification must be done in a manner which is not embarrassing or psychologically unacceptable to the user.

4. The system must be uncomplicated.

5. The system must be capable of identifying an individual across the entire spectrum from a relatively simple function such as cashing a check through the relatively sophisticated function of limiting access to a computer.

6. The machine must be capable of operating as a stand-alone device, as well as in a system, and in both cases allow a comparison to be made between the encoded information on an ID card or badge and the individual presenting such a badge or ID card to the machine. A stand-alone device can be used as a lock or an on–off switch.

7. The system should be commercially consistent with the necessary evolution within a company from a simple paper system to an automated computerized system.

The problems of positive personal identification has increased as we have become dependent upon automation to perform many of our daily tasks. We can expect the problem to become even more acute in the future. To a very large degree, the future of some of our most sophisticated and ambitious plans to control the looming paper work explosion and the need to protect the privacy which we as individuals so dearly cherish will depend upon a highly reliable system of identification and verification.

These problems have been known for many years. For example, Mr. Richard W. Freund, a vice president of the First National City Bank, stated in December 1967, "One of the major hurdles checkless banking must clear is a fool-proof method of customer identity verification."

Just a year earlier in December 1966 the American Bankers' Association Personal Identification Project Committee report was published. This report indicated that 83 per cent of the 244 respondents believed that a uniform nationwide personal identification system would be helpful. Seventy-four per cent saw a need for an acceptable, efficient method of verifying the identity of individuals to demonstrate that the person is really the one he purports to be. The respondents to this survey included government agencies, utilities, banking institutions, insurance companies, hospitals, and retail organizations whose files cover over 440 million individuals.

COMPETITION: TYPES OF PERSONAL IDENTIFICATION DEVICES

The field of personal identification can be divided into three basic types of identification:

1. Identification of something a person carries.
2. Identification of something a person remembers.
3. Identification of a personal characteristic of the person.

Each of these exists in both attended and unattended versions and often different systems are combined for greater security. Examples of attended and unattended systems are given below:

TYPE	EXAMPLE
Type 1 (attended)	Department store.
Type 1 (unattended)	Ordinary lock and key. Identimat 200
Type 2 (attended)	Passwords. Identimat 200
Type 2 (unattended)	Combination lock. Identimat 200
Type 3 (attended)	Police fingerprint system. Kleen-Print ™.
Type 3 (unattended)	Various Identimat models.

For the purpose of evaluating the competition to Identimation's products, all six categories must be considered as the customer always has the choice.

Type 1 (attended)—Identification of Something a Person Carries

IDENTIMAT 200®

Theater tickets, airline tickets, train and bus tickets, etc.

Employee badge; if it contains a picture or fingerprint, it also fits #3 (attended).

Official badge, police, M.P., postal, etc.

Credit cards.

Bank passbooks.

Social Security card.

Draft card, drivers license (also may contain personal characteristics—#3, attended).

Uniforms—police, military, postal, United Parcel, etc.

A check either made out to, or made out by, the person often, but not always, requires additional identification.

Letter of credit.

Check made out to bearer for cash.

Ordinary lock and key.

Optically or magnetically coded ID card—

Card Key Systems:	Card Key
Selectro Corp.:	Badge Reader
Digital ID Systems:	DIGI-LOCK (with Identikey)
Detex Corp.:	DENTCO
Western Industries:	GUARD-KARD

Time card.

Subway token—this does not identify who the person is but rather establishes that he belongs to the class of persons entitled to use the subway.

Type 1 (unattended)—Identification of Something a Person Carries

A multitude of sophisticated and simple lock and key systems.

Type 2 (attended)—Identification of Something a Person Remembers

IDENTIMAT 200

Passwords or phrases.

Telephone credit card numbers.

Person's name ("I am Joe Doe").

Group or category name ("This is the police"; "Avon calling"; "This is your operator").

Telephone number—given to operator for charging purposes on many calls.

Telephone number—given for identification purposes in conjunction with other systems such as check cashing.

Room number at a hotel dining room.

Membership number or name at a private club.

Type 2 (unattended)—Identification of Something a Person Remembers

IDENTIMAT 200

Numerous dial combination locks.

Push-button combination lock—Permaloc Security Devices, Inc.

Litton Systems (ACCESS ™)—Combines with Type 1 (unattended).

DeLaRue check cashing—Combines with Type 1 (unattended).

OMRON check cashing—Combines with Type 1 (unattended).

Holobeam, Inc. ("SPACS" system)—Combines with Type 1 (unattended).

Card Key systems (Memori-Lock ™)—Combines with Type 1 (unattended).

Security Controls, Inc. (Securiti-Panel)—Combines with Type 1 (unattended).

Varicard, Inc. ("Vericard")—Combines with Type 1 (unattended).

Computer access control using passwords or numbers within the computer memory.

Type 3 (attended)—Identification of Personal Characteristics of the Person

Police fingerprint system (also FBI, military and industrial)

Personal recognition (where the person is known)

a) based on appearance

b) based on voice

Voice print—computer plus expert analysis. The goal here is an unattended system which has not yet been achieved.

Comparison to photograph or other information on badge or ID card (combined with Type 1 attended)—Polaroid ID card, Litton "Laminex" cards, R.D. products "IDENTI-PROOF", AVANT QUAD CAMERA, closed circuit TV.

a) remote badge comparator

b) stored photograph on guards display—Mardix Security System VIDEOGUARD.

Signature—on check or other document.

Bertillion system.

Type 3 (unattended)—Identification of Personal Characteristics of the Person

IDENTIMAT 2000

KMS Industries fingerprint system*

Holograph Fingerprint System.*

IBM photograph system*—computer recognition of photograph.

Voice Prints.*

Signature patent.*

*Not commercially available.

Perspective on a New Company's Problems

A good competition section will go a long way toward making a business plan credible. Many venture capital firms will tell you that one of the leading failures of most business plans is the inability or unwillingness of the entrepreneur-inventor to define the exact nature of the opportunity *and* problems to be faced.

After all, the new company is walking onto a stage of free enterprise that is four or five hundred years old. The industrial revolution is two hundred years old. The technological and information explosion is fifty years old. Nevertheless, many business plans describe their product, personnel, and opportunities as if they were going into business in the time of the cavemen. In a situation where the statistical likelihood is that they will fail rather than succeed, they come off looking like naïve dreamers. Successful entrepreneurs always utilize the dreamer aspect of their personality but combine it with a realism which is apparent to all those from whom they seek investment.

Discussion of Contingent Plan

Perhaps the most serious blunder made by persons preparing market surveys and business plans is the failure to develop and communicate contingent plans. Many venture capital firms will tell you that few start-up companies can avoid getting into trouble because of the vicissitudes of the American economy, the high aptitude and quality of the competition, and the inexperience of the new top management. Because this *is* the case, problems and prior incorrect judgments should be stated, to add realism to the business plan. Failure to do so makes the promoter of the new company appear to not have thought his business situation through.

The Plan as an End in Itself

Business plans are now prevalent enough as a means of communication between the new company and the venture capital group to court the danger of institutionalizing the business plan and making it an end in itself. Like the psychological test, it can be exaggerated in importance. It may mistakenly become the main basis for an entrepreneur's judgment on whether to go into business or the venture capitalist's decision to invest. The professional planner inside a medium-sized or large company has been doing his work long enough so that his plan is slick. The danger is that his planning may become mechanical, routine, and (like a too-commercial play or stage show) intent on generating a certain response from the audience rather than on reflecting basic meaningful realities. In the *Harvard Business Review*, David W. Ewing has written, "New directions are needed to avoid the danger that this function [planning] will take the low road while top management travels the high road."[4] There is surely no evidence that the better and more eloquent writer and planner is a better businessman or more likely to succeed. For many businesses, the exact reverse may be the case. In fact, the entrepreneurial situation is such that major advantage may lie in unforeseen events, rather than those that are ordinary, foreseeable, and plannable.

Independent Evaluation

The beginning new company usually shuns extra expenses. However, some form of outside independent verification can add credibility to the proposed enterprise in the mind of the potential investor. "Can I afford it?" "Maybe

4. David W. Ewing, "Corporate Planning at a Crossroads" *Harvard Business Review*, vol. 45, no. 4, July-August 1967, p. 77.

he will tell me things that will kill the whole deal." "Whom should I hire?" These considerations are both a burden and an opportunity, and consulting an outside firm can in some cases prevent several years of anguish and false hope. If the outside firm is reputable, independent, and prestigious, the new company will have moved far along.

Identimation hired the Stanford Research Institute (SRI) at a cost of about $10,000 to make an independent study of the technical feasibility of using hand geometry as a means of personal identification. SRI is one of the handful of technically oriented management consulting firms whose name and reputation have wide acceptance. The summary part of their report illustrates the credibility that can be added when the independent consultant comes to a positive conclusion. On other occasions, inventors should consider abandoning or putting on the shelf, product development projects whose analysis by an independent agency show feasibility to be tenuous or non-existent.

Personnel Identification by Hand Geometry Parameters

I. Summary

Stanford Research Institute was requested by the Identimation Corporation to evaluate the theoretical feasibility of establishing personnel identification by hand geometry measured to reasonable tolerances. The lengths of fingers II, III, IV and V (index, middle, ring and little, respectively) of the right hand, measured from adjacent crotches, were selected as reproducible and measurable parameters for this task.

The initial evaluation was made utilizing available statistical data, which included pertinent finger length measurements, developed by the U. S. Air Force. This data was developed from a sample of over 4,000 Air Force male flying personnel. An additional evaluation was performed by acquiring finger length data from a random sample of approximately 100 SRI personnel——both male and female.

Using these data, the normal distribution of finger length parameters was modeled by a computer. Sets of four finger lengths, comprising one hand (except for the thumb), were randomly chosen in pairs from this model, and their respective lengths were compared to see if all four finger lengths of one set fell within the four finger lengths plus a given tolerance, of the other set.

As anticipated, a somewhat lower error rate for a given tolerance was found in the SRI sample as compared to the Air Force data. The inclusion of females as well as males, and the random subject selection among SRI personnel presumably provided a more representative sample of the adult population than the relatively homogenous Air Force sample.

The analysis of these data . . . indicates that the reliability of identification for a measurement tolerance of ± 0.06 inch (± 1.5mm) is on the order of

99.5 percent, and for a measurement tolerance of ± 0.03 inch (± 0.75mm) the reliability of identification is on the order of 99.95 percent. In other words, with the tolerance ranges of ± 0.06 inch and ± 0.03 inch, the probability of a match or cross-identification *(i.e.,* two people having four finger lengths of one hand that are identical within this tolerance, permitting one person to be- improperly identified as another person) is about 0.5 per cent and 0.05 per cent respectively.

Manning the Plan

One of the traps of a business plan is the qualification and selection of key personnel. For example, an executive who can boast a Harvard M.B.A. is likely to impress more investors than an equally capable graduate of the Business School of the University of Oklahoma.

Realizing the susceptibility of investors to this kind of halo effect, it becomes difficult for the business planner to refrain from stacking the cards. He hires individuals on the basis of how they look on paper rather than how they will perform in fact, and this tendency creates a schism between the business plan and reality. A "paper team" that seems to pack a tremendous wallop because of its qualifications may be highly ineffective in reality. But as long as venture capitalists operate on the basis of conscious or unconscious biases, there is likely to be a restriction against some economic, national, racial, and religious groups.

In some cases, there is a legal problem of who an individual or a group of individuals works for. One company now on the American Stock Exchange was started by five individuals making up a complete department of United Aircraft. The rumors in the financial community suggested that they were actually working for themselves while still getting paid by United Aircraft.

Another group of individuals negotiated the purchase of a technology from the prominent new-products consulting firm of Arthur D. Little Co. and were accused of negotiating while still employed by Xerox Corporation. The front page of their first public offering under a usual section, for new and start-up companies, "Risk Factors to be Considered" (by the investor), was a copy of a letter from Xerox Corporation to Little Co. indicating that while it was the opinion of Xerox's management that these people had been working on their own while employed by Xerox, Xerox had decided not to sue them at this time but reserved the right to do so in the future.

All the problems of ordinary organizational planning are likely to appear in the business plan: What type of structure shall the new organization adopt? Should the hierarchy of line units be loose or rigid? At what point should line and staff interrelate? Who should report to whom? How much autonomy should different elements of the organization have? What is the likely timing of organizational additions? Who will service the product when it is out in the field?

And basic financial policy must also be covered. For example: What is the worst point on the cash-flow? How conservative should one be in estimating cash requirements? What is the best timing of various financing moves? What is the estimate of the size and pace of earned income?

An Eye on Reality

Keeping in mind not only the ordinary woes that organizations are heir to but also the changes in operation and prospects that develop as the venture moves ahead, it becomes clear that the best-laid business plan must be viewed as only tentative and as continually subject to reexamination and adjustment.

Ideally, the first draft of a business plan and subsequent redrafts should be based upon operating events that are occurring while the plan is being written. Here again, it is dangerous for the plan to become an end in itself because it will deceive both the company's management and the venture capitalist.

Increasingly, venture managers are becoming concerned about the difference between running a department or division and running a company, even if it is exactly in the same business. After a great deal of frustration one top executive in a start-up firm said, "I would not have believed running your own company could differ so from running the department of a large company, even though I am selling exactly the same products." Harry Truman had an apt sign on his desk: "The buck stops here."

It's not only the element of responsibility but also that of perspective that makes the top job in a new company different. The difference of total perspective and ultimate risk taking must be reflected in the business plan.

From Shadow to Substance

Since the business plan is a projection into the future, to some degree it must be tentative. New developments, strengthening or weakening the plan, will suggest—or even demand—alterations of approach and action.

Essentially, new-company management operates in a climate of both uncertainty and opportunism. One might say this is the prevailing atmosphere of the business scene in general. True; but both these qualities are more important for the infant firm than for the established one.

In operating terms, new-company management must try to ride two horses at once, and even, judiciously, try to leap from the back of one to the other as circumstances seem to dictate. Since the business plan represents countless hours of considered research and analysis, evaluation and judgment, it cannot be treated lightly. At the same time, to adhere to a business plan—no matter how well thought out—in the face of unanticipated situations can clearly be suicidal. Some of the considerations involved in going from planning to action will be covered in the next chapter.

Chapter 6

Concretizing: Implementing the Business Plan

Pinocchio was only a puppet until the Good Fairy made him into a live little boy. Similarly, a business plan is an inanimate thing until the breath of life is blown into it.

The activities proposed in a business plan seldom have a strict chronology. Its development is not like a building, which requires that the first floor be constructed before the second floor, but more like a jigsaw puzzle. In assembling a jigsaw, one works on a corner, then another, then possibly along an edge. A small triumph with one group of pieces may suggest where to operate next. Coming up against a blank wall in one place may lead to a temporary abandonment of that area, and a search for pieces whose position one can be sure of because of a unique shape—a corner piece, for example. In short, implementation of the business plan tends to be opportunistic.

Although one cannot give a definite chronological series of steps in which concretization takes place, it is possible to sketch out the steps that eventually must be taken, and in a sequence that in many cases represents their actual order:

1. Organizational readiness: "We're ready to go—aren't we?"
2. Top executive selection: "Who's going to run things?"
3. Charting and manning: "Who else do we need?"

4. Headquartering: "Where do we locate?"
5. Function development: "What activities must we perform to grow?"
6. Gap-spotting and filling: "Do we really need salesmen in Tierra del Fuego?"
7. Organizational review and rounding out: "Do we have one of everybody and everything we need?"

Each of these steps is discussed below.

1. Organizational Readiness

This is the trigger step. During product development, and after the business plan has been drawn up, someone says, "Go!" It may be the inventor, the promoter, a key money man. And always, it's after an injection of cash makes concretization practical.

Three things are usually brought together to create the initial spark: the development of the product to the point where it is ready for commercial and marketing considerations; the cash to pay for the people, services, and production that the approach to the market requires; and a climate of readiness.

2. Top Executive Selection

The outcome of the recruitment of the top two or three men for the enterprise is critical. A so-so product with a good man behind it can succeed. An excellent product with a poor top executive will probably fail.

It's when the top executives are found and hired that the business plan begins to come to life. One authority puts it this way: "A plan remains only a plan until a head man, regardless of his title, takes over."

The first step in the selection of a key man is finding enough candidates for the one or more jobs for which there is an opening. While executive recruiters seem to have become more professional, they are usually too traditional and too expensive for a small company. I have had excellent results, with some exceptions, from recruiting people who are known to employees or someone else close to our company.

When additional candidates are required, advertising in the *New York Times* Sunday business section has drawn several hundred responses each time it has been used. The following is a typical example:

technically oriented
MARKETING
MANAGERS

Sibany is a rapidly growing leader in creating new businesses through new product development. We are looking for determined self starters with proven managerial talents capable of undertaking complete direction of technically oriented marketing divisions or new start up companies. We offer excellent opportunities for capital gains to imaginative candidates willing to accept challenging responsibility.

Positions are located in Northern New Jersey or Southwestern Connecticut. Salaries are commensurate with individual qualifications.

Reply in confidence in full detail to:

Sibany Manufacturing Corp.
6 Neil Lane
Riverside, Connecticut 06878

**Interviews will be held in
New York City on Monday,
January 20, 1969**

An Equal Opportunity Employer (m/f)

The large number of résumés and letters can usually be reduced to a few dozen by a quick perusal of most and a detailed reading of some. Ten or fifteen candidates for each open job is typical, and each of these people is called and talked to at some length. The candidate's résumé will have told you the essentials. A telephone call can give the interviewer an impression of the applicant's personality, aggressiveness, eloquence, and other factors. Half or more of the candidates for each job usually survive the telephone conversation and are given a personal interview. It is important to interview all the candidates within a short time span so that you can compare them with each other. Therefore, all the preliminary interviewing for a particular job is done by one person; it usually takes not more than an hour for each candidate and is accomplished in a single day.

The applicants who survive the initial interview are run through other patterns that have proved effective over the years. Sometimes, references given by prospective employees are checked. The evidence presented by the candidate himself, however, is considered much more important. An investigator's report on key candidates is used to determine whether they have a criminal record, what their neighbors think of them, their financial history, and so forth. And because women seem to be good instinctive judges of character, the interviewer may arrange a dinner including the prospective employee's wife and his own.

Because the candidate, too, is taking a significant risk in a new venture, a serious prospect is brought into a great deal of personal contact with other people already on the job who have made a decision similar to the one he is contemplating. In short, he is given an opportunity to weigh his own motivations and ask questions concerning the motivations and attitudes of potential associates.

For those making the selection, an array of questions must be faced and answered:

WHAT KIND OF MAN?   Since very few executives, even the most experienced, have had the chance to start up a corporation, how can one judge from a typical work record how well a candidate is likely to perform?

Is it better to recruit a man with a considerable amount of big-company experience, one who has probably been exposed to management development courses, possibly the Harvard Business School type of background, to ensure his knowledge of theory of management? Or would it be better to get a man who has proven himself as a successful "small businessman" because that is the initial type of situation he will be facing? Or, is a "hungry" young man with less experience preferable?

HOW BALANCED HIS QUALIFICATIONS?   And how does one decide between the qualities (initiative, imagination, and drive) required to get an organization over the early hurdles of its existence and the set of virtues (judgment, ability to develop people, ability to think in long-range terms, and so on) required to maximize the operations of a going concern?

No one has been able to determine any pat answers to these questions. There do seem to be patterns that individual companies can evolve that serve their own interests, even if they are not universally applicable. For example, people with a two- or three-year pattern of changing jobs or whose experience has been only with large companies are usually not able to make the adjustment to the atmosphere of the small organization or the embryonic company. Also, as prejudiced as it may seem, candidates for top jobs who think of themselves as assistants or staff to other people are usually not considered. The generalist is preferred to the specialist. Finally, there is little concern for whether the candidate has specific product knowledge, because by definition, the product has to be either revolutionary or dramatically different from anything presently on the market, or the venture management company would not be interested in the first place.

Despite all the help from the experts, practical or professional, in recruiting a top man for a new organization, the problem of choice eventually comes down to individual people, and here the person or group making the final selection must proceed on the basis of intuition and personal appraisal instead of just on such standards as education, work experience, and other means of measurement.

WHAT ABOUT TRADITIONAL RATING METHODS?   The trait approach to executive evaluation can be helpful and misleading. Certainly, in getting a broad picture, some materiality is added to the executive image if attributes such as initiative, energy, and global vision are considered, but when these traits are used as rating scales, unreality creeps in. For example, one says, "We must have a man strongly capable of independent action." But Boy Scouts as well as executives are capable of "independent action." The *nature* of the independent action is crucial. And in attempting to state these specifics, one runs the danger of stating as an attribute the goal you want to achieve. For example: "He must be able to get results." To reduce this approach to its ultimate form, one looks simply for "a successful executive," whatever that means, which brings us full circle.

WHAT TYPE OF EXECUTIVE?   One basic choice that usually must be made is whether the top executive should be an "inside" man (whose essential duties will be to complete development, get production going, and so on), or whether he should be picked for his "outside" capabilities (developing the marketing and related functions). If the latter, he must be able to sell himself, his product, his business concept, and his company.

Once this basic choice has been made, of course, the man selected will pick his opposite number. An inside man hires his outside counterpart or vice versa.

Let's say you have begun interviewing. Here are the suggestions of one experienced new business promoter:

> You check out the candidate's resume, references, knowledge, attitudes. Evaluate his personality as to how it relates to yours. Determine the reaction he will have on you and other key employees. If you have found him knowledge-

able, aggressive, optimistic, but not unwilling to argue, not particularly impressed but not disdainful of your exalted position and background or the accomplishments you have made so far, then hire him.

If, however, he seems to be a nice fellow, acquiescent, eager to agree and please, one who will follow wherever you lead instead of devising his own operating maps—in short, bland, even though he may be expert in his field—end the interview reasonably soon. It won't work out!

Another entrepreneur has this to say about the search for the top man:

You may meet a man you think could do very well but you suspect that he is so strongly self-propelled that he eventually may move to take over the company. I would hire a man like that. Remember, you are not going to succeed with average people. You need the stars, the brilliant performers, to make the venture successful.

Don't be afraid of a bright guy. He may be the top manager; but if you play your cards right, you are still the owner. And if you have made the proper arrangement in terms of compensation, it will be worth his while to stay with you rather than drop it all and start a new company. In any case, you have him as long as he stays.

Another quality to look for is "blow-away-ness." If a person has high "blow-away" strength, he will *not* be blown away by the many difficulties he will meet when trying to take an idea and build a business around it. The employment investigation always includes a detailed discussion starting with a question such as, "What will you do on those days when you look in every direction and up and down and only see blackness, irresolution, failure, and criticism?" The ability to bounce back from apparent defeat and not give up is one that is prized especially in people who have to wrest success from a competitive and uncompromising environment.

A person's attitude both about money and personal responsibility gives insights into his character. If he treats the capital he will manage with the same discretion he would if he had obtained this money from close friends and relatives, then the chances are he will utilize the company's money in the best way.

People from a combination of medium-sized and large corporations who have the entrepreneurial urge and have not been able to satisfy it may under the proper circumstances become enthusiastic owners and managers of embryonic companies. To stress the point that they are being paid for their ability to succeed, the Risers' program is structured in such a way as to require the man to make a crucial personal decision. He is given a great deal of authority and in return must, after a period of learning, make a strong personal commitment, sometimes including his own funds and usually those of his friends and relatives, in the new company. Risers' is also utilizing women as venture managers.

If his experience with the product, the market, and the financial community is such that he will not do everything he can to obtain investment from his friends and relatives (assuming they are able) based upon his belief that he has an outstanding opportunity and that they will share in his success, he should not continue in a top position of the company. This approach is rarely resented and serves to add other people to whom the key man *will feel responsible to succeed.*

In a sense then, it is a game. If he accepts the money that has been given to him by relatives and friends, then he is accepting responsibility and making a personal commitment to succeed. If he is unwilling to invest his own money in himself and his product and to encourage his friends and relatives to invest with him, because the potential risk is too high, then he probably lacks the motivation to overcome the various problems that will occur as he builds his business.

How Does He Start?   In many cases the new manager has been responsible for, or at least involved in, the planning process. If not, he must be shown the plan early. One promotional group used its business plan as a hiring tool, showing it to the top three candidates, and evaluating their ideas and reactions with respect to it. The new leader's motivation to make the business plan a success is high because he usually has participated in the creating of the business plan.

How Much Authority?   If the new manager has not had an opportunity to participate in the planning, he should be given the right to modify the business plan, since he is responsible for building the organization and for its fate.

As a matter of fact, there is good reason to specifically tell the newly appointed top man that he has the authority to modify the business plan even in important respects. Of course, if the changes he suggests seem illogical to the overseeing group, there had better be a discussion to see whether there is an understanding and agreement on basic objectives.

The Care and Feeding of Venture Managers   Reams of material have been written about what managerial style venture teams and entrepreneurs should use. The fact is that nobody really knows the full answer to this question, though it is of great importance to the success of new ventures. Therefore, the problem is worth trying to solve, however imperfectly. Once the characteristics, needs, and desires of the entrepreneurial businessman are reasonably well known, one can make some reasonable assumptions about the appropriate climate for success. In theory, the climate is not too difficult to describe; in practice, it is harder to achieve.

The proper environment for the successful management of venture managers and venture teams seem to be these:

1. Provide a situation characterized by moderate risk in which his own personal actions can measurably affect the results.
2. Do not allow the situation to be so unstructured and nebulous as to preclude meaningful and clear feedback regarding performance.
3. Provide performance incentives which are appropriate to his desires and which he considers adequate to provide him with desired payoffs.
4. Provide reasonable but not unlimited freedom in decision making and action implementation, but insist on knowing the results of decisions and actions.
5. Build into the managerial relationship a structure of accountability for results, having the structure based on some kind of plan, however crude it may be in the beginning.
6. Hold frequent analytical review meetings about the progress of the venture to give and obtain clear feedback on the results attained.
7. Don't abdicate the responsibility for overseeing the venture. Many ventures have floundered because the venture manager was unable to determine the rules of the game he was being asked to play.
8. Be prepared for various forms of failure and set up a system to detect and diagnose problems quickly and accurately. Many ventures headed for failure have been saved by an early warning system.

While these ideas are certainly neither exhaustive nor novel, they do seem to be at the core of the kind of managerial climate in which entrepreneurs and venture managers do best, a structured yet independent relationship which only comes into play when necessary—that is, when results are not up to par.

3. Charting and Manning

The reliance on organization charts in business is controversial. Many people think they are misleading or useless. Others feel it is impossible to plan for the growth of an organization without one.

It has been our experience that the use of an organization chart at least gives the employee the sense that management is spending time on the planning function. In an embryonic company, where so little is specific and concrete, this is an added benefit. Thus, policy, in all its forms, including organization charts, is regularly offered in writing.

But regardless of the virtues, real or imagined, of organization charts for going concerns, a new organization can be planned far more systematically if a chart, even of the most vestigial kind, is used for the basic departments that are being contemplated. Even a simple diagram affords some idea of what corporate functions are being mobilized, who is in charge of each, and to whom these departments report.

The usefulness of an organization chart is that it helps the top executive work out the lines of authority and the basic activities he plans for his fledgling company. Once the chart has been set down on paper, the top executive and others can set about looking for the people to fill the vacant squares.

Peopling the organization effectively is critical, second only in importance to the appointment of the top man. As was true of the top executive, individuals joining a small or start-up company require special qualities. One promoter advises, "The men and women who come in on the ground floor should be self starters, able to accept responsibility for their particular areas of activity."

At the start of recruitment a president or general manager faces an array of questions. How does he find the right type of people? What qualifications does he look for? How does he pin those qualifications down? Does he read articles and books on selection of personnel? Does he use psychological testing, or does he depend more on individual interviews?

One guideline: The people sought for a new company should be psychologically attuned to work in untraditional and unstructured environments. If these words could be printed in red ink, they would deserve that attention. To the uninitiated, the lack of structure can be devastating. The ability to adapt to an open-ended and fluid situation seems to be the key requirement for the new manager in his situation. A successful minority have shown fortitude that even the individuals often did not know they possessed. They rise to the occasion. The majority unfortunately leave the new venture embittered and made aware of their inability to operate in an unstructured situation.

Unlike the employees of established companies, people in growing organizations will not be called on to maintain the status quo. They cannot be caretakers: they must be innovators, doers, and users of experimental approaches. They should be venturesome rather than conservative. And in terms of personal activities, they cannot be nine-to-five people; they must be nine-to-whatever-hour-is-required people.

Even specialists should have a catholic outlook, with interest, if not experience, in all facets of the business. Since both apathy and pessimism can stymie the new enterprise, the new people should be energetic and optimistic—in a sense, naïvely confident.

One entrepreneur looking back over his successful manning operation says:

> To attract the type of people you need, structure the opportunity you offer in such a way that in effect you ask each key person to bet on himself.
>
> If each man is willing to bet on himself first, because of the opportunity you present to him and second, because of his belief in his own capability, then you have the type of individual who will be a definite asset.

Many entrepreneurs agree to the idea that it is wise to be generous to other managers. The magnanimity generally takes the form of ownership of the company. The new key man will usually be desirably motivated by a percentage of the company, with his reward resulting from the price appreciation of the company stock. This makes the entrepreneur's and the top executive's goals the same. The executive is no longer under pressure to convince you that he is performing satisfactorily. His aim is to make the venture succeed for his own enlightened self-interest.

The ownership offered should encourage the executive to think of himself as an owner. One specific benefit: In seeking subordinates he will worry less about possible personal competition and hire the most effective people he can find.

With this ownership approach, it is possible to attract key people from larger companies, individuals who are anxious to take over, instead of being supervised—who want to run their own show.

As a result of the top executive's strong motivation, he becomes highly result-oriented. His hours on the job will begin to outweigh his hours at home. His wife and children will react adversely to the new situation.

The outcome of this conflict naturally depends on the personalities of the individuals involved, but according to one observer, "Families soon realize that if the top man is happy, even though he may not be available as much, they too have reason for contentment."

Another entrepreneur observes, "A job-satisfied husband who is available part of the week-end and most evenings to join in family life, even though he works a 70-hour week, is more of a loving husband and father than a 40-hour man who is dissatisfied with his job."

In addition to the stock and/or stock option given to the top man, the top executive should have available similar ownership incentives to attract other managers. In all cases, stock options should be offered right down the line to stenographers, secretaries, typists, maintenance people, salesmen, etc. Mutual stock ownership engenders a feeling of mutuality of objectives. Added to the job is a new element, both a feeling of involvement and the feeling of adventure. As a result, every employee regards company activities like a mother hen. They view the activities of a competitor as an attack on the common home.

At the germinal stage of corporate life, a detailed and complete clarification of job content, responsibility, and so on in traditional terms is undesirable. But it *is* essential for basic operations and objectives to be spelled out.

One businessman who has been through the mill suggests, "Let the marketing man develop his marketing and sales strategies. Let your inside man build up the internal organization that is needed."

One type of direction is undesirable: day-to-day supervision of the top operating executive by the entrepreneur, financial people, or promoters. "Insist that major decisions and policies get prior approval but otherwise let them go," is the advice of an investment banker.

Executives who will be in charge of divisions or functions should be required to plan their own suborganizations on paper. To do so they should become familiar with the overall business plan. They should then enlarge on their own segment, recommending how they will produce or sell, and what distribution channels, markets, prices, service policies, depreciation schedules, and so on are planned. In other words, from the business plan which may have seemed detailed originally, subexecutives must refine the details still further, so that objectives become clearer, along with ways to achieve them.

4. Headquartering

Archimedes said, "Give me where to stand and I will move the earth."

A physical headquarters provides several immediate and essential benefits for a new firm:

- A mailing address
- A telephone
- A feeling of being in business

To individuals unfamiliar with start-up company operation it may seem unexpected that all the above benefits may be derived from as little as rented desk space. They do. At an early stage there is so little to identify with and show that every bit helps considerably. A letterhead, business card, some office and engineering supplies, a copying machine, a typewriter, a desk, a chair, a bookshelf—all of these things give the struggling souls a greater sense of identity and existence.

Whether it's the entrepreneur or his appointed executives, the actual start-up of a company is usually signified by renting or purchasing some kind of physical headquarters. In making this move a number of questions must be answered:

"HOW EXTENSIVE?" Desk space rented in someone else's office may suffice for the new company. But in cases where more than one, indeed several people, may already be on the company roster, one or more office rooms may be required. A key factor in making the space decision is the amount of time required to get the company rolling.

The well-planned move at this stage is usually one where there is sufficient flexibility for the fledgling firm to expand as needed. In other words, a rental should give the new company the option to increase its space usage or, if this is not feasible, to commit itself for six months or a year so that it is not hampered by inadequate facilities if and when the operation begins to grow.

"HOW EXPENSIVE?" Two factors generally determine the degree of luxury that is advisable. The first one obviously is the amount of money in the till. Regardless of other considerations, if the money isn't there the interior decorator with his desirable bag of tricks won't be either.

The second factor is the use to which the headquarters will be put. If prospects or customers will want to visit headquarters, then the decision may be strongly pushed in the direction of an attractive, even impressive, physical setting for the new company.

"LOCATION(S)"? Where there are both production facilities and sales or marketing facilities in existence at an early stage it may be desirable either to have these together or to separate them. For example, Company A, set up to produce a new type of plastic container aimed primarily at the cosmetics field, decides to have attractive and expensive offices in the downtown section of a large city with its pilot production facilities out in the less expensive suburbs. For one thing, there's no need to show prospects what the production equipment looks like; they're willing to buy on the basis of samples.

Company B feels it is important that prospects actually see the production facilities to understand not only the advantages of its new process, but also the reason for its efficiency and low price. Here the sale can be favorably influenced by a plant tour. Accordingly, sales offices and plant join one another in a reachable and affordable suburban area.

Many start-up operations have been stymied because of a poorly selected site. Rapid growth catches the company unaware and, moved by expediency rather than foresight, the company continues to expand. The result is not helpful to operations. Cramped facilities in an inaccessible spot will hamper company growth.

In opening headquarters, the wisest decision is one based on compromise between the broadest possible extremes: "If we really don't get rolling for a year or so, our facilities costs will be relatively bearable," and "If things go the best possible, we'll be able either to expand here or move to another location easily."

A final consideration may be the availability of labor. One company started with a combined corporate office and laboratory in Connecticut. Finding that not enough engineers and technicians were available, they moved to New Jersey where qualified employees were more readily available.

5. Function Development

As every business school graduate knows, a typical corporation features a number of basic functions: finance, engineering, production, marketing, and sales. Just exactly when and how these functions are formed into recognizable differentiated activities is an individual phenomenon specific to each company.

In the beginning, the top executive, with assists from his backers, board of directors, or employers, will probably take care of all the functions himself. Somewhere along the way he will require a marketing and/or sales executive. Similarly he will acquire men to head up the other functions as the need for them becomes apparent.

The crucial aspect of function development is that functions just starting up are not the same as those in established corporations. The operation of a going sales organization is highly complex, with considerable differentiation. A sales function of even a moderate-sized company requires a hierarchy of individuals: a vice-president in charge of sales, a general sales manager, regional managers, product specialists, national accounts specialists, and on down to product line salesmen.

In the start-up company, the sales operation doesn't have the advantage of either this extensive staffing or refined task differentiation. The man hired to start up the sales function will certainly begin by doing it all himself: manager and salesman, and so on. Then, as experience and success dictate, he will start building a staff based on his judgment of requirements. He may take on a salesman with considerable experience in selling to a particular region or in a particular type of market, or one who has had extensive experience in selling products that are the same as or similar to those of the new company.

In this situation it is up to the top man not only to hire the people to start up the corporate functions, but also to see that tendencies toward empire building are kept under control. He will not, for example, let an aggressive production executive invest more heavily in men and equipment than he feels is warranted by company prospects. This is especially true if the investment tends to hamper the development of other functions which may have a more logical cash need but which are not presented as articulately because the executive heading up the function is less aggressive.

In other words, the top man must keep the functional development in balance, where smooth operation will keep the entire organization moving in the most desirable fashion and at optimum speed.

6. Gap-Spotting and Filling

Somewhere in the early days of corporate life (and before a general review, which is the last step in this process) the top man should start among his executive staff an investigation that serves to identify and fill operating and manning gaps.

The purpose of this step is to eliminate a question raised in the next one. In step 7, organizational review, there is a *general* reconsideration of progress. But before this can be made there should be no reason for anyone to say things like, "We cannot really say how we are doing because we haven't fully explored a given market or tried a possible production method."

Step 6 requires a careful tightrope movement. It has already been suggested in step 5 that an "edifice complex" may push certain functional heads in the direction of overstaffing and overactivity beyond a desirable balance with other functions. Yet in step 6 the top executive must ask the question that *seems* to invite this response. He asks, "Do you think we should spend another $25,000 in advertising in order to make sure we've given plan A a fair trial?" He asks, "Should we invest another thousand dollars in a more powerful machine to make sure that our production costs and quality are stabilized?"

And even though he is the one who is asking the questions, he must not only listen to the answers he gets from his subordinates, but also must evaluate their answers. In others words, even though they may say "yes," he, having raised the question, may still have to say "no."

What is important here is his overall objective. He wants to make sure that the new company is moving along the best way possible and is not missing out on overall results because of inadequacies at one or more points.

7. Organizational Review and Rounding Out

This is the acid test of progress. Are the objectives and goals of the business plan being met on time and within the cost-frame forecast? If not, why not?

Have you (the top manager or investor) been kept aware of *all* the important failures and successes that have occurred since you started? When things go wrong, has your man known why? Does he make the same mistakes twice? Does he have contingency plans for most emergencies? Are these in writing?

How do you keep your key people aware of your concern and interest? There seems to be a need for people to know they are being watched. They seem to want it, and to operate better for it. From young children, the call of "Mommy, Daddy, watch me!" is omnipresent. A common statement from juveniles arrested for indiscretions is, "They don't care what I do" (meaning, "They don't love me enough to concern themselves with what I do or think. I am a nonperson to them"). Similarly, religion gives people the comfort and discipline of being held accountable for their actions.

By the same token, managers have to *feel* (as well as *know*) that they are being held accountable for their actions. Their superiors, or board of directors, or stockholders, *do* care and *are* watching. How, then, is it possible to give someone the needed sense that his superiors are concerned and ready to help when he needs it, but also the assurance that the superior will not butt in, offer gratuitous advice, or change well-conceived and well-thought-out plans? First, the problem can be avoided by not appointing to key positions any men who are afraid or unwilling to make decisions. There are also various other approaches:

SCHEDULE REVIEW MEETINGS   These are either held periodically —biweekly, monthly, etc.—or on an occasional basis (e.g., quarterly reports, presentations to venture capital groups or large potential customers).

REQUIRE FORMAL WRITTEN REPORTS   These should cover what has happened, how these happenings compare with the plan, and what should be accomplished during the next reporting period. The most important report relates to the budget. At a minimum, there should be a monthly budget review, as close to the end of the previous month as possible, to determine what was done and how it compared with what was planned, for better or worse. Cash receipts and expenses are the single best item of information for determining whether the company and individual departments are performing well or poorly.

UNSCHEDULED SESSIONS   This is probably the worst way to provide the feeling of being watched. It substitutes conversation for commitment, and form for substance. Unless the conversations are taped or put into black and white, they are usually too general and gently waft away. But this laissez-faire approach can work and work well if the results of the discussions are written down and presented in a format comparable to the written report.

Next Step

Inevitably, the entire start-up company, or important parts of it, will not succeed, or will succeed only partially. Or, inspection and evaluation of various aspects of its performance will suggest modification. The next chapter takes up the considerations involved in the reshaping or reorganization of the new company after a reasonable trial period.

Chapter 7

Shakedown of the Company: The Next Effort

When do you stop or change a program? When will patience and a little more time and money allow the program to succeed? This is the second of the three most tenuous judgments in the venture management business. The first, the judgment of which companies will make it and which will not, has been discussed in Chapter 4, Venture Capital: Investing in New Companies. The third, determining what consumers and industrial companies will buy, or market research, will be discussed later, in Chapter 9.

There are really no universally valid ways to make these three difficult judgments, because the decision maker *always* has insufficient information. No wonder that it is safer to work for the established automobile company introducing a new model with only a style change, or an entrenched soap company introducing a new liquid soap. No wonder that AT&T and IBM become investments for "widows and orphans." No wonder that a great deal of good money is spent after bad. No wonder that we will never know about products and companies that might have made it if someone had been a little more patient and daring.

Yet, like so many other circumstances, difficult to analyze, the choice of stopping, changing, or going straight ahead can be assisted, if not totally resolved, by more information and proper understanding of the information.

Recognition that major problems exist is the first step in the process of understanding. Having planned the company and participated in its implementation, the venture manager and the investor should both keep themselves intimately aware of what is going on. This will enable them first to recognize when major problems exist and second to become intelligently involved in their solutions. Recognition of major problems and their solutions is the substance of this chapter. Also, this chapter stresses that the chief executive officer is the dominant factor in this process.

Recognition of Major Problems

The implementation of a new program or start-up company is relatively smooth as compared with the turbulence of the planning and venture capital stages. Many different kinds of people with different values have reviewed the situation and decided to invest their time, money, and talent. These diverse people share an optimism about the risky situation. Each decision to join, by each of the different participants, adds supportive strength and hope to the project in the eyes of each of the others. Success seems to require only a little more time. You can almost taste it.

This emotionalism is both an asset and a problem. The recognition and admission of major problems cause turmoil that is difficult, and, for some, impossible, to accept.

Richard Nixon has described this natural human reaction very well:

> I learned that the real emotional pitfalls lurk not in preparing to meet a crisis or in fighting the battle itself, but rather in that time immediately afterward when the body, mind, and spirit are totally exhausted and there are still problems to deal with. Those who have known great crisis . . . its challenge and tension, its victory and defeat . . . can never become adjusted to a more leisurely and orderly pace. One of the most trying experiences an individual can go through is the period of doubt, of soul searching, to determine whether to fight the battle or fly from it. It is in such a period that almost unbearable tensions can build up, tensions that can be relieved only by taking action one way or the other. And significantly, it is this period of crisis conduct that separates the leaders from the followers. A leader is one who has the emotional, mental, and physical strength to withstand the pressures and tensions created by necessary doubt and then, at the critical moment to make a choice and act decisively. The men who fail are those who are so overcome by doubt that they either crack under the strain or flee to avoid meeting the problem at all. On the other hand, if one is to act and to lead responsively, he must necessarily go through this period of soul searching and testing of alternate courses of action. Otherwise he shoots from the hip, misses the target, and loses the battle through sheer recklessness.[1]

1. Richard M. Nixon, *My Six Crises* (New York: Doubleday & Co., 1962), p. 19.

It is so much easier to continue what you are doing. "Maybe the problem will go away." "Perhaps I am being impatient." "The changes may be worse than what I have now." Rationalization or fact? You have to decide on the basis of your own unique situation.

Unique, but perhaps analogous to other situations. One pitfall to avoid is looking inward and excluding the outside world. Be in the center of the situation (and, in particular, be in the middle of what is happening in the emerging company), and you will realistically and more accurately know where it stands. Recognize that you're in a continuing cycle with many patterns occurring simultaneously. Inoculate yourself against completely relaxing, against assuming that the last problem has been understood and solved. Minimize what you take for granted. Differentiate between what is major and what is minor—a detail that will be corrected, or is not important, anyway.

It is at this shakedown phase of a new venture that the four key *ingredients* in a new company are particularly clear. Understanding them is difficult; it provides the hints and signs of major problems. Thee ingredients are:

1. The chief executive officer and his top subordinates
2. The marketing and sales plan and its carry-through
3. The financial plan and its implementation
4. The budget and how it is being followed

Because of their importance, the second, third, and fourth ingredients have been chosen for discussion in greater detail in the last five chapters of this book. The main theme of the balance of this chapter involves the chief executive officer: the focal point of the implementation and shakedown of the plan, the recognizer of its faults and of new opportunities that were not planned, and the solver of the problems.

The Chief Executive Officer

The chief executive officer, the president, should carefully evaluate his new team, its planning as well as its implementation. He will continually ask evaluative questions like these:

- Do team members have objectives and goals on a month-to-month, week-to-week, day-to-day, hour-to-hour basis?
- Do they admit mistakes? Seek advice? Learn from mistakes?
- Do they keep the president informed on matters of importance and not bother him with details? Do they do the same for their office associates? For the investors?

- Do they have enough conviction about what they are doing and about their chances of succeeding so that they are willing to specifically commit themselves in writing?
- Are they keeping accurate records of whom they have seen, what happened, for what purpose, and what action they are going to take in the future to bring about a desired result?
- Are they insistent about knowing what is going on in other parts of the embryonic organization so that they are informed?
- Are they more interested in accomplishment in their area of responsibility than in trying to show how much better they are doing than their colleagues?

These questions and similar ones are important to the president. They are also the obvious questions and are discussed more fundamentally and in more detail in standard textbooks. The following subtle questions and insights, which provide equally compelling evidence on how the new venture is proceeding, are rarely discussed:

1. A poor worker blames his tools. If the president sees that subordinates are blaming circumstances and other people for poor performance, it is likely that the employee is in trouble.
2. There is a dichotomy between the "if only" syndrome and "the next time" syndrome. The employee who is constantly pleading "if only this or if only that" also sees himself in trouble. The subordinate who thinks and acts in terms of "The next time I will . . ." recognizes the problem, is prepared to meet and deal with it, and will probably be successful.
3. A person who is constantly running off to the next deal before solving the problems of the present deal is a candidate for trouble. This approach probably indicates a lack of maturity and decisiveness.
4. Managers who do not defend "the company" to their subordinates are almost always incapable of administering their job. Regardless of their personal opinions, managers must support the policies and objectives of the people above them. They may take exception at policy meetings, fighting vigorously for their views, but once the decision has been made, they must support it and do everything possible to ensure its success. If they cannot support policy decisions, they should leave the company or be asked to leave.
5. The employee who is brazen and seemingly unaware of the problems around him shows a lack of reality that is subject only to education. If this fails, he is a candidate for leaving the company.
6. The yes-man is a business legend. Less well known is the "no-man." He is usually against everything, making it as difficult to un-

derstand what he believes as what the yes-man wants. He is unlike the yes-man in that when the same subject is discussed at different times, he is on both sides of the issue. It may be deduced that he really does not know which way to go and feels safest giving two decisive answers.

7. The compulsive type with the "need to win" is also well known. More subtle, and much more difficult to perceive and understand, is the employee with the need to lose. He will snatch defeat from the jaws of victory every time. It is such an illogical pattern that the president must see it on numerous occasions before he comes to understand the case.

8. The man who has just lost, but who otherwise has a pattern of success, is probably the best man to bet on. He is likely to have a compulsion to prove that he can win again and will show that he knows how to do it.

9. The "expert" syndrome. One of the prime and most subtle self-destructs is the manager who is always seeking an expert or some other single factor that will save the day. He seeks the answers to his problems from a book he never quite finds; a key customer he never quite sells; a new product he never quite develops; a new investor who never quite invests; or some expert who will ideally solve the problem at hand.

10. People who do not trust their own ability and judgment are rarely able to trust others and therefore are incapable of delegating responsibility.

11. Subtle problems relate to those employees who are for "God, mother, and country" but are not meeting the specific objectives of the company. During product development, tooling of a new product, and the marketing phase before the selling of a new product, it is a conflict in terms to apply a standard of success based on profits or a positive cash flow. A successful selling program can only be based on a successful marketing plan. Paradoxically, profits or a positive cash flow may indicate a lack of aggressiveness. Leasing instead of outright sales may be the best program for the company, yet it may yield a lower cash flow or greatly increase interest expense. The point is that a good manager is meeting the immediate objectives of the company and not necessarily maximizing operating results at a particular time.

The president is not alone in seeking and questioning. A good board of directors is going through a similar process. The manager of venture capital and the investors he has brought in are watching the president. Sideways, managers are watching each other and subordinates. Upward, the subordinates are watching the managers. In the established company, the relatedness of these people to each other has been documented in an organization chart. In the start-up company, this chart is likely to be more nominal than actual. Everyone is wearing many hats and an informal methodology has grown up to supplement and in many ways improve chances for the new venture.

In these early operations, the business plan is not a static document, but a guide. It suggests where to go, how to get there, and what routes to take, and it includes timetables.

As in any major undertaking, even when objectives are known and the route predetermined, there are many detours and changes in plans, often made on an *ad hoc* basis. These detours should not change the business plan materially.

Yet, as has also been explained, a plan is not fixed nor unalterable. It usually must be modified as conditions change. During the crucial first phase, the president and his colleagues must be flexible. The environment, the economy, the technical problems, the marketing difficulties, the delays on shipments, the seemingly never-ending evaluations by potential users, the difficulty of getting the right people together and motivating them to actively undertake the work ahead, the moving of families or offices, and myriad other things that happen in both an ongoing and an embryonic business venture must be taken into account during the evolution of the company to an operating business.

What if the president, the central figure, goes wrong? If he is blown away? If he panics and stays? In a small company that is on its own, without outside venture managers or venture capital investors, such an event usually means the end of the venture. In a small company with strong vested interests outside the company, he is replaced.

Three cases are given below that illustrate companies with problems almost entirely based on the attitudes of the president. The story about President Casey shows the chief executive officer who is so happy and busy being president that he never really takes the trouble to get his company into business. President Wrigley is an intellectual; he is going to school and learning more and more about his industry, without ever getting into his industry. President Stubbs is unable or unwilling to make the decision to take advantage of peripheral business to survive.

A LATTER-DAY CASEY STRIKES OUT

A company was set up to capitalize on a revolutionary electronic product. The organization was established and Sam Casey was hired to run it. Casey's previous experience was heading up a division of a large corporation. He had developed procedures, set up guidelines, formed his business on paper, and started to bring in key executives. His initial objective was to advance product development through the engineering stage and place models in the market for field testing and market evaluating.

Casey quickly built an organization to handle the marketing problems, the engineering difficulties, and the manufacturing. But in the excitement of building and staffing and talking to prospective suppliers and interested customers, he was losing the sight of his original, overriding goal, which was to market the new product.

President Casey discussed advertising programs with advertisers, and established financial and corporate public relations with outside firms; he met with venture capital people to obtain funds that were not needed at the time, and he traveled to meet with manufacturing organizations to see whether or not acquisitions and mergers might be a possibility. He concentrated on many things which had no relationship to his primary goal of developing units for field testing and marketing.

Casey delegated the production and testing of product units to Frank Hess, a middle manager who was technically oriented. Hess was asked to engineer the products, find customers who would be willing to participate in field testing, evaluate these tests, modify the equipment, and freeze the design so that commercial production could be undertaken. Hess had a lonely job, since Casey was rarely available for consultation. Casey was very busy being "president."

President Casey appeared to be an aggressive, dynamic, forward-looking, and a hard-charging leader. In actuality, he was playing a game unrelated to the basic realities of his situation.

The company began to come apart at the seams. The venture capitalists and potential customers lost interest because they were unable to see working units of the product. Suppliers who had been providing engineering service gratis in hope of being able to supply parts for this new product cooled off because there were no machines in the field. And the morale of the employees started to decrease because they saw much flurry but little concrete accomplishment, and because they sensed the dire results of this discrepancy.

Sam Casey did not accomplish his main objective, and the venture failed. Millions of dollars of investor money were thrown away. The people who had been providing funds for the preliminary work saw that an organization of more than forty people had been built up and had accomplished practically nothing. All the people had to find other jobs because of the chief executive's failure. They will never know whether the product line was any good.

WRIGLEY THE INFLEXIBLE

George Wrigley was hired and was handed a product that had been engineered to the point where it could be demonstrated and used in the field. Initial research and the development engineering had been completed, and the product was ready for marketing. The product lent itself to hand fabrication and assembly, and it required no tooling. The per-unit cost of three units was almost the same as for 100 units. Wrigley's chief objective was to produce and market the unit.

Wrigley was an electrical engineer, bright, technically oriented, with experience in management consulting and administration. But apparently neither his training nor experience helped him avoid the pitfall of misdirection. He became intrigued by the technological aspects of his product; he fell in love with his technology. He also was a perfectionist and felt that to discuss his product with prospective customers he would have to be as knowledgeable in their fields as he was in his own. He started to educate himself. The few moves he made toward his assigned aim were merely direct implementation of the business plan handed him without regard to timing or relevance.

He spent 95 percent of his time keeping up with his industry's advances, reading the technical journals, attending seminars, becoming friendly with executives and managers and technicians in the industry. Unfortunately, he was not selling; he seemed almost to feel it was beneath him to sell. He was not making proposals to tailor the product to satisfy specific needs of customers. He had to be replaced by a goal-oriented executive who realized that sales do not simply happen, that programs must be undertaken, and that hard work is required to convert a business plan into an effective commercial operation.

In shaping and reshaping an organization, a frequent candidate for shakeout is the inflexible person. Come what may, he sticks to his business plan —and fails. The executive who insists on implementing the plan on paper even though the environment has changed, and even though other changes have taken place, is also headed for disaster.

STUBBS THE STUBBORN

A company was established to capitalize on a new method of optical measurement. The initial development was successful and field tests were underway, with interest from prospective customers. But the economy turned down, and the customers who had been interested in the concept and at one time had the funds available, now were not purchasing new things which immediately required a larger outlay than competitive equipment, even though this could save money in the long run.

A great deal of technological expertise had been built up in the optical scanning area by this company. Engineering jobs were offered to them by firms which felt that their ability to develop the optical scanning concept indicated an ability to solve the customers' problems.

However, the president, Robert Stubbs, felt that this type of work was a dilution of effort. He held to his course of trying to sell a new product to an economy that could not afford it. The company went bankrupt.

If adhering to objectives and principles will result in bankruptcy, then one must cast around for other ways to remain solvent. One entrepreneur in the industrial goods area told a friend that he would buy a pizza shop if it would help him survive, even though pizza shops could in no way help build his industrial products business. Properly, he felt the overriding immediate goal was to survive—to be around when the world was ready for his new product—and he was willing to take almost any steps to increase the chances of survival.

Managers may see elements of their own attitudes and operating performances in the three case histories given above. Success instead of failure is a matter of degree. The president *should* enjoy and feel comfortable being at the top. He *should* have a basic and detailed understanding of his industry. He *should* concentrate on his product line and avoid other tempting opportunities that come along. But with no book to go to that will advise on his unique set of circumstances, the determination of degrees must be intuitive and timely.

Is his method of operating in his own peculiar circumstances a dilution of effort and not appropriate to meet objectives? Does he really have the will to win? Or is playing the game an end in itself? "Dilution of effort" and the will to win—let us discuss them for a moment.

Dilution of Effort

If the immediate goal is profit and the chief executive sees his company falling behind, changes to bring about more profitable operations should be considered. If a key goal, however, is to first establish an organization which will be the nucleus of the business for the next five years, then short-term efforts to achieve profit may weaken the organization. Periods of unprofitable operations may have to be accepted. If sales are the goal and they are not being achieved, then the organizational structure should be modified, ways to increase sales should be explored, and efforts to obtain this particular goal made. If the goal is to place a certain number of products in the hands of customers to gather field test and market information, then profit, sales, and structure may be diversionary. In short, dilution of effort must be avoided if significant accomplishments are to be made. Yet, one must be able to distinguish between dilution of effort and fruitful digression.

The Will to Win

How does one explain the will to win? In a negative sense, it is not letting down when a basic problem has been solved. In the embryonic company, there are still many other basic problems. It is not blaming others for mistakes and taking credit for success. It is not concentrating on what is fun to manage and delegating the unfamiliar and difficult.

The will to win is a dedication and commitment of thought and action that will compromise and adapt to reality but never really believes it can lose.

A particularly bad series of circumstances were besetting the head of a young company. He discussed his many problems with his wife. "Why don't you quit?" she asked, with sympathy. After he thought for a moment, his answer was, "Because it has never occurred to me."

When the doubts are frequent and long-lasting, perhaps the will to win has been lost. Those who concentrate their thoughts and action on their doubts are incapable of leading and probably of winning. They will never make a total commitment, because they draw back from failure, and their many doubts are the early proof of the possibility of failure. The rationalization, never quite on the surface of their mind, goes as follows: "If I don't make the total effort and fail, I will later be able to tell myself that I really could have succeeded, if I had tried harder. Maybe I will get lucky and succeed, even if I don't make the total effort. If I make the total effort and don't succeed, I will not be able to live with myself."

Having explored the recognition of problems and, in particular, major problems in relationship to the role of the president, it is appropriate to discuss the solution to major problems.

Solving Major Problems

The solutions to problems that are less than critical are too varied to go into in this chapter. We have discussed many of them from the standpoint of being in a position to recognize them. Recognition is at least half of the battle.

When critical problems threaten the existence of the company or project, at the simplest level possible and very early in the continuum, you stop the operation. I once stopped an early product development when the same product appeared in a Sears catalog. If the project had been further along and had had more going for it, I might have continued. A new start-up company was also stopped after the second meeting because it was judged to be a dilution of effort. Here are the notes of the second meeting, to indicate the frailty of the idea:

Subject: European Venture Capital Deal

This is a meeting to discuss assumptions and follow-up items for a potential business deal involving venture capital investment:

(1) It is assumed that there are a continual number of good real estate investments in the United States. These fall into the categories of nursing homes, raw land, office buildings, shopping centers, etc.

(2) It is assumed that [manager] and the rest of management have to approve any arrangements.

(3) It is assumed that a working capital investment of between $50,000 and $200,000 would be required to put together a plan and for initial start-up.

(4) It is assumed that the venture would be on some type of joint basis between us and the [other American] interest.

(5) It is assumed that in some manner European management can be attracted by giving them ownership in the new company. Consideration should be given to any SEC consequences of any of the dealings.

(6) We should remember that [major brokerage firm] in Brussels indicated a large availability of venture capital in Western Europe.

(7) We should also bear in mind the position of [a German businessman].

(8) It is assumed that real estate investment in the United States is to be a bread-and-butter business only. The business of the company is ultimately to be a European version of our U.S. company.

(9) It is assumed that 12 to 15 per cent return can be made on rather conservative investments as a return on investment.

(10) Shames will check with corporate counsel about Europeans investing in American companies and the tax consequences. Perhaps a European company that is partially or totally owned by an American company is best.

```
(11) It is assumed that [our inventor] can be made a
permanent part of the new company.
(12) It is assumed that the program, after it is well
defined, will start relatively small so that we can
learn the tax factors, motivation factors, pitfalls, and
prove out the concept.
```

In addition to simply stopping the company or project with critical problems, other solutions include: selling the company, putting it on the shelf in the hope that something basic will change, and, finally, making basic changes in the direction of the company. Because of its complexity and possible insights, one of my experiences in changing the direction of a company will be discussed.

Changing the Direction of an Operation

Identimation required basic changes about a year after it started. It actually required changes earlier, but the need was not recognized at that point.

In this instance, three Sibany employees were moved from Sibany to similar positions in Identimation: the president, the executive vice-president, and the director of operations.

The requirement to move people and other assets from one operation to another when trouble occurs is not unique. When this flexibility is not available because a new venture has been started on its own, separated from other new ventures, the venture probably has less chance of succeeding. Others involved in venture management concur and lead to the prediction (discussed in more detail in Chapter 4) that the next major peak of the venture capital industry will include much greater intimacy between the managers of venture capital and new ventures.

My approach to strengthening Identimation was as follows:

My basic problem related to the fact that I did not know what was going on in detail and I was not totally qualified to judge the people I had working for me.

I determined that I was going to concentrate on three goals:

(1) The company needed a very firm hand. This was tremendously resisted, because it had previously operated in an open-ended manner.

(2) There was basically no communication among people and this had to be improved. In particular every employee had to understand what his job was, whom he reported to, and the goals of the company and where his job stood in relation to those goals.

(3) We had to obtain operating results because of the practical need for income and to give each of the employees the sense that we were able to accomplish something.

During the first month, an organization chart was completed and discussed with each employee individually. A series of policy and procedure memos were sent to employees under the running title, "Identimation Operations Procedures." Each employee was told where he worked, for whom he worked, the functions and goals of his job, and how they fitted into Identimation's short- and medium-term goals.

I came to realize that the company had six or eight managers; each had a vested interest in making himself look as good as possible and to censor information in a manner that he thought would make me happy. They wanted me to believe that prosperity was just around the corner.

These defensive attitudes created confusion in the judgments of what was true and what was being distorted. In all honesty, I cannot tell whether many of these people who were subsequently fired were deliberately confusing me or were simply unrealistic and passing along their own lack of realism.

I began doodling and behaving in other ways which I have learned satisfies my style of decision-making. I came to important conclusions. Unfortunately, these conclusions were not immediately implemented but rather were carried out over a period of nine months. It was a basic mistake on my part because my preliminary analysis was subsequently proven correct. But because of fear that I did not have enough information to prove that certain things were being improperly handled, I proceeded to make changes cautiously.

While many of Identimation's previous people were still in office, a new division, the Technology Group, was organized to supplement Identimation's basic business of exploiting its personal identification technology. It was hoped that contracts could be received for new-product development, and production and facilities problem solving by the Identimation engineering department, to make it a profit center. Contracts totaling approximately $150,000 were received within six months, the first operating income Identimation had ever received.

FINE POINTS OF INTANGIBLE SELLING

Technology Group contracts were intangible sales. Identimation's own products in development required tangible selling. This meant that special techniques were required for internal sales training:

```
Memo:    To All Concerned
Subject: Intangible Selling
```

1. An intangible sale is made when the seller has left a nagging doubt in the mind of the buyer, and the nagging doubt is worth more to the buyer than the cost you ask of

him. Almost never is an intangible sale made to an
enthusiastic buyer. Those used to selling tangibles have
to change the road marks they are looking for during the
course of the sale.

2. Intangible sales will automatically be killed if there
   is any semblance of talking down to the customer, or
   glibness, canned talkiness or patness. You must give the
   buyer the sense that he is being customized, or that you
   had him in mind when you started the whole thing.

3. When you have hit the prospect with all your barrels and he
   yawns, begin to suspect that you have not related your
   talents to his needs, as he sees them.

4. When a company needs a prototype, or more work done on
   their product, and they ask you about a joint venture,
   they are likely to be telling you that they have no
   intention of giving you any money, or have none.

5. If you find yourself compulsively making telephone
   calls, having meetings, demonstrating equipment and
   sending letters, you are processing leads, not selling.

6. It is a fiction that you cannot close a contract in one
   meeting. "Our study contracts have run between $600 and
   $4600 and this problem looks like it would run about
   $1500." "That sounds reasonable; why don't you go ahead!"
   "Good! I'll schedule it and send you a confirming
   signature letter." If you believe it will necessarily take
   three or four meetings, the belief will become
   self-fulfilling.

7. A turn-down by a reasonable person should be followed by
   putting the man on the Identimation mailing list. Sometime
   in the future he may buy.

8. If you cannot get in the door or get a call back, something
   audacious may do the trick. Send him a telegram, or the
   like.

9. "No" from a customer is an abrupt end. "Yes" is a continuum
   requiring a great deal of patience from the salesman.

In order to obtain immediate results, the sales program concentrated on
companies which were known to us. Lack of credibility is a major deterrent to
intangible selling. By concentrating on these companies, the sales situation
was reduced to the much simpler question of whether or not the potential
customer has a new product, facilities or production problem that is greater
than what we would charge to solve the problem.

MORE ON RECONSTRUCTION

I made sure that I had very high visibility to each employee, both in person, and in writing. I challenged, cajoled, inspired, swore, yelled, and implored. At all times I tried to keep in perspective the priorities of the goals on the one and and the priorities of the problems on the other hand. For example, even after determining that all of the key people had to be replaced, their actual replacement was on a priority basis.

In the second month, one of the most important problems in a start-up operating company based on high technology really began to plague us. The technical orientation of so many of the employees leads to the wasting of time. The technical people waste each other's time by splitting hairs on issues of little consequence. The business and sales people are overwhelmed, so that they do not know if an engineer has taken advantage of them, or if he is simply incompetent.

Changing everything overnight would have hurt more than helped. Basic changes were instituted which were characterized by impersonalness and slowness at first, and personalities and comprehensiveness, after a few months. Two directives issued that second month are good examples:

```
Memo:    To All Concerned
Subject: Glossary of Terms at Identimation

    Identimation—a company to be profitable with a high rate
      of growth. . . .

    Identimation Board of Directors—a distinguished body of
      members checking the activities of Identimation's
      management vigorously and individually doing everything
      possible to insure the success of the company.

    A Sale—that transaction in commerce of which it is our
      policy to make instead of having a good meeting. . . .

    Demonstration of the Identimat®...—a meeting of only
      one Identimation sales employee and one or more potential
      customers only after a customer has been qualified.

    Identimation Distributor—an independent company devoutly
      to be sought and made a business associate in order to
      increase sales.

  Training—the investment of a quantity of time in the
    expectation of a many-fold return on the investment.

  Communication—that which is sought between two or more
    individuals and not avoided.
```

Policy—an important decision of the management of
    Identimation that is communicated to all concerned,
    and followed. It is always arrived at carefully, and not,
    because of a vacuum, quickly.

Cavalier Negativeness—a tongue-in-cheek practice of some
    Identimation employees that it is our policy to
    immediately stop. (Not to be confused with honest
    disagreement).

Delivery Date—a solemn promise to Identimation's best
    friend.

Unemployment—the present condition of former
    Identimation employees not getting results.

Vacations—that which there will be none of until after
    we get our head above water.

Family—former associates of Identimation employees.

Memo: To All Concerned
Subject: Saving the Time of Identimation Managers

1. Acquisitions

    Identimation should not be interested in acquisitions
    for diversification purposes. The time required to look at
    and investigate acquisitions can become burdensome.
    Therefore, no potential acquisitions should be considered
    unless a judgment is first made that the acquisition
    would save time in setting up an operation that was going
    to be set up anyway and that the cost of the
    acquisition is no greater than doing it ourselves.

2. Legal and Accounting Matters

    All accounting, legal and contractual matters for
    Identimation should be coordinated through the
    controller. All contracts require the approval of
    Identimation management, and Board of Directors,
    through the controller.

3. Communications

    There are basically three ways for each of us to
    communicate with each other. It is important that we
    follow the priority of writing instead of phoning and
    phoning instead of personal meetings.

4. Accessibility

   The manager is responsible for insuring that his
   secretary can reach him at all times.

5. Participation in Meetings

   Participation in meetings should be limited to only
   those essential to the meeting, even if this means that
   some questions are asked that cannot be answered on the
   spot.

6. Operations Meetings

   Operations meetings will be conducted to discuss and
   answer the specific problems and plans of participants
   that require a sounding board. Each meeting will start
   with a summary of a maximum five minutes' duration of the
   participants' activities. Each of us will have to take
   the trouble to make the summary concise and to the point
   and stay within the five-minute maximum.

7. New Product Developments

   Only projects that are currently active will be
   considered active projects and a Project Manager will
   be assigned to each. The first active projects list is
   enclosed.

8. Project Objectives

   The goal of each project will be to move it along, kill
   it or put it on the shelf as soon as possible. Until
   our present number of potential opportunities is
   substantially reduced, it will be our orientation to add
   no new things, unless a customer will pay the costs of
   a project, plus a reasonable profit.

   Concurrent with administrative changes, a series of "Sales Program
Things To Do" was initiated and made the subject of implementation:

1. Modify Identimate® 2000 design to both severely reduce
   mechanical complexity and reduce its cost.

2. Set up mailing list.

3. Set up daily sales reports.

4. Set up regular press release program.

5. Set up a sales manual.

6. Set up Identimat® distributor programs.

7. Set up a competitive file.

8. Sales brochures on the Identimat®, Scanamat and Technology Group.

9. Set up regular product application mailings.

10. Set up competitive and industry pricing and discount file.

11. Set up Technology Group distributor program.

12. Set up manufacturing license or farm out ability.

13. Have internal consultants make a product study of the Identimat® and disposable products.

14. Set up factory-determined price lists and discounts to avoid inconsistency and insure prices are set cooly and by Identimation management.

15. Set up definitive costing program, as part of a pricing program.

16. Review copies of all existing or outstanding proposals and all previous proposals that have been turned down.

17. Follow military sales status.

18. Implement Honeywell service program.

19. Follow Travelers re insurance and whether the rates would go down to the user of the Identimat® system.

20. Review inventories of parts for all products.

The implementation of any of these sales items within the oganization was made specifically and aimed at taking nothing for granted about the knowledge and wisdom of each of the recipients. A good case in point was the first directive concerning the sales manual:

Memo: To All Concerned

Subject: Identimation Sales Manual

Each of you has received several memos concerning Identimation Operating Procedures.

We are now instituting a sales manual program which will be
coordinated by Mona Newman. The first policy is that we
will have limited distribution of this manual to only those
who are receiving this memo or are later sent it. Mona
Newman's manual will be No. 1 and is defined as the
coordinator's copy. Arthur Zemad's will be No. 2 and will be
defined as the office copy. Smithton's copy will be No. 3;
McKnight, No. 4; Shames, No. 5; Jack McGee, No. 6; Tony
Garden, No. 7; and Larry Doolittle, No. 8.

Since we are new at working together, and because the
Technology Group's going sales programs have to be
cordinated with the new organizational effort, we will each
start with a blank sales manual. The persons not included in
this memo will be added to the system if and when
appropriate.

The new Identimation Sales Manual will have sections to be
defined as we go along. The first section should be
Identimation Operating Procedures and should include the
first two operating procedures that you have already
received, and this memo. Beyond that there will be sections
on price lists, specification sheets, institutional and
other type fliers, and press releases. The information will
come to you with three holes, prepunched, so that you can
make appropriate arrangements for filing accordingly. In the
beginning, when there will be only a few pages, and sections,
I would suggest you carry the sales manual with you at all
times. Later on you can begin dividing it into that part of
your sales manual which remains at your desk and that part
which you carry with you in a portable fashion. I should
appreciate any additional suggestions any of you may have
for making this tool as useful, coordinative, communicative,
and directional as possible.

As contracts for our bread-and-butter business, the Technology Group,
began to be received, Identimation, for the first time, faced the problems associated with having made sales. After months of the problems relating to
only spending money on product development, the joke became: "How are
you?" "I have a problem!" "What's the problem?" "I got an order!"

Specific problems were identified and solutions attempted. Some worked
the first time, others required modification and remodification. The following
memo is an example of the approach that was taken in solving some of
these problems in the Technology Group sales program:

Memo: To All Concerned
Subject: Sales Coordination and Follow—Up System

At the sales meeting it was agreed that:

1. People need to know that someone is monitoring their efforts.
2. Coordination is needed and should improve efficiency.
3. Our goal is to produce valid proposals.
4. The proposals should agree with the order subsequently accepted from the customer.
5. The internal paper work implementing the order must agree with the proposal and purchase order.
6. An accurate and complete end product, which may be a report generated by an Engineering Study or a prototype piece of hardware must be delivered to the customer.
7. All of the above efforts should result in profit.

   To implement a simple, easy-to-use system, the following items were decided upon:

(A) Salesman for Technology Group contracts:

   (1) L. Doolittle (Scanamat/Technology Group)
   (2) R. McKnight
   (3) J. McGee (Identimat®/Technology Group)
   (4) W. Shames
   (5) M. Smithton (ATS/Technology Group)

(B) Transactions which must be reported to Shames at the time of the first and then subsequent contacts:

   (1) All proposals (two copies).
   (2) Salesman's call reports (standard forms to be procured and issued by Shames). Two copies are to be retained by the writer for his use; two copies are to be forwarded to Shames.
   (3) All face—to—face sales meetings. (Use call reports.)
   (4) Important phone and letter contacts. (Use call reports.)

(C) Sales Procedure:

   (1) All problem statements are to be committed to writing—one copy forwarded to R. McKnight, prior to proposal meetings.
   (2) R. McKnight will be available at Northvale on Thursdays from 9:00 a.m. to 1:00 p.m., and on Mondays from 1:00 p.m. on, for proposal meetings or any coordination needs; meetings to be called by salesmen involved.
   (3) All proposals must be in writing, one copy to R. McKnight upon issue.

(4) All proposals must have concurrence of salesman and McKnight prior to release.

(5) Any reproposals or modifications to proposals are subject to the same requirements as new proposals.

(6) Creative meetings when required are called by salesman and scheduled through Shames.

(7) We will accept only official purchase orders or signature—line letters from customers.

(8) Salesman and McKnight must agree that P. O. accurately represents the proposal previously agreed upon.

(9) A copy of the P. O. or letter should be sent to McKnight as authorization to proceed. He will use it as his internal "work order."

After a year we had four important accomplishments. First, we received approximately $200,000 in business, by way of contracts from 11 companies. Second, we changed the company to being an operating company. Third, we had a contract with the U.S. Air Force for the test and evaluation of the Identimat, the basic business of Identimation. Fourth, the cost and mechanical complexity of our basic invention had been greatly reduced.

In addition, each employee now has a sense of what his job is and what the company's goals are and how they relate to each other. While there are still organization problems, some of them important and difficult to solve, there is no longer a sense of wandering without any purpose, either by the company or the individual employees.

We entered the new year, with very specific numerical and other goals and a great deal of confidence that they could be accomplished.

Many people think that the president of a company has unlimited power and can do pretty much as he likes. This is not the case, because of the consideration that must be given to the "whims"—fancies as well as insights—of each of the people that are being paid to participate in management. I understand much better and am more convinced of the wisdom of Plato's *Republic* than in any previous time. The head of an organization must be a benevolent dictator.

In a given week, perhaps there are several issues that arise in which you disagree with one of your subordinates. Theoretically, it is assumed by lay people that you simply tell him to do it your way. In practice, that is not the case because a bright hard-working person who is handling a certain matter will soon become disillusioned and have greatly reduced morale. Therefore, you have to array the importance of these disagreements and intercede only occasionally to give him the sense that you have really delegated responsibility to him.

Guidelines

One may or may not agree with the means used by Identimation's top management to get set for its second effort. For example, it's possible to question the management style, or the insistence on the primacy of organizational goals over personal goals, or the practicality of a production company going into the business of hiring out its staff capabilities.

But the Identimation case has the virtue of illustrating some of the basic problems of start-up companies—unresolved employee roles, inadequate communication, confused goals, and vague performance standards.

Thus, in this chapter we have reviewed, in principle and practice, one of the four basic ingredients of a start-up company, the chief executive officer, and one of the most tenuous judgments in venture management, when to drop a program and when to be patient and follow the predetermined plan.

The basic ingredients of the start-up company, marketing and financing, will be discussed in the next three chapters.

Chapter 8

The Marketing Problems of a New Company

Marketing a new product is like rowing a small boat into the fog of the future, without a map of the waterways and with the limitation of being able to look only backward. It is comparable to walking into a vast art museum in search of a particular painting, whose appearance, coloring, title, and painter have been described to you only fourth-hand or fifth-hand.

The problems that General Electric would face in marketing a new chocolate pudding or General Foods in marketing a new light bulb would be roughly parallel to the problems a new company faces in starting an untried product through the maze of modern marketing. However, when General Electric introduces a new light bulb or General Foods a new chocolate pudding, they're on familiar ground and can proceed with a certain confidence. They design the product and go through a succession of market research stages and testing that substantially increase the likelihood of the success of the product.

Their decision-makers have years of experience in analyzing the light bulb and food industries, the likely future markets, the additions to the present organization that will be required, the advertising strategy, the quality control necessary to assure consumer acceptance, the optimum distribution pattern, the appropriate pricing, time factors, and budget requirements. If the new product seriously deviates from comfortable commercial standards, it is dropped. As the idea becomes a project, then an organized activity, and finally gets to the marketplace, thousands of pieces of information are analyzed and organized in a more or less experienced manner.

Even so, most products introduced by large companies fail.

To the entrepreneur of the new company, marketing is often the vital challenge. Pay him little or nothing for his efforts, but provide the possibility of a huge tangible and intangible return for success, and he will strive to move products forward with few, if any, signposts on the road.

As he would if employed by a large company, the entrepreneur breaks down the overall problem into as many component parts as he and his associates have time to handle. He then substitutes for the experience and resources of the large company as many analogies as he and his associates can find in their own experience.

If there are 1,000 components of the problem, he may find analogies for only 100. He seeks to solve the balance by intuition and guesswork.

Depending on his background, the entrepreneur may be more comfortable with the components of the overall problem that are related to finance or budgets. Or manufacturing. Or marketing and sales. Or engineering and design. The new company will come to grips with its problems in a descending order of comfort.

If marketing and sales considerations are uncomfortable, the new company increases its likelihood to fail. Many studies have set out to determine why some companies succeed while others fail. One such study undertaken by the Bureau of Business Research of the University of Michigan investigated ninety-five small Michigan manufacturers over a three-year period. By the end of the third year:

Thirty-seven of the ninety-five new companies were still successfully operating.

Thirty-three companies had gone out of business.

Twenty-two were marginally successful.

Three were dormant.

The study further clarified the fact that insufficient working capital is *not* the main reason why smaller manufacturers fail. Only two of the companies failed mainly through lack of funds. *Lack of marketing knowledge and initiative* was the single most common characteristic of both the outright failures and the marginally successful companies.

The truth seems to be that while ignorance of marketing can cause failure, knowledge, while not necessarily causing success, at least may *prevent* failure.

Marketing and sales programs are special to the product and to the company marketing it. The common problem of marketing, to the established company as well as the new company, is determining in advance what consumers and industrial companies will buy. Earlier, this judgment was characterized as one of the three most difficult judgments in venture management. It will be discussed in the first part of this chapter, followed by a description of marketing as an organizational goal and finally, by a discussion of other marketing problems.

Finding the Right Product

Finding the right product or service to facilitate the success of the new company seems to be so difficult because most purchasers do not know what they want until they are actually presented with a new product in the same manner as they are normally accustomed to buying.

Market surveys, panel tests, and market tests are necessarily an offer to a potential purchaser of only a fraction of the real-life sales situation. Nevertheless, they are usually better than nothing, and in some ways very valuable. Their particular value lies in pointing directions—by orders of magnitude—to packaging, pricing, design, and the extremes of acceptance or rejection of a new product. The first market survey is the problem statement, which is conducted in your head.

THE PROBLEM STATEMENT   Problem statements, as indicated earlier, can come from anywhere. They seem to be a function of a predetermined attitude. In my personal experience, some of the most fruitful sources of problem statements, in addition to customers, are the following: the United States Patent Office's *Patent Gazette*, where one can see what other people are doing and draw analogies; exposure to people in the venture management business; outgrowths from other new-product concepts; and, most important, creative meetings in which one person acts as a catalyst in a freewheeling discussion.

THE INVENTION   The inventive process is purely an art. Inventors look at the world differently from other people. They see the essentials of an object rather than the way it is defined by common use.

MARKET FEASIBILITY   After the invention, the inventor goes through a process of inexpensively checking technical, patent, and market feasibility.

Depending on the nature of the potential new product, he attempts to communicate in person or on the telephone with a cross section of appropriate people. They might include shareholders, wives, friends and acquaintances, employees, vendors, other inventors, managers in the industry of the particular product, and other persons who are available inexpensively. At this early stage, until preliminary feasibility is apparent, expenditures are minimized. Experience seems to be an important ingredient in the gaining of this early "feel." If the pattern of reaction by the same person interviewed is consistent, even when the product changes, forget him. A person with experience seeks particularly the inconsistent, the unstereotyped, the extraordinary response.

PANEL TESTING   A panel test is a formal or informal sampling of a small group of individuals. For small companies panel tests tend to be informal and to include a representative sample of individuals as discussed in the previous section.

Panel testing of products by mass merchandising companies is more formal. Usually there is an established place and procedures that have been sharpened over many years. The number of participants varies from 5 to 200. Emphasis is placed on price, appearance, convenience, and the number of different places in a home that the consumer might use the product. The quality is more important than the quantity of interest.

MARKET AND FIELD TESTS   As used in this book, "market testing" means the testing of user acceptance of a product and "field testing" means the testing of a product's physical attributes. Market testing is a universal practice of consumer products companies. Typically, a market area that is considered typical of the need for that product is selected. Although only a sampling is being taken, all the facets of the new product are planned as if the product were being sold nationally. The consumer in the market test area feels as if he or she is buying a product that is being sold to everyone else.

Field testing is important to companies marketing a product which requires high technology and which must be handmade at a cost of several thousand dollars per item. Field testing is the first occasion on which the product can be used by potential customers, none of whom are "in love" with the product. The field tester may be charged for the product or not, depending on individual circumstances. He is asked to use the handmade product as if it were a fully commercial product. His expectation of the product is similar to, but not exactly the same as, his expectation of a commercial product.

He expects a field-tested item to have more bugs and breakdowns than he would expect of an item sold on the open market. For a high-technology product selling for a few hundred dollars to a few thousand dollars, a field test cannot be considered successful until at least twenty-five to fifty copies have been used for a period of months. (These numbers are intended to be only a guideline, as each market sampling has to be based on its own circumstances.)

The selection of the problem statement is the first market analysis. From the idea to the market or field test a new product may undergo a dozen or more informal and formal surveys. Some are as simple as asking the opinion of a top company executive. In the final analysis, the new product's marketing credibility moves along in a process where "no" is sometimes an abrupt ending, and "yes" is a point on a continuum.

Most problem statements are failures because they are simply based on what is quantitatively around us most of the time—the automobile, the telephone, and daily inconveniences. Since in a sense everyone is an inventor, these everyday reminders of new-product needs also suggest themselves to thousands of other people. Furthermore, these industries are not noted for dealing with outside inventors or companies, and when they do, they tend to drive a hard bargain.

We cannot leave the subject of finding the right product without discussing the value of patience. E. B. Weiss has pointed out that a large number of new products failed on initial exposure to the market, and he goes on to say:

> Some of our greatest contributions to civilized living were "failures" from the standpoint of initial sales reaction when originally introduced. Clearly, those who pioneered the early autos had every reason to conclude, on the basis of early sales efforts, that the horseless carriage would never be more than an unprofitable novelty. And if they had doubts on this score, the research experts of that era (there were a few even then!) could have easily proved beyond call that Old Dobbin would always rule supreme. Henry Ford failed with his first two cars; by present-day standards of market testing he should have given up.
>
> My recollection is that the telephone and the incandescent lamp hardly set the world on fire when they were initially marketed. Any student of marketing in the first quarter of this century (before market testing became the dictator) could easily compile a sizable list of enormously important products that "failed" when they were first marketed, in that initial sales held out just no hope for profitable operation.[1]

Marketing as an Organization Goal

In its early stages a company is new-product-oriented and has a high ratio of technical to nontechnical staff. It is small, lean, and hardworking, and is usu-

1. E. B. Weiss, "Try Re-testing those Discarded New Products," *Advertising Age*, Oct. 1, 1958.

ally quartered in a "garage" facility. Typically, it is less than five years old and has fewer than fifty employees and less than $1 million in capital. It has few customers and they in a sense are insiders. One dissatisfied customer and the firm may face disaster, and so it must try harder to please.

Because its market is limited, the new firm often produces on a custom basis. The typical inventor is still a prime mover in the company, but lacks managerial skills. Orienting the company to marketing may be the greatest challenge, at this early stage of its development, for the top management of the company.

With his market survey as the first step, and the wealth of information that can then be derived from preliminary assumptions, the entrepreneur can begin to turn his company in a marketing direction.

He faces quite a battle. He would like to make a new-product development project into a company. The technical people want to add just one more feature that will make the product perfect. The entrepreneur cautions against an increase in price because it may limit the market or reduce profits. The technologist fights budgetary control and other systematic attempts to organize the company. After all, the technical people are happiest in an environment without constraints. Reporting, planning, and controls threaten to limit their creativity still further.

Top management has to shut the door quickly and decisively. The systems and controls will immediately be tested by the technical people in the company. Any vacuums that are found will be immediately occupied by lack of direction and misdirection. If possible, schedules will be avoided, and communication will be oral and rarely in writing. In a word, the tremendous virtues of the product will be used to explain away any limitations, cautions, or attempts to be businesslike. However, since no product sells itself, and since profit is unattainable without strict discipline, the battle must be won by a market-oriented and business-oriented top management. Otherwise, the company has no chance of success.

The market survey and business plan can now be effectively used by the entrepreneur as a tool. Because of the market analysis, the fears of the inventor have now been partially mitigated and can be further diminished by giving the product-development project dimensions other than the technical. Many of the marketing and sales tools required by a typical sales program should be instituted rapidly. They will have a quantitative effect on the new-product-oriented people, as will initial sales leads. The sense that there are early indications that "someone else cares" will assist in gaining a market direction.

While use of the marketing and sales tools may vary from product to product, they are, in general, the same.

SALES BROCHURE

In the embryonic stages of a company, everyone on its roster may be selling at the same time. It is important that all aspects of the new product's description be thought through logically. Sales brochures and canned sales letters can be used to define what the company wants to say about its new product as a matter of policy, safely away from the firing line of the sales situation itself. In this manner presentations and descriptions of the new product, no matter where they take place, can be aimed in the same direction. Sales policy can be directed from the central office. The sales brochure should feature a description of the product, especially the features which distinguish it from other products. It should explain how the potential customer may deal with the company, and should give the customer a sense of the credibility of the company selling the new product.

SALES MANUAL, PRICE LISTS, AND DISCOUNT SCHEDULES

In addition to the sales brochure, the new company should develop a sales manual and pricing information. Typically, the sales manual should include sales brochures and other product sheets or flyers that describe the product or product line; price lists for the standard product; prices for optional equipment; and, if appropriate, differentiated discounts for the small and large user, distributor, and the purchaser, for use in original equipment manufacture (OEM). In addition, photographs, background memos, training material, and sales techniques that have worked in other places should be continually added to the sales manual.

COMPETITIVE INFORMATION

The sales department of a new company should be as conscientious in acquiring competitive information as in creating information about its own product line. Routinely, competitive sales brochures and product sheets should be accumulated in a consistent and convenient manner. When information is obtained about a competitor that is likely to create a major problem or opportunity, it should be immediately passed on, with a detailed explanation, to all persons who call on customers. Salespeople should be requested to add to their sales reports information on competitors gathered from customers.

SALES REPORTS

To the experienced sales executive, routine sales procedures are accepted as a matter of course. But lapses, undesirable in any case, can lead to chaos in new-product marketing. For example, everyone who talks to a customer on the telephone or in person should be required to file a written sales report. It should include the method by which the sales lead was gathered, the problem the customer is attempting to solve, the highlights of the conversation or meeting, and things for the salesman or company to do as a follow-up to the meeting or conversation. The sales report should be routed so that the office of the head of the sales department is a clearinghouse for the information. It will assist in judging the success of the overall and individual sales effort, and in reshaping sagging or unsuccessful policies and procedures.

MAILING LIST   All potential customers and other VIP contacted by salesmen and others in the company should be added to a mailing list. The proper use of a good mailing list can yield returns at a minimum advertising and public relations expense. A communications program based on the new mailing list can cost as little as a few hundred dollars per month. Until the list grows to include thousands of people and companies, such mailings are usually better handled on the outside. A copy of the complete list should be in the hands of the sales manager.

Mailings to the list should be regular and diversified. At a cost of a few cents per mailing to each potential customer the industry can be kept abreast of the activities of the company and the progress of the new product. Over a period of time, a basis for acceptance of the new product can be created. The company will learn how to describe the advantages of its product in a more graphic way. The credibility of the new company will increase as time goes by, decreasing the resistance of the sales prospect.

PRODUCT APPLICATION SHEETS   The sale of any product is made when a potential customer decides that the cost of the product intended to solve his problem is less than the consequences of the problem. As the early sales effort continues, a surprising number of new applications will materialize. Some will have been forecast; others will be totally unexpected. Product application sheets should be completed on a regular basis. The specific problem of the customer and its general application should be detailed. Its cost to the customer should be explained and compared to other situations. These sheets should be prepared by following sales reports, proposals, and shipments to customers. They should be distributed internally and should be made the subject of regular mailings to the company's mailing list.

PRESS RELEASES AND ADVERTISING

A high percentage of trade publications will print a synopsis of a professionally prepared press release. New products are news to the industry served by the trade publications.

The cost of a public relations firm is less than even a small advertising campaign. The costs of the two can be compared only by talking to both types of agencies.

The advertising programs of most new companies are limited to trade publications. One company in the data communications field used six monthly full-page ads in three trade publications to introduce the company and the special features of its product line to its industry. Its out-of-pocket cost was approximately $15,000.

The sales activities of start-up companies are often directed by the president. As financial, manufacturing, and corporate development functions are broadened, the president must expand his activities. The marketing plan for organization and the implementation and decision making of the various sales functions must be developed. Definition of the functions and organization of the marketing department of Metrodyne, as originally planned, is a case in point:

METRODYNE'S MARKETING DEPARTMENT

This department, headed by a vice-president of marketing, has the principal responsibility for sales growth. Primary functions carried out by the Marketing Department are: sales, field service, market research, product advertising, application engineering, and public relations.

The markets to be served by Metrodyne's weighing systems are:

General manufacturing industry

Transportation industry

Construction material and equipment industry

Highway toll booths and truck weighing

Agriculture (raw material processing) industry

State and local law enforcement agencies

Lumber industry

Processing industry

The most immediate markets to be penetrated are general manufacturing and the transportation industries. In the year 1 to 3 period, domestic sales from these markets will be generated through a network of sales engineers, distributors and manufacturers' representatives. The manager of marketing and his regional staff will establish contractual relationships with selected representatives who have backgrounds in systems marketing of industrial electronic instrumentation and sophisticated material handling equipment. As the company's ability to satisfy customer requirements is increased, the company plans to give marketing and engineering emphasis to the total system concept. Application engineering, systems marketing, and systems engineering people will be hired in years 1 and 2 to augment the company's capability to offer totally integrated systems. Only a small percentage of the total system will then be manufactured by Metrodyne. The balance will be purchased and modified as required.

Other more specialized markets, such as the construction material and equipment industry, will be covered through agreements with marketing companies experienced in those areas. For example, the company has discussed exclusive marketing franchises with several material handling and independent scale distributors.

The company has not budgeted for full-time sales offices during years 1 and 2. Return on investment will be the yardstick for establishing leased sales offices and a full-time direct sales organization in any geographical area. Based on an assumed annual operating cost of $50,000 and an intended profit return of 25 percent before taxes, a field sales office must generate $200,000 in sales before it can be economically justified as a replacement for commission agents.

A corporate international sales function is being considered. However, at this time its total function is not completely clear. More consideration must be given to both one-way and cross-licensing agreements for marketing and/or manufacturing rights, especially in the industrialized countries of Europe and Asia.

FIELD SERVICE

The field service function is more than an accommodation to customers. It is also a sales-revenue generating mechanism, and logically is the responsibility of Marketing. The field service encompasses repair and service on customer equipment both in-warranty and out-of-warranty at customer facilities. During year 1, costs for the field service function are included in operating costs (sales expense). However, by year 2, field service is expected to operate at the break-even point.

Inordinate, in-warranty, field service costs will be an instant barometer to undetected quality control problems in manufacturing. Thus, the field service reporting responsibility through the Marketing Department is designed to be part of the overall checks and balances required to meet the objective of delivering a quality product at a reasonable price with a reasonable return.

All services and repairs on equipment returned by the customer will be the responsibility of the Manufacturing Department.

In general, the company plans to encourage equipment users to do their own maintenance. Through the combination of maintenance bulletins, maintenance training courses for customer personnel, and spare parts provisioning, many users will be able to cope with their own service problems. Customers' in-house skill level will determine need for outside assistance.

During year 1, demand for field service will be satisfied by company technicians. Beginning in year 2, a field service manager will be hired and additional field service engineers will be added to the staff during years 2 and 3. These will handle user service problems, and also train customer personnel in the use and service of the equipment, and train outside contract service organizations to handle service contracts.

As field sales offices are opened in the post-year 3 period, field service personnel will be assigned to them.

APPLICATION ENGINEERING

As the company adds to its sales activities of off-the-shelf products and concentrates more on problem-solving through systems, the sales function will require additional technical-marketing support.

The application engineer will accompany the salesman in direct contact with the potential customer and will serve as technical liaison, for customer requirements, between sales and systems engineering. In addition to his assignments on new installations, he will assist existing customers in upgrading older systems. The first application engineer will be brought into the Marketing Department in year 2.

MARKET RESEARCH

The company is already challenged by the sales potential of static weighing systems, automatic inventory control, and in-motion weighing. However, there will be need for market data in the years 1 through 3. Outside market research organizations can provide this specialized service on a retainer basis, during years 1 and 2.

The market research function is normally closely related to long-range planning (3–10 years). The market researcher with knowledge of the company's growth objectives will concentrate on either new markets for existing products or new products for ready markets. Forecasting will also be performed by market research. The responsibility will continue when the position is filled by a full-time staff member in year 3.

ADVERTISING

Advertising will be performed by an outside agency. A full program has been planned and budgeted without the need for in-house staffing, at least through year 3.

Institutional brochures, product brochures, and product advertising will be produced on the outside. The company is intent on developing an institutional image as opposed to a product image and will therefore carry a common theme (print, color, logos, etc.) throughout all of its advertising and product design.

Approximately 7 per cent of forecast sales have been budgeted for media advertising in the first year and 4 percent and 3 percent respectively in the second and third years.

Trade publications will be utilized for space advertising in years 1 and 2. Other tools will include: direct mail, trade shows, and regional meetings.

PUBLIC RELATIONS

The objectives of a public relations program . . . are twofold:

Increase acceptance of the corporation's products and services.

Create a corporate image; tell the company story.

The company expects continuous public relations involvement with shareholders, financial community, customers, suppliers, community and the Federal and local Government agencies.

The company will retain the services of a competent public relations firm to assist in projecting its image to the press, the general public, and the potential investor public. The format will involve continuous dissemination of articles and press releases covering company progress. Institutional advertising, either through brochures or media, will be coordinated by the public relations firm and produced by the advertising agency.

Company management, through involvement in community civic affairs and fund-raising drives, will bear responsibility for projecting the company as an asset to its community.

Customer relations activity are the responsibility of the Marketing Department. Good supplier relations will be fostered by combining sound purchasing practices and minimizing undue delay in payment of supplier invoices.

The company does not expect to hire a full-time public relations director in the near term. Based on the magnitude of responsibility, this assignment will be given to a professional public relations firm.

Special Marketing Problems of a High-Technology Start-Up Company

The substitution of cleverness and workability for customer need is the most important marketing problem of high-technology companies.

To some extent, there will and should never be a final solution to a problem. It is likely that a market-oriented inventor will not be a very good inventor. With a few notable exceptions, this seems to be the case. A successful inventor, like an artist, sees the *essentials* and not the *order* of things. As soon as you have described something as being *definite,* you have rendered yourself blind on the subject. You will stop seeking information and insights. The purchaser of a product or service to satisfy a real or expected need has defined his subject. He is not only blind, but worse. He will defend his choice because he has made it part of himself.

But all is not lost, perhaps. In an ongoing company the independent inventor often acts to engineer the product into being. To a large extent, much of the engineering is "subinvention." The inventor, when acting as an inventor, can be surrounded, in front and back, by more marketing orientation, without any loss in creativity. The informal policy should be that problem statements will originate from a customer or a market-oriented person in front of the invention. Furthermore, the inventor, when he is being an engineer, is closer to the realities and considerations of the customer—in back of the invention.

REINVENTING THE WHEEL   The process of inventing is introspective. It is unrealistic and naive. It is therefore susceptible to answering a question nobody is asking, solving a problem not enough people may have. And the dangers can at least be limited, as indicated in the suggestions in the previous section. In addition, the company should have a good patent attorney for patent searches and should stay informed on the state of the art of its industry.

LOVE AND THE LABORATORY   In the laboratory the product is being worked on by men who are in love with it. A psychological and practical phenomenon is that they conduct tests that invariably come out in favor of the product. Their pricing and bills of material invariably are short so that the product will look cheaper and include fewer parts. They underestimate the total costs of the project and the amount of time it will take. Requirements for an industrial or consumer product will be found only by a field test outside the laboratory. A prime and early goal should be to get a product out of the laboratory without prejudicing minimum standards.

NOT EVERYBODY IS TYPICAL   It's an accepted axiom that everything that passes for market research is not really market research. Biased tests, unscientifically conducted tests, tests with a poor design, or tests using inappropriate subjects will yield useless results. Such tests are another fact of life on the marketing scene; they may seem innocuous, but they are actually harmful for two reasons: first, because they are widely prevalent, and second, because they are often given undue weight. A typical example: "I took the two packages home and showed them to my wife," says a business executive. "She preferred the green one." This executive's wife may or may not know what she's talking about. But it is likely that her judgment, without further qualifications, will carry considerable weight in the councils having to do with the packaging of a product.

TOO MANY HATS, NOT ENOUGH HEADS   An executive in charge of research and development for an electronics company says:

> If we talk about how to make a particular electronic circuit in a general meeting, half the people will not even comment and will leave it to the "engineer." However, let the discussion turn to a matter of features for the product and all of the engineers will willingly participate and give their views. It is difficult to convince them that their "vote" is not as valid as that of the experienced marketing people.

This executive, who feels very strongly on the point, continues:

> An eloquent engineer may make a suggestion that seems plausible to even an experienced sales executive. The fact that it may not have much validity may be lost. Another problem with giving engineers or development people too loud a voice in marketing councils is that this tends to make the "group-mind", technically oriented. Accordingly, the group will seek management judgments on the basis of "truths" reflecting technical premises. But the choice made by a marketing or sales manager tends to be involved with the understanding of people.

In new companies the problem is particularly acute because there is always a shortage of qualified people, and the ones available are disproportionately technical.

Another aspect of the "engineering mind" versus the "marketing mind" appears in market planning. A market strategy, like an invention, is a very fragile thing. The manager is theorizing about what the response will be if his company does this and what the response will be if his company does that, at many levels. By the time the plan has been completed, he has made assumption upon assumption and is walking on very thin ground, indeed. The eloquent technically oriented person who asserts himself in a very positive way may very well distort the vision of even the experienced sales management person.

The final aspect of this problem is the fact that many of the technical decisions about the product have nothing to do with technology, but rather with what the customer will accept, what price the customer will pay, how the customer will use the product, and what psychology of use for a new product there will be in the everyday life of the user.

Other Marketing Problems of a New Company

A company that is pioneering in a new industry is statistically unique. It has been estimated that of thousands of new businesses formed every year to commercialize technological innovation, almost 80 percent die during their first year. An additional 10 percent fail during their second year. Fewer than 1 out of 100 survive to the fifth year and beyond.

Volney Stefflre believes that these statistics can be improved by better "support processes":

> Statistics like this on business failures can be compared with two other types of figures to be put into perspective (1) the success rates of large manufacturers' new consumer products, and (2) the success rate of the more successful franchises such as MacDonalds Hamburgers, Dunkin Donuts, Colonel Saunders Kentucky Fried Chicken.
>
> Statements like "95% of the new products developed by American manufacturers are failures" abound in discussions of the new product development process. While the figures here, as in all these other anecdotal statistics, are a matter of conjecture and sensitive to details of their definition (i) "new" (ii) "developed" and (iii) "fail," for example, the general trend of the evidence suggests that large American manufacturers are no more successful (statistically) at introducing new consumer products than individual Americans are at successfully starting new businesses.
>
> A second type of statistic, however, presents a somewhat different picture. Some of the successful franchisers—national companies inviting local investors to run local offices/branches/stands—report success rates of 80%. Much higher than those found in either small new businesses or in the new product development activities of large manufacturers.
>
> The net result of the above, in our opinion, is simply that (i) given the current state of the art, new business ventures have a quite high probability of failure, and (ii) it looks like it should be possible by providing new business with the kinds of well-prepared support processes used by successful franchisers to sharply increase their chance of survival and/or success.[2]

These insights may not be totally applicable to all new businesses, particularly those intended to be operated on a larger scale than a local hamburger stand. Nevertheless, the franchisers have totally solved one important problem of the new company: knowing what business you are in. How do you know when to deviate from your business plan, and when to follow it, explicitly? How do you know *for sure* what your business is?

Any new company will have many temptations for other business opportunities thrown at it. Feature stories and press releases will provide persons and companies with new opportunities that look good and are tempting.

2. Stefflre Associates, Inc., *The Small New Business,* prepared for the Office of Economic Opportunity, Executive Office of the President, pp. 1-2.

Their investors will add additional opportunities. Preliminary sales efforts will point to new and previously unknown markets for the product.

The franchised company is provided a total package. Decision making is kept to a minimum. Lack of marketing results can be pinpointed to a narrow number of reasons, analyzed, and often corrected.

Other types of new companies are likewise involved in planning, concretizing, and making changes at dozens of decision levels. Some of these cycles are unrelated to other cycles. Others are intimately related.

Defining the type of business is a function of time, money, and the attitudes of the founders of the new company, and the people who have bet on the new venturers.

It is essential that the new company limit itself to a range of marketing effort consistent with its personnel, time, and financial abilities. Yet, the factor that is always misjudged is the time it takes to accomplish a given goal. Failure to project enough time for these activities to sort themselves out can lead to disaster. Some new companies solve this problem by financing their operations for a longer period of time than they project. Others acquire an existing operating business at an early stage in their development, to provide current income. Still others sell the services of their employees and license the rights to their products to existing companies for market and geographical areas that they will not be able to handle themselves in the near future.

This quandary when more fully analyzed is found to be semantic instead of real. If you say, "Concentrate your efforts," everyone will salute. If you say, "Survive!" they will again salute.

Until customers buy enough of the new product at a price that at least equals its total cost, the new company has to continue to struggle with the problem of knowing its business. Accomplishing everything else in the new company but not surviving, because the economy is in a downturn, makes no sense.

Everyone in the new company is learning how to work together. The people and products in a new company are on a shakedown cruise. The bouncing ball to be followed by the eye of the new company is survival. Concentrate on selling whatever you can, until you are both reasonably cerain of what your business is *and reasonably certain that you can afford it.*

NARROW PRODUCT LINE   Another typical marketing problem is inefficiency of selling time. "While I'm calling on this guy anyway, I wish I had other products to sell him." If this problem has not been solved at the market planning stage, there are likely to be unplanned and hasty choices.

The timely solution is the one developed at the planning stage before many sales dollars are spent. Each element is subject to analysis, after which a marginal choice has to be made.

How many sales calls, letters, and telephone calls to how many customers will yield a sale of how many dollars? What is the cost of those "how many's"? What is the gross profit of the sale? How much are the total general, administrative, and selling expenses, including the start-up costs that are still occurring? The answer to these questions leads to the conclusion: We can (or cannot) afford direct salesmen.

Does the industry use manufacturers' representatives or distributors? How much supervision will they require? Can we get their attention and motivate them to sell our product? Should we give them a larger discount or commission? Can we afford it and still make our profit goal?

Planning when there is still time to survey and experiment will provide the *right* answers for any particular company's marketing situation.

WHICH COST IS APPROPRIATE IN PRICING?   The curve of product costs (Figure 8-1) is similar for any company making a product. The price should be set on the basis of the marketplace. The cost curve is then divided at one of the points where it begins to flatten. Quantities and costs to the left are start-up costs. Quantities and costs to the right show first a breakeven, and then a rising, profit margin. The manufacturing costs are then overlain on the pricing pattern determined by the marketplace, and a decision is made about whether the new company can afford the start-up costs.

An outside vendor may be considered, to pay for the start-up costs. This vendor will have to make an investment judgment about whether, in effect, to bet on the new company. Typically, if he decides to bet, he will want part ownership of the new company and/or the right to apportion the start-up costs over the first quantity he will supply. Or he may want an exclusive right to manufacture for a period of time, assuming the vendor remains competitively priced.

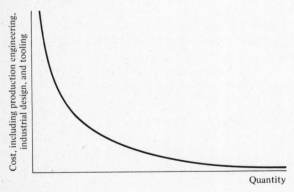

FIGURE 8-1

One company in the Northeast has offered this type of service regularly for many years. The outline of its proposal is very informative about the items that should concern the new company and that will concern a vendor asked to invest.

AGREEMENT

between

MANUFACTURING COMPANY, of Greenwich, Connecticut, hereinafter referred to as MFG., and NEW COMPANY, of Stratford, Connecticut, hereinafter referred to as NEW.

****

WHEREAS, both parties intend to mutually benefit from a long-term association in which MFG. will manufacture products for NEW providing, thereby, favorable financial assistance to NEW's growth objectives; it is agreed that:—

1. NEW will be fully responsible for all its product designs. MFG. will provide Engineering Change Requests as a means of assisting NEW to maintain its responsibility in maintaining its files of bills of material, drawings, etc.

2. NEW will carry on all necessary marketing effort to insure the growth of the Company. MFG. will assist only to the extent of assuring NEW's customers of conformance with necessary delivery schedules.

3. NEW will continue an active program of Product Research and Development and expansion of its product line. MFG. will assist only in a consulting capacity.

4. MFG. shall have the right of first refusal for all of the production of all NEW products through _____, or for _____units of various products, whichever shall be achieved first.

5. At the expiration of this agreement, MFG. shall have the first refusal right to additional production for NEW provided it meets the average price of the three (3) lowest qualified bidders for new business.

6. MFG. will provide the following services on a no-charge basis:
   a. production engineering
   b. finalizing part drawings

    c. development of economical processing
    d. tooling designs
    e. cooperation in design of test equipment
    f. make or buy decisions
    g. economical inventory additions

7. MFG. will finance inventory and tooling acquisitions for NEW and bill its product to NEW as shipments are made on a net 30-day basis.

8. MFG. will consider extended credit to NEW at prime interest rates plus ½ of 1%.

9. Tooling, and test equipment, acquired for NEW by MFG. will be amortized over the first _____units built and will become the property of NEW after full payment has been made to MFG.

10. NEW shall have access to MFG. test equipment and test laboratories, at nominal fees, with extended credit terms, if it should so desire.

11. NEW shall have the privilege of renting office and factory space from MFG. at nominal rates including all utilities except telephone.

12. MFG. will guarantee the quality and workmanship of its products and will certify to the products meeting NEW's prints and specifications once accepted by MFG.

13. A pricing formula of factory cost plus 8% G & A plus a 15% profit margin is acceptable to both parties. A fixed price for each product shall be negotiated to the satisfaction of both parties, as soon as prints and processing are available.

14. It is agreed that initial production shall be only to order and that no finished product shall be built for inventory. Monthly, a meeting of MFG. and NEW representatives will provide a review of sales and forecasts and re-establish production plans and schedules.

15. MFG. will take the necessary steps to protect NEW's patent position and proprietary designs, for_____years dating from the initiation of this agreement. NEW will have the right of first refusal to any patentable devices or processes, developed by MFG. in the production of NEW products. If NEW does not wish to exercise its rights, MFG. will have the right to file patent applications in its own name.

16. In recognition of the MFG. contribution to the ultimate success of the NEW effort to grow and prosper, NEW will, on a no-charge basis, transfer_____of its then outstanding shares of stock, to MFG. at a date _____days after initial production deliveries from MFG.

17. In return for MFG.'s efforts, MFG. shall also have an option to purchase _____shares of NEW's stock at a price of _____up to the amount of total financial accommodation by MFG. to NEW. This option shall expire at the conclusion of this agreement.

18. In the event NEW should be sold, merged or acquired during the term of this agreement, its successor will be obligated to the continuation of this agreement or MFG. shall be paid either the cash sum of _____outright or_____% of the accrued MFG. sales to NEW during the useful period of this agreement, whichever is the lesser.

19. In the event of any failure on the part of NEW to make full payment to MFG. MFG. shall have the right to all patents and designs of NEW, and to produce and sell equipment utilizing these patents and designs, at its discretion, to insure liquidation of its inventory and reimbursement of the amounts due.

20. Both parties recognize the probable need to modify this agreement from time to time. Such changes as might be made will be reduced to writing and filed after signature of both parties, as formal letters of understanding or addenda to this agreement.

21. In the event of dispute between the parties hereto it is agreed that both parties will abide with arbitration in accordance with A.A.A. rules rather than resort to costly, lengthy, legal procedures.

22. MFG. shall have the right to designate at least one member of the NEW Board of Directors.

Signed this _____day of _____.

_____	_____
Witness	MANUFACTURING COMPANY
_____	_____
Witness	NEW COMPANY

SURPLUS MARKETS   What do we do with surplus markets? A surplus market is one which you will not have time or money to exploit in the plannable future, usually five years. Xerox had a surplus market—the overseas market for its copier—and formed a very successful joint effort with the Rank Organization.

In addition to surplus markets for geographical areas, a product may have product applications for diverse distribution channels or lend itself to a series of other products in the same industry.

If planned for, the problem becomes an opportunity. Surplus markets can become assets.

NOT WANTING TO KNOW   The transactions involving only "yes" or "no" decisions, such as asking a customer to buy, are difficult among the optimists in a new company. In a sense, there is always a tendency to postpone these ultimate truths to avoid reality. The best solution is recognition of the problem, because it is usually more latent than active.

KEEP EVERYTHING IN SIGHT   One of the themes throughout this book is the complexity of judging such things as where you plan to go, how you plan to get there, and where you presently are.

This problem is particularly noteworthy in the marketing and sales area because these areas are the primary source of income, and along with financing, they pose the most critical problem of the new company.

The process of judging "where you are" is particularly difficult for the people who "were standing on the lot while the building was built over them." The new salesman has similar problems, in addition, to the selling problems of any company, and he does not know how the new company got to the point at which he joined it.

A broader training program is required. Training is an investment of time in order to make a profit. The new salesman in an embryonic company needs a knowledge of the rationale for starting the company, as well as product knowledge.

As already cited in the discussion on sales tools, all sales policies should be in writing. These decisions should not be left to the whim of the salesman or distributor. They should not be left to the pressure of the sales situation itself.

The sales manager of a new company should keep score. By way of a blackboard or sales control sheets, which he himself updates, he can remain fully *conscious* of the stages from suspect to prospect to customer to servicing to resale. He can modify or change sales policies. He can intervene in a negotiation, he can know when, to what extent, and how intervention is appropriate.

Other marketing problems will be solved by the experience of the marketing and sales manager. The marketing and sales area proliferates with consultants. Some one-man shops are effective. Many small advertising and public relations firms specialize in the problems of the new company. Many will invest in new companies by charging less money and perhaps by becoming partners or shareholders.

This chapter has attempted to isolate the less obvious marketing problems of the start-up company.

Before the financial problems of the new venture are discussed in Chapter 10, three market surveys will be discussed in Chapter 9.

Chapter 9

The Market Studies of Three Start-up Companies

The market survey of a start-up company marks its coming to grips with the real world. To this point in its corporate existence, the new company has groped its way through the choice of its product or service. Previously, it is likely to have used informal market research, word of mouth, published papers, literature, personal contacts, and reports in its field. If it is a technically oriented company, it may have arrived at the decision to develop and market its product solely on the basis of uniqueness, with little marketing consideration. "It works!" is a satisfactory substitute for, "Someone will pay money for it!"

If the company is formed to exploit a new technology, as in the case of the two market studies in this chapter on Identimation and Metrodyne, then the survey is normally done concurrently with the development of the new product. If the company is not based on a new product or invention, but on the harvesting of a natural resource (as is International Oceanographic Corporation, the third market study in this chapter), then the survey is usually done as the first step by the entrepreneur.

The market information that was required by Sibany to continue to back the Identimat® was a function of the amount of money we were spending at a given time. More information, quantitatively and qualitatively, is always required as a project moves forward. Like all product development, cash outlays tend to increase like an upside-down pyramid as time goes on, and more and more is spent to learn about less and less.

Before the market survey on the Identimat, the marketing attempts by Sibany were typical of new companies. The product was discussed with likely potential customers in the most general way, because we hesitated to disclose how it worked for fear of its being copied before we were off the ground. We scanned published papers, newspapers, trade publications, and other literature to determine whether anybody else was interested in the field of personal identification by personal characteristics, and also to determine the extent of competition. A summary of competition has been discussed in Chapter 5.

Sometimes, as with the Identimat, the market potential seems to continue to be valid, but the product development has to change. Sibany substituted the measurement of hand geometry for fingerprints. The following summary sketches the steps that resulted in the first commitment to the personal identification industry and the primary reasons for switching products to meet the same market need:

1. Basic assumptions of problem statement:
   a. The need to personally identify people is common in an industrial society and grows as that society becomes more complex.
   b. The need for personal identification will continue, independent of the evolution of the social, political, and economic trends of an industrial society.
   c. The cost of labor is increasing, so that the ideal personal identification system would eliminate the need for people to make the identification.
   d. Fingerprints are an ideal approach because they have been popularized by the Federal Bureau of Investigation as being the most secure means of identification.
2. Problem statement: How can a machine identify the human being by measuring his fingerprints, without requiring an attendant?
3. One of the first goals of product development was building a machine that worked and performed all the functions required. This first reduction to practice was accomplished and allowed Sibany, with outside vendors, to guess at a "ball park" selling price for the product. This was determined to be approximately $5,000 per system, or approximately $125 per month rental during the first year or two of marketing; perhaps this might be reduced to approximately $30 per month within five years.
4. Literature in the field, and in particular the sentiments of the *Personal Identification Committee of the American Bankers Association,* indicated that banks believe that they cannot afford to

pay more than $15 per month for a personal identification product. Banks are seeking to move us into the "cashless society." American Telephone and Telegraph states that they have learned that a mass market for one of their products depends on a rental price of $10 per month or less.

5. Sibany concluded that a new approach to positive personal identification was required.

Since no one else had ever marketed a positive personal identification system, this judgment was made entirely on the basis of analogy to comparable products presently on the market and the *apparent* desire of potential customers.

Fortunately, the concept of using hand geometry had been invented just after Sibany's invention of its fingerprint identification system and before Sibany's decision to put the fingerprint system on the shelf. The market data that had been accumulated over approximately eighteen months were determined to be as valid for hand geometry as for fingerprints.

Inventor's Irrationality

Those involved with the creation of a new product have an urge to show it to other people, not only to determine its marketability, but—let's face it—to show off.

This desire, combined with the fear of someone's stealing his idea, can lead the inventor to irrationality, but it need not do so. Some products, such as Metrodyne's Dyne-A-Mat® can be shown without disclosing the invention. Others, such as the Identimat, are disclosed as soon as they are shown. Sibany chose to get around this problem by showing a product analogous to the Identimat at a trade show. At the same time, through publicity and direct mail, we tried to attract as many people to Sibany's booth as would come.

The primary market for personal identification, discussed in the media, related to the "cashless society." It was decided to show a machine that dispensed cash. To activate the machine, the user had to insert the identification card he was given as he walked into the trade show.

The show served several purposes. It gave Sibany the opportunity to publicize what was hoped to be a new industry, identified Sibany (later Identimation) with that new industry, and most important, provided the opportunity to discuss with representatives of about fifty companies who came to the booth their interest in buying the Identimat when it was available.

At the time of the show, Sibany had already chosen the word "Identimat" as a trademark, but there was no separate Identimation Corporation. It was a product development project in the Sibany laboratory.

Market surveying in the field of personal identification had problems not faced by either International Oceanographic or Metrodyne. How should we market-research personal identification when it was not an existing industry? When the words themselves were not in current usage? When we were unwilling to show or disclose the product for reasons of secrecy?

Sibany decided on a market study by an independent market research company not related to Sibany, primarily to take advantage of someone else's reputation and professional knowledge. The choice had been between hiring an independent company and continuing to do it ourselves, but because of a decision, already made, to hire SRI to make a *technical* study of the feasibility of hand geometry, it was decided that Sibany could not afford to also pay for these additional marketing services.

However, good fortune permitted a detailed and professional market survey without any cost. Several dozen government agencies and companies had been dealt with in the course of research efforts. One of these companies, a large chemical company, was interested in personal identification and decided to do the survey. All the information and insights previously acquired by Sibany were turned over to the chemical company. Another excerpt from the article in *Business Week* that was cited earlier tells the story:

> From posh headquarters in New York, Allied Chemical Corp. executives direct a worldwide operation with 35,000 employees and sales that top $1.2 billion. Exactly 42 miles north, in Riverside, Conn., are the small, cramped quarters of Sibany Mfg. Corp., a 70-man company that develops new products. Its total income for 1966 was $35,821—and only $747 of it coming in the first six months.
>
> Yet for the past six months, giant Allied has quietly spent around $100,000 to study the technical feasibility and market potential of a Sibany-invented automatic system for indentifying individuals. In return, Allied has an option to manufacture and sell the system. The deal, if it goes through, may simply be a licensing agreement by which Allied pays a royalty to Sibany. But Sibany hopes to have Allied set up a separate, jointly owned company in which profits and management would be shared.
>
> LARGE HOPES. The identification system on which Sibany is pinning its great expectations is able to spot an individual after he inserts a card or key; if the holder loses his card and someone else tries to use it, the machine will refuse to identify the person. In short, the machine is triggered by a card, but identifies the person directly. More than this neither Sibany nor Allied will say.
>
> The system may be sold for as little as $300. Applications include automated banking, industrial and military security, and a host of others where foolproof personal identification is a necessity.

Allied has been doing market research, and is said to believe that the system is "not just a new product, but a whole new industry—a la Xerox." Not wishing to disclose its plans, Allied is naturally reluctant to talk. "We've participated financially in its development, and we're evaluating it. We just don't know yet," says Robert Reed, director of corporate development.[1]

After considerable time and expense, Allied Chemical eventually turned down the option on a joint venture. They believed that the product and market areas were too unrelated to their business, which was understandable. What was less understandable was their indication that they confirmed Sibany's estimate of the need for about $3 million by the joint venture, but felt that that amount was *too small to avoid competition:* "After all, many companies can invest $3 million in a new project. Only a handful can compete with us in those areas requiring investments of $100 million." Like the market analysis, Allied's other comments were basically positive, and Sibany continued to commit resources to the field of personal identification.

Here are excerpts from the market analysis that resulted from Allied Chemical's survey:

Markets for Positive Personal Identification Mechanisms

Possible applications were considered in the market study for the Sibany ID system. The Sibany system usually was not disclosed. Prospective purchasers were given a description only of what the system would do and the price.

Security Use Within Department of Defense (D.O.D.)

The Sibany system was not revealed during interviews with Army, Navy and Air Force personnel. The persons contacted were responsible for specifying required security measures only in general terms. They felt a final decision on whether to use the Sibany system or guards would be left to the base commanders.

Representatives of the Army estimated that about 20,000 units could be used by their branch of service. They listed several areas of use, including cryptographic facilities in the Army; arms rooms; and classified weapon (mostly nuclear) installations. If the system rented for about $70/month, they felt that an actual cost savings could be shown.

Also contacted in the D.O.D. were officers responsible for security in the Defense Automatic Support Agency, U.S. Army. While the system was not disclosed to these men, they indicated there would be applications in their group for a personal I.D. system, if it performed as claimed. For example, this group is located within a single corridor at the Pentagon. A security guard is stationed at each end. If the system were acceptable, one of the two

---

1. Excerpted from "Inventions for Hire, But Not for Sale," *Business Week*, Mar. 25, 1967. Reprinted by special permission of the copyright holder, McGraw-Hill, Inc.

guards could be replaced with a turnstile operated by the ID system. Since their guards are obtained through the General Services Administration, at a cost of about $500/month, an identifier unit with a rental cost of $70/month would offer substantial savings.

The potential demand for the Sibany system in military applications is estimated at 20,000 units, . . . somewhat conservative when the Army alone apparently could use about 20,000 units.

Security at D.O.D. Supplier Facilities

To determine the potential in this area, a representative of the Defense Contract Administration Agency was interviewed. Again, the system was not disclosed. He was told the system was capable of matching an individual with an ID card and that if the card were lost it could not be used by anyone else finding it.

In the official's opinion, there would be many applications for such a product at costs in the neighborhood of $70/month. He estimated that about 20,000 units could be used within the facilities of D.O.D. suppliers.

Security at Miscellaneous Government Installations

The primary applications in this area would be with the Atomic Energy Commission (AEC) and the National Aeronautics and Space Administration (N.A.S.A.). Their purpose would be to restrict access to confidential information or to provide safeguards at hazardous areas.

The system was disclosed to the Atomic Energy Commission, which proved interested and anxious to test prototypes of the system.

Other departments of the government which might use the Sibany system are:

State Department, for use in identifying couriers and other persons traveling between embassies in foreign countries.

Treasury Department, for controlling access to mints or specific areas within mints.

Central Intelligence Agency, for identification of agents or couriers.

Various agencies making substantial use of computers to which they want to limit access. These include Internal Revenue Service, Social Security and the FBI.

We estimate the total demand will be about 5,000 units for security at all these miscellaneous government installations.

Security at Industrial Installations

This marketing application includes controlling access to plants, laboratories and areas within plants (e.g. tool cribs or supply rooms). This control of access could relate to guarding information or to protecting employees against safety hazards.

In investigating the potential in these areas, contact was made with a vice president of an electronics firm. The company markets a radar device for security applications in retail and industrial firms. The unit, which detects motion in the store or plant after hours, sells for about $900. The firm also conducts extensive security surveys for customers and recommends devices and services. It would be in a position to recommend Sibany's system to customers.

The executive was enthusiastic about the system. He estimated that at a price of $1–2,000 each, he would be able to sell about 30,000 units for industrial use. Tempering this optimistic projection somewhat still assigns a potential of 20,000 units to industrial security markets over a nine-year period.

Also contacted: 14 Directors of Security for large corporations. These men were very interested, though the system was not fully disclosed. Cost was given as $50–80/month; performance, 200 people during a 15–20 minute rush period. The group visualized applications in controlling access to laboratories, supply rooms, tool cribs and certain hazardous in-plant areas. The system was considered less applicable for perimeter control of entire plant sites, where guards supply a more complete surveillance.

The system would be useful in plants or laboratories with more than 50 employees and most useful when employees-per-plant exceed 100. There are about 60,000 plants and laboratories in the U.S. with more than 50 employees. Over the next 10 years, about 10,000 of these plants and laboratories could install two identifier units for tool or supply room control and for traffic control through high-security areas.

The number of security guards employed by industrial concerns also gives an indication of the potential volume in this area. There are now about 250,000 guards manning 60–80,000 guard stations. On the basis of improving guard efficiency and lowering the total cost of security, we believe 1/3 to 1/4 of these guard stations could use the Sibany system.

Identification of Credit Card Holders

Interviews with executives of credit card companies indicate a high degree of interest in the Sibany system. They are currently spending large sums to combat fraudulent use of their cards. Most of this is spent on making and distributing their "wild card" (lost, stolen, or overdrawn cards) list. If the system allowed for positive matching of an individual with the card, these companies estimated they might install about 5,000 units for $1–2,000 each. These would be placed where transactions were large, (e.g., airline ticket counters). These units would not cover all points, but some executives felt they could mix the actual units with dummy black boxes to get apparent total coverage. There are about 40,000 locations where airline tickets are sold, all of which accept credit cards.

Among the major credit companies, the auto rental companies and some of the major airlines, about 5,000 units could be leased within a nine-year period.

Identifying Persons in Banks

The largest potential market for an identification system is probably in conjunction with "automated banking" or the so-called "cashless society." As commonly described, a person takes his bank ID card to a retailer. The retailer, to collect for a sale, puts the card in something like a "touch-tone" telephone. By dialing the amount charged for the merchandise, the retailer's bank account is automatically credited and the customer's debited. The same type of instrument could be used at home for payment of installment bills. Obviously, such a system requires positive identification of the cardholder. Based on the number of banks and various types of retail establishments, it is estimated that such a system could absorb 1.5 million "identifier units."

In security markets it is an advantage that the Sibany system operates without being tied into computers. Operation remains simple. However, that advantage will not apply to its use in automated banking to which computers are essential for accounting purposes. A computer itself can identify a person, for example, by comparison of a prerecorded code number with one given by the person. Assuming that computers are necessary for accounting purposes, the identification function may be performed at marginal cost; considerably below what the Sibany system could be sold for at presently projected costs.

Banking industry needs suggest an identifier unit renting for no more than $10–15/month. This appears possible with touch-tone telephone, which might be the instrument for communicating with the computer; for both identification and accounting purposes.

There are additional banking-industry applications for the Sibany system; for example, identifying a person cashing a check at a distant bank. The system could also be used to control access to safe deposit boxes, vaults, night depository area, and so on.

There are now about 30,000 banking offices in the U.S. Five thousand of the major offices might use a system of the Sibany type to a limited extent.

Miscellaneous applications could absorb 5,000 units such as the Identimation ID system within the next 10 years:

Hospitals (baby I.D.: identification of unconscious patients, etc.)

Colleges (student I.D.: dormitory access)

High-rise apartments (access key to front door)

Private clubs (Gaslight, Playboy, VFW, etc.)

Passport & Visa Verification

Calculation of Revenues

During all marketing interviews, researchers discussed prices of $1–2,000 or rental prices of $60–70/month for the Sibany system. Only in the area of banking, where the respondents thought in terms of several identifiers in a given location, were there objections.

However, these prices would be justified by improving security-guard efficiency and possibly reducing the number of guards required; reducing fraud losses by credit card companies; or reducing loss or theft of supplies.

Most marketing calculations are based on a rental value starting at $70/month ($840/year) in years 1 and 2, decreasing to $25/month ($300/year) by years 7 to 9. This sharp drop in part will be caused by competition. The effect of using rental values vs. sales value is to lower total revenues during the first four years and to increase them during the last four years. The interviews indicated acceptability of both approaches.

Management's Summations

Starting from market research, for the first time, Identimation's management could project all aspects of its business.

After the discussion of projected revenues, the market survey detailed the estimated revenues by units and then in dollars for a projected nine-year period from start-up. From this information and the costing of bills of material and operations sheets, it was possible to calculate projected costs of goods sold and gross profit.

From the estimated shipments, by market areas, a fair idea of the nature and extent of the marketing and sales organization could be projected on paper. Using the information in the report, plus general information on typical companies in the security and data processing industries, general and administrative expenses could be approximated. Later, this information was translated into pro forma profit and loss statements and balance sheets and estimates of cash-flow.

Market Survey of an Existing Industry: Fishing

The marketing of a new product often represents one segment of a general approach to the market. The history of one company's appraisal and goal selection of its markets provides a revealing case in point.

One founder of a company started with the insight that he needed a bread-and-butter business as a base operation. He had no new product to focus on, and felt he could not afford one. He wanted to start with an operating business, with sales and income.

The entrepreneur spent the better part of a year becoming an expert on the nature and economics of the fishing industry of the United States. From this accumulated information, he deduced that his first operating business should relate to specialty and higher-priced fish products. From this analysis he also decided to first enter the shrimp business. The decision was implemented. The new company operated a freezing and processing plant and a fleet of shrimp boats in central America.

A review of the facts and assumptions that became the basis for this operating company's marketing operations makes some interesting points about the practicalities of new-product marketing, and about the nature of the marketplace in general. The case has been excerpted from the company's business plan:

General Review of the U.S. Fishing Industry

The fish market in the U.S. is strongly competitive because of three factors: First, there is no product differentiation; second, buyers and sellers tend to be small and numerous; and third, a variable resource base causes intense short-run fluctuations in supply.

Competition is not only intense within the U.S. industry, but it also exists among fishing, meat and poultry industries, and between the U.S. and foreign industries. While fish consumption has remained relatively static —about eleven pounds per capita for the last 50 years—meat and poultry consumption per capita have increased steadily. In addition, imports of fish have gone from 30 per cent of total U.S. consumption in 1956 to over 60 per cent in 1968. In absolute terms, the U.S. has gone from number two-producer (behind Japan) in 1956 to number five producer in 1968 (behind Peru, Japan, China and the U.S.S.R., in that order). It is clear that the U.S. fishing industry is failing to keep pace with other competitive products or foreign fishing industries.

In the middle of the '60's, steps were taken to remedy this situation. The Anadramous Fish Act of 1965 and the Commercial Fisheries Research and Development Act of 1964 both aid in the funding of R. & D. programs. The Fishing Fleet Improvement Act of 1964 offered federal subsidies for the construction of fishing vessels. Results to date indicate that more needs to be done in the areas of basic research and investment in backup industries for the U.S. to compete with foreign industries.

As yet, no national protective measures, in the form of tariffs, have been taken to restrict the importation of fish products. It is doubtful that federal measures will be taken unless a price war threatened a sizable segment of the U.S. industry.

Economics of the Fishing Industry

The economics of the industry are useful in understanding its problems. Three basic factors affect fish consumption per capita: price, income and competing products. In general, the price elasticity[2] of fish products is below unity; that is, a one per cent change in the price of *all* fish products will result in less than one per cent in quantity of fish consumed. When prices fall in a period of glut, consumption does not increase proportionally, causing a decrease in total revenues.

However, price elasticity for individual fish products or species may be high. This is true when consumers substitute one kind of fish for another in response to relative price changes. As a whole, shellfish are less price elastic than finned species. Inasmuch as shellfish are a luxury product, the substitution between shellfish and non-shellfish is limited.

In terms of income, buyer demand for fish, like all foods, is inelastic, constituting a smaller percent of income as income increases. Elasticity of demand for shellfish is much higher than for other species but is still below unity.

Cross elasticity between fish, meat and poultry has been found to be below unity. Hence, as meat and poultry prices change, the percentage change in fish consumption is less than the percentage change in the prices of the competing items.

The U.S. consumer regards fish on a "take it or leave it" basis. Demand is fairly steady over the long run, but weak in the face of short term changes in price, income and competitive product conditions. The challenge to the marketer is to establish species and then brand loyalty in order to avoid the vicissitudes and unattractive demand characteristics of the industry as a whole.

The U.S. consumes 80%–90% of the world's supply of shellfish. The figures on shrimp, lobster and oysters presented below refer to the U.S. market. As a producer, processor, or marketer, International Oceanographic will be selling to this market almost exclusively.

Shrimp—A Whale of a Market

More than 70 per cent of the shrimp sold in the U.S. goes to restaurants, hotels and clubs, where shrimp cocktail is the most popular appetizer. The growth in per-capita consumption of shrimp was greater than 70% over the past ten years. This has resulted in increased restaurant revenues and the general establishment of shrimp as a luxury food.

2. Elasticity of demand is an aspect of product marketing. Demand for bread is relatively inelastic. People will continue to buy bread at about the same rate despite price fluctuations. Pleasure boat sales, on the other hand, are highly elastic, and major price changes create large shifts in demand.

Imports of shrimp have grown steadily over the past ten years to 54% of total U.S. consumption in 1969. While this is certainly a larger percentage, it is noteworthy that the U.S. industry seems to be defending its position better with shrimp than with any other species of seafood.

While the U.S. fleet expands and improves its efficiency, it has not been able to grow as fast as domestic demand. New shrimp grounds are being developed around the world which increase production at a very fast rate. In the Caribbean area and off the coast of South America, American nationals and boats are producing for the U.S. market. The Japanese continue to play a more and more important role in the international shrimp picture. They are developing resources off Southeast Asia and the West African coast as well as in the Caribbean.

Shrimp prices change relative to several factors. As a commodity, the market prices fluctuate seasonally with supply and demand. No individual or group of buyers dominates the industry. Similarly, no individual or group of producers control enough volume to affect market prices.

Studies show that the shrimp market is characterized by an inelastic demand with regard to price and an elastic demand with regard to personal income. A 10 per cent increase in price reduces sales 3 per cent to 5 per cent. However, income elasticity of 1.0 to 1.5 yields a 10 per cent to 15 per cent sales increase with a 10 per cent rise in personal income.

There is a general upward trend of wholesale and retail prices over the past three years (1966–1969). It is interesting to note that prices for shrimp and seafood in general have not grown in pace with the general inflationary trend. An average annual price rise of 4.5 per cent has occurred during the 1960's, compared with 5–7 per cent for beef products.

The market value of shrimp and shrimp products has grown at a higher rate than prices alone. This is due to the combined effects of increasing prices, increasing per-capita consumption and increasing population.

The United States market for shrimp appears to have no end to its growth potential. To maintain per capita consumption at the 1969 level of 1.81 pounds, heads-off weight, sales will have to increase 8 million pounds, per year, just to keep pace with the expected population increase. If per capita consumption should increase in line with its long-run average, 20 million more pounds of shrimp will have to be sold per year.

Factors affecting the future market for shrimp products include the growth of personal income, price trends, population growth, and per capita consumption. Recent reports by leading economists in *Fortune Magazine* and *Business Week* project a "real growth" in personal income of from 2.5 to 5 per cent annually. With a 1.0–1.5 elasticity factor, the effect on the shrimp market should be 2.5 to 7.5 per cent annual growth. Continued inflation and short supply should yield price growth of 5 per cent annually. This will reduce demand 1.5 to 2.5 per cent. Population and per capita consumption should grow 3 per cent to 5 per cent per annum respectively.

Computer studies made by DuPont indicate that at the projected growth of population and per capita consumption, the market for frozen seafood will climb more than 150 per cent in the next ten years.

After the Survey

All start-up entrepreneurs have the same problem: the need to analyze, evaluate, and plan their market, integrate operations with marketing requirements, and so on. However, some companies avoid some of the problems, and others have additional problems. The point is that each start-up company, each market study, has its own individual problems. The foundation for studying the market for a certain product is first to gain an understanding and then later to seek a solution to the unique market-study problems involved. Gerber had several unique problems. The weighing industry does not turn up on anybody's list of industries in which to diversify. No engineering student makes the judgment that he wants to enter the scale industry. Being an old and established field, the manufacturers, distributors, and users of scales have a well-defined and conservative attitude about the realities of their business. They already have all the answers.

Gerber had to use terms unfamiliar to the old guard, such as "electronic weighing" and "mat scales." The mat is equivalent to the platform of a mechanical scale. At a trade show of the scale industry, one distributor, who had just seen several demonstrations of the product, actually picked up the flexible mat to see if a platform scale were underneath. Potential customers, such as an airline or a truck fleet, had to be educated before they could be surveyed.

Like Sibany and the chemical company, Gerber had to devise better ways to communicate. Working with an artist, he developed drawings of what his final product would look like in various commercial applications. He wrote descriptions of his product, comparing what was by now called the Dyne-A-Mat, with existing products. The drawings, combined with text material, evolved as he was making his market survey, usually in response to a specific problem of communication. These enabled Gerber to make a market analysis. Because of the maturity of the industry and its highly traditional nature, the market analysis was unique.

Gerber begins his market plan with a retrospective analysis of the weighing industry.

The Scale Industry

The weighing scale was conceived in 5000 B.C. to help the buyer and seller of a commodity consummate a fair transaction. Since that time, the *commercial scale* (defined by National Bureau of Standards Handbook 44 as "a device for establishing the weight of quantities, things, produce, or articles for distribution or consumption, purchased, offered, or submitted for sale," and for official weighing used by law enforcement agencies) has been continuously used in commerce. Today, the commercial scale is controlled by federal, state and local weights and measures officials.

The total domestic scale market has increased over the years, percentage-wise, roughly in relation to gross national product. In 1968, weighing industry sales were estimated to be $149,000,000 having increased in fairly equal annual increments from $76,000,000 in 1958.

Today's scale has changed little in the past 100 years. Conventional mechanical levers, springs, and pendulums are used in the overwhelming majority of applications, with load cells making small inroads.

The industry is stale, its management generally unprogressive and unable to attract young, aggressive technical and managerial personnel. Manufacturing facilities are usually antiquated, leading to high manufacturing costs and low profit margins.

Nevertheless, the scale market will continue to expand and the industry will continue to grow, in spite of itself. Traditional types of scales, however, will become obsoleted. Example: in some applications, the load cell is now being used where the lever and beam were previously used. While the load cell is still heavy and cumbersome in heavy platform applications, it is less cumbersome than levers and will continue to capture a small share of the market.

The scale marketplace is anxiously awaiting a better idea. There is no evidence of a technical breakthrough other than the Metrodyne DYNE-A-MAT.

The Historical Market

The domestic scale market is served by about 50 manufacturers, many of which have been in business for over 50 years. Detecto, Fairbanks Morse, Howe Richardson, Hobart, and Toledo produce approximately two-thirds of the scale volume.

[All] of these companies until recently were family controlled. . . .Though they have been in existence many years, none of them is thought to be highly profitable. Toledo, Fairbanks Morse, and Howe Richardson have profit and loss statements that are combined with their parent companies, Reliance Electric, Colt Industries, and Robert Morse Corporation, Ltd., respectively. . . .Hobart does report publicly, with New York Stock Exchange listing, but only a small percentage of their business is in the scale industry.

The sales of the domestic industry, for the years 1959 to 1968 [Figure 9-1] shows continuous growth, with the exception of 1967. The 1968 scale market for American manufacturers was estimated to be $149,000,000. [Figure 9-2] shows a breakdown of the market by scale types. Though not reflected in the charts, manufacturers of the present day

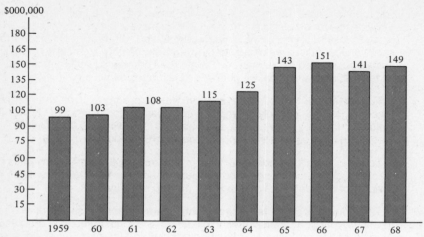

FIGURE 9-1   Scale industry sales, 1959 to 1968.

electronic (resistive load cell) scales, who have been in business for nearly 20 years, managed to capture only 11 per cent of the total scale market in 1968.

Future Market

Today's scale industry management is heavily populated with old timers and descendants of old timers—operating with facilities that show only modest improvement in recent years. With this fact as possibly causal, the industry lacks imaginative design (technological innovation) and aggressive marketing.

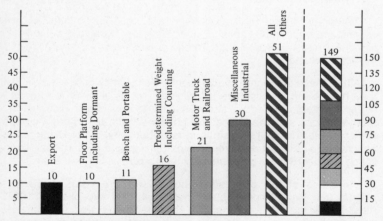

FIGURE 9-2   Scale industry sales, 1968 (by scale type).

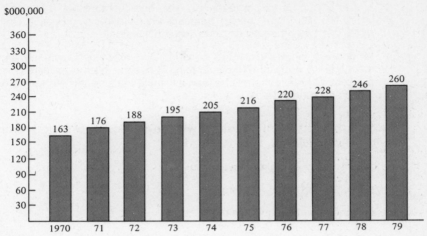

$000,000

FIGURE 9-3   Scale industry forecast, 1970 to 1979 (without new technology).

Nevertheless, the industry has managed to maintain or slightly improve the percentage growth curve of the Gross National Product without the introduction of new and revolutionary electronic weighing devices. We expect the industry to continue to keep pace with the predicted increase in the GNP.

[Figure 9-3] reflects a 1970 to 1980 sales forecast for the existing industry. During this same period it is expected that profit margins will decline and that industry consolidation will take place, considerably reducing the number of manufacturing companies. Further, existing electronic (resistive load cell) scale manufacturers will continue to make small inroads into the mechanical scale market but will probably not create new requirements and markets.

New technology will be introduced to the potential weighing market in the next few years. The new technology, with its simplicity and cost advantages, will open up entirely new markets. In addition, the suppliers of this new technology will be able to capture major shares of the existing scale market, now served by conventional products.[3]

Examples of specific new markets which will become available to first-generation new technology scales, such as the Dyne-A-Mat, are:

Check-weighing platform scales (for freight and cargo carriers). The railroads currently perform only a spotcheck on shippers and freight forwarders shipments. Because with conventional scales it is not cost effective to weigh all shipments, the carrier believes he is losing 5 per cent

[3]This rapid growth is not without precedent. During 1945–1965, while GNP increased at an average of 2½ per cent annually, Polaroid, 3M, IBM, Xerox and Texas Instruments, to name a few, grew at an average annual rate of 17 per cent. This was accomplished by introducing improved technology into markets that were being served by conventional products.

to 15 per cent of freight revenues. This potential user will buy a low-profile portable scale that can be positioned at all receiving docks. Currently there is nothing available to serve this market.

Wheel/Axle Scales (for road construction vehicles). Downtime and maintenance costs due to overloading is becoming an ever-increasing problem. Currently there is nothing available to serve this market other than very crude portable wheel scales.

Existing markets which will expand with the introduction of devices, such as the Dyne-A-Mat, are:

a. Motor truck and aircraft weighing

b. Freight and cargo weighing

c. General purpose industrial

In all of the markets the evolution o the Dyne-A-Mat- type system presents additional market potential through the sale of special purpose electronic data processing equipment such as remote readers, scoreboards, printers, and special purpose computers.

[Figure 9-4] shows the total potential market, expanded through the introduction of new electronic weighing systems. For comparison, we have also shown the forecast of scale industry bookings without new technology [Figure 9-3]. It is dramatic to note that new technology alone may be responsible for a 25 per cent increase in the market by 1979.

The scale industry market analysis led Gerber to his first major business decision: to concentrate on the scale industry as his first operating business.

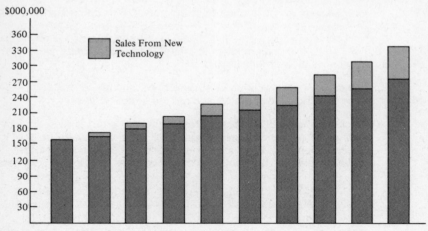

FIGURE 9-4   Scale industry forecast, 1970 to 1979 (with new technology).

The foreword to Metrodyne's business plan included the following explanation:

> Metrodyne's unique technology[4] points toward the creation of two new industries in the fields of automated inventory counting and control and inmotion high speed dynamic weighing and the extension of an established industry. The company intends to pioneer in these new fields from an operating base by first entering the existing scale industry with its DYNE-A-MAT systems. Success in this industry will enable the company to test and tighten its organization, facilities, financial requirements, technology, and other operating requirements as discussed in this business plan.

With respect to each of these three cases—Identimation, the fishing company, and Metrodyne—each of the market projections is presented in an optimistic and obstacle-minimizing tone. This is the rule rather than the exception. It is to be expected. People who start companies have to be optimistic, or they would not begin. This built-in bias is particularly strong when the inventor, innovator, or developer participates in estimating the marketing potential of a new product.

To balance the rosy-colored hue of many marketing projections, we must keep in mind that almost every new-product launching is preceded by just such an appraisal, the *failures* as well as successes.

Some 75 to 90 percent of new companies fail in the first two or three years, just as eight out of nine new oil well drillings fail. It is less well known that the new products of large companies fail at similarly high rates. Of course, while statistics such as these are always subject to the definition of the words "fail," "new," and so forth, there can be no question that new companies and new products are risky ventures.

Much of the direction of new ventures is dictated by what the inventor and the entrepreneur can afford. All surveys indicate that in the eyes of the people who started new ventures, the overwhelming proportion agree that they failed because of lack of capital, typically because they did not have enough money to live on while the start-up company struggled to survive and grow. But lack of capital is poor planning, poor management. In the following chapter we will look at the problems of financing the new venture.

---

[4] The first United States patent for its Electronic Weighing Device, No. 3,565,195, was issued on Feb. 23, 1971.

Chapter 10

The Financial Problems of the New Venture

In 1970 the managements of many small companies were startled but gratified by a financial event: American Telephone & Telegraph, the largest corporation in the world (it has the most employees, the most investors, and the highest investment) announced corporate financing of $1.3 billion. For years AT&T had been making a net profit after taxes of over $1 billion, yet here was one of the most profitable corporations requiring additional financing.

While engaged in a struggle to find enough money to properly finance an embryonic company, one gets the sense that most other companies are in perfect cash position. The AT&T need for financing put corporate cash needs into a somewhat more realistic perspective.

To the student of finance, the AT&T requirement was routine. A rapidly growing company that leases its products and services will have cash shortages from time to time. AT&T has chosen a strategy of financing that includes the payment of a large part of its earnings to its shareholders as a dividend. Other companies pay to their shareholders a smaller percentage of earnings each year; and still others pay only a nominal cash dividend, or none at all. The dividend policy and the strategy of large companies in handling their finances clearly affect their cash position and needs.

AT&T's requirement for $1.3 billion was equivalent to a company with $25 million in sales and $2 million in profits requiring $1.3 million, or a company with $2.5 million in sales and a $200,000 profit having a cash requirement of $130,000. An influx of money is a requirement of the successful company just as it is of the new company attempting to grow.

In a falling stock market, with the Dow-Jones average hitting its lowest point in seven years, the AT&T financing was completed in a few days. Others seeking venture capital, at the same time, were almost all turned down.

Compare the AT&T experience to the struggles of those entrepreneurs who eventually became immensely successful: Edwin Land looking for several hundred thousand dollars in the midforties to finance his instant photography process. The early businessmen-flyers C.R. Smith, Eddy Rickenbacker, and Juan Trippe with the dream of an airline industry, eventually to become, respectively, American Airlines, Eastern Airlines, and Pan American World Airways.

Alexander Graham Bell got almost no financial support from the existing companies already in the communications industries. Carlson, with the first prototype of a dry copying machine (now Xerography) had no money except that which he scraped up from friends and relatives.

And consider Philo T. Farnsworth, far ahead of the technology of his time. During the First World War, he had to learn to blow glass to make the television tube bottle. Then there was Thomas Edison with a light bulb that could not be used practically until a large section of lower Manhattan had been equipped with generating equipment and electric lines. Money —immense sums—was required by these innovators.

These are typical of inventions in which investors would make new fortunes, many others would lose all their money, and still others would have many frustrations because they could not be sure their situation would pay off.

Paradoxically, the entrepreneurs and inventors who *do* make it follow a pattern similar to the many more who *do not* make it. But for both groups the need for cash input is continuing and crucial.

The most critical financing problem of the new company is financing the venture well enough to move it along according to plans. (This aspect is covered in the first part of this chapter and will be followed by a discussion of the other financing problems of the new company.)

Reviewing a few of the successful new ventures helps clear up the murk and distortions that mark the view of a struggling company, day by day and week by week. If only one could see next week's newspaper!

Carlson's poor copies from the first dry-process Xerox machine showed "Carlson . . . Garden City, Long Island, 1938." The first Xerox machine was not on the market until twenty years and almost $100 million later.

Let us respect the patience of Alexander Graham Bell, with a product that almost no household or office wanted until a lot of other people had the same product. Graphic Sciences, Xerox, and Magnavox are pioneering the facsimile industry, with a problem analogous to Bell's today.

Let us acknowledge the frustration of Clarence Birdseye, who, after developing a revolutionary quick-freeze process, had to start almost all over again to invent and design a freezer so the storekeeper could store frozen foods and the housewife could buy them. From the investors' standpoint, who looks like a Carlson, an Edison, or a Birdseye?

A handful of these pioneers start with a lubricant to grease the way: money. They were born to it, or married into it. Or, every once in a while, someone finds his "J. P. Morgan," his angel, at an early stage of his cash requirement.

However, almost all new companies follow a pattern of struggle to get the money they require. A typical though hardly universal pattern, in today's world of high technology, starts with financing from relatives and friends. In the last third of the 20th century, as compared with the entrepreneur-inventor of the 19th century, the company seeking investment finds a fairly understanding and cooperative environment—tough as it looks, from the middle of it.

All of us have heard that most of the products that will be on the market five or ten years from now are not available today. The number of companies and their backers that have made it have been popularized by the mass media, and many of us want to participate in this new phenomenon that seems to be both exciting and potentially very profitable. The new industry, venture capital (discussed in Chapter 4) has made the method of getting investors more regularized and sources of capital more numerous.

One Company's Financial Experience

The traditional sequence of financing for the typical new venture proceeds in this way:

Home financing: "First money" from relatives and friends.

Private financing: The second round is normally received from a limited number of "sophisticated investors" who are strangers to the management of the new company.

Public financing: The company gets its cash from a large group of strangers, via public sale of stocks.

Relatives and Friends as Investors

To tell the story as it develops for the company, the case used is essentially that of Sibany. It has been modified at some points to eliminate idiosyncratic elements and to present a more typical picture of small-business financing.

Before you seek cash from friends, relatives, and their friends, you believe they are the easiest people to sell on investing in your company. But two circumstances make it difficult. First: you have been raised in the same house with them or they have known you since you were "this high." Accordingly, how can they believe you are another Thomas Edison or Tom Watson?

Second, you are not prepared for the difficulty of asking someone you know to do you a favor. At this early stage of financing, the reactions of those you ask to invest are little different from reactions to being asked to donate to the Red Cross.

The idea of a Sibany started in September 1961. As previously discussed, it was based on a new bowling game concept considered revolutionary. However, since better product ideas were soon developed, the product which sparked the beginning of the company was never worked on and never reached the marketplace.

We talked to friends and relatives about putting money into the company. Even though they were close to us, it was obvious that we must have something concrete to show them.

The two founders invested $7,000, all they had. We built a prototype of our first product, a hand-held roving telephone with which one can answer an office or home telephone when he is within a half-mile range. It's like taking a regular telephone, severing it from the wall, and shrinking it so that it fits your pocket.

Then we worked with a friend who charged us very little for a brochure which discussed what the company was and what business we were trying to go into. Armed with our prototype of a remote telephone and our business plan, we sought investors among our relatives and friends.

Someone wanted to invest $100 and we found this was unacceptable because we could solicit only a limited number of potential shareholders. We learned, at that point, that a modern-day new company is very dependent on the counsel of a competent attorney. If we had gone beyond that limited number, the Securities and Exchange Commission might have decided that we had made an unregistered public offering. We might have had to offer to repurchase the shares purchased by the investor. And so we decide to ask for a minimum investment of $1,000. This became $5,000, then $10,000, within a period of 2½ years.

The first person to say "yes" presented another problem! He wanted to know how large a part of the company he would own. We needed the answer more than he did. Discussions led to the conclusion that we needed $80,000 for which we were willing to give up 40 percent of the company. Within six months we raised $56,000, so that our investors owned 28 percent of the new company and we, the founders, owned 72 percent.

Some people we were sure would back us invested not a nickel. "I have to put braces on my son's teeth" is symbolic of those whose rejection hurt us deeply. Others, from whom we expected little or nothing, invested a few thousand dollars, and as they saw us struggling over the months, invested additional amounts of money.

Those people, in the early 1960s, were given the investment opportunity of a lifetime. We did not realize it at the time. An investment of $1,000 in Sibany in 1962 grew to a paper value of $150,000 in November 1968 and was reduced in value to $1,000 in 1973.

We realized that $56,000 was not going to finance the remote telephone to the point of getting it on the market. We adopted a second method of financing and marketing: licensing to an existing company. During the day we wrote letters, made telephone calls and had meetings to find a licensee. At night we held meetings with potential investors.

Eventually, we found licensees for the first two products we developed: the remote telephone and a hermaphroditic electrical connector. There was a sense of accomplishment and relief. But again we ran out of money. Unfortunately, that became a pattern. Sometimes it was solved by a new shareholder, this time for $10,000, which we had by then set as a minimum investment. We had made some progress and we wanted that to be recognized, if possible. We arbitrarily raised the price, in the second and third year, to twice the original price and then 3½ times the original price. Other times we borrowed small amounts of money and lent it to the company to be returned when we got the next investor. Somehow we survived, and in some ways we even thrived.

If we had been interviewed when we first started the company and had been asked the specific question: "How long will it take for one of your products to make a great deal of money for Sibany?" our answer would have been, "About a year; two years at the most."

By this time, we had learned better. We had begun to learn that almost everything takes two or three times longer than you expect. We had learned that developing a product from the idea stage is actually risky, rather than routine. We had learned that the most difficult part of our planning was: "When will we have cash income, and how much?" Therefore, predicting when we could pay back a loan would be next to impossible. We adopted a policy of selling only equity in the company and not borrowing. There was one small exception, a $25,000 convertible bond issue, where the investors were all existing Sibany shareholders and informally agreed to convert the bond at the company's direction into Sibany shares, instead of expecting to be paid back the loan. We continually told ourselves that until we were able to have continuing operating results, we would not change this policy.

Investment by the Public

In one way, Sibany did not follow the normal pattern of investment. Most companies are able to find and sell sophisticated investors as a second stage of financing. The major reason we did not was that the year 1965 in the venture capital market was poor for high-technology companies—a bad financial climate for Sibany.

Since we did not know any people directly or indirectly who could invest or find us investors for the several hundred thousand dollars we then needed, we decided to do a public offering. Knowing no underwriters, we did it as a self-underwriting, the company selling its own stock. The founders were back on the financing trail to individuals in their homes. We found that, like most other new companies based on product development, we had to spend a great deal of time financing. This took away from the time we should have been spending solving the considerable number of everyday problems of the new company.

This time we had an offering circular that had been reviewed by the Securities and Exchange Commission in New York. This provided an important advantage of giving us the right to accept *any* amount of investment because we were selling shares that could be traded publicly. But the SEC also posed a major problem: Before we could receive any money from this public financing, we had 120 days to sell $50,000 worth of stock and before that had to put all the money into escrow. If we sold only $49,999 of stock, we would receive none of the proceeds. At the time, we resented the escrow. Later, we came to realize that this requirement was one way of protecting the small public investor. The minimum investment by an institutional investor or a small investor should be an aggregate amount able to accomplish the purposes of the company in which the investment is being made. The investment of a lesser amount than that required by the company adds even greater risk for the investor.

We needed the money so badly we could taste it—a feeling that continued. We wanted to go into our latest new product, a small air conditioner. In addition to the financing from the public offering, we were seeking arrangements with the Small Business Administration (SBA) in Maine; an investment group of local businessmen in Lewiston, Maine; and a bank. The

SBA, the Maine investment group, and the bank would put up 95 percent of our financial requirements for capital goods. The public offering would provide working capital.

Finally, on the very last day, we delivered the last check, making a total of $50,000, to Chemical Bank, the escrow agent. They gave us a check for $50,000 on the spot, and we made out a deposit ticket. We were in business for a little while longer.

The first public offering raised a total of $127,000 for Sibany. It financed the activities of the company for thirteen months. The earlier sale of stock privately to friends and relatives had raised a total of about $100,000. The $100,000, combined with about $75,000 of revenues from the first two licensing agreements, had financed the company for two years. To the objective observer, Sibany was showing a pattern of some success and much frustration.

A year later we again needed several hundred thousand dollars, this time to begin the financing of the Identimat, a machine that could identify people by measuring their personal characteristics. (By 1973, $2 million had been invested in what was by then Identimation Corporation.) A year later, four things were better for us:

- We were somewhat experienced in selling a public registration.
- The venture capital climate was gradually becoming better.
- We had been around for four years and had more to show than in the earlier financings.
- Our technique for presenting ourselves to interested people had become more professional.

This time we sold the entire public offering and actually had more people who wanted to buy our stock than had been registered with the SEC. We were not certain, at the time how long it would last, but the $300,000 we received financed us for 15 months.

A pattern had emerged. Instinctively, and then later consciously, as a matter of strategy, we had financed ourselves project by project, goal by goal. We had raised several hundred thousand dollars from investors and had retained ownership of about 60 percent of the company. If we had raised all our requirements for several years at one time, we would probably have been required to give up a higher percentage of the company. However, we had spent about a quarter of our time in raising money—a severe penalty. Later, we were accused by some in the financial community of having gone to the well too many times. We were finding that these financing decisions, like other critical elements in the new company, were becoming 51 to 49 percent decisions, whereas earlier in our corporate existence, they had been 98 to 2 percent decisions. We were still about two years away from deciding that our basic business is venture management and we decided to continue to finance project by project.

Investment by the Sophisticated Investor

We had been dealing with investors with whom we were either friendly or acquainted, or with people who were friends of friends. We did not have to provide solid and incontrovertible proof of our competence, honesty, or experience. To a great extent at least, our honesty and experience were taken for granted.

But at some point, we knew we must take the first step toward the more sophisticated and more questioning investor. On vacation I met an investment broker with whom I hit it off. Because neither of us likes to mix business with pleasure, we waited until the last day of the vacation to talk about Sibany. He was both interested and skeptical. We were friendly with each other and agreed to see each other socially when we got home.

After my vacation, back in the office, I found several telephone messages from him. Another vacation so soon? No! We were in luck. A three-page article had just appeared in *Business Week* with my picture plastered all over it. If I had written the entire script, I could not have done a better job of pre-selling the broker.

I had not mentioned *Business Week* to the broker or anyone else because eighteen months earlier *Business Week* had written a story and taken hundreds of photographs, but the story had never appeared. When the reporters came back to update the piece, we were afraid to believe that this time the story would appear. But it did! And the broker was convinced that Sibany was worth an investment of his time and perhaps later the investment of his customers' money.

Although we had sold stock that could be publicly traded, there was no public market for the shares of Sibany until the *Business Week* story appeared. Then several people started making a market[1] and our 700 shareholders and the general public could sell and buy Sibany. More important, an objective value was placed on our shares. We now found ourselves, in a sense, in an election; but one that never ended. There was no election date, but the voting continued.

At the beginning of 1968, a third public financing of Sibany took place, this time underwritten by the broker. To this point we had had four rounds of financing totaling three-quarters of a million dollars—a lot of money by our standards but, we soon learned, not much for a new company in the business of high technology.

In the spring of 1968 the price of Sibany stock suddenly took off, for no apparent reason.[2] From the spring of 1967 to the spring of 1968 the price had

1. The over-the-counter market.
2. This is a pattern. In the short run, the trading price of the stock usually cannot be identified with the activities of the company.

been in the range of $4 to $11. By the late spring, it was $30. By the end of 1968 it was selling in the high 40s. We were both pleased and mystified.

But there was a reason: High-technology companies were the rage in 1968. Within a year they were to become much less popular, and within two years they became a drug on the market.

We had reached the point where we needed a lot of money by anyone's standards. Our plans suggested a requirement for $1.2 million. Mostly, it was to start our own subsidiary companies, to exploit several product developments.

This kind of financing was too large for the stock brokerage firm that had done our previous offering, and we sought a new underwriter. Unbelievably, it was easy. We received a positive response from the first Wall Street brokerage firm with which we talked. They suggested that private financing from a limited number of sophisticated institutional investors would be more appropriate than a public offering. We agreed because we did not understand the significance of either method and our main concern was getting the money. They also told us that if our projections indicated that we needed $1.2 million, we ought to seek more money because we would probably need it and because the stock market might get worse. Both suggestions were persuasive, and at the closing of the private financing we received a check for $2.4 million. Included in the new investment group were insurance companies, banks, and other investors whose names had been legendary to us throughout our business careers.

We started the new companies and invested the newly acquired money according to our plans. The companies were organized to continue the product development and begin marketing and sales. Progress was slow, and again, everything took longer than projected.

The cash we had raised carried Sibany and the new Sibany companies for 2½ years. However, we were again seeking money for the next stages of the development of the Sibany companies. Because venture capital was almost unavailable in 1970, we were back to the public financing route. In 1971 public offerings were completed for two Sibany companies, and by 1973 the two companies were no longer new ventures and their financial problems were those of a more established company.

This outline of Sibany's financing history has shown a new company's financing pattern at three levels: (1) a chronology of events, not presented as being the same as other new companies, but presented rather as being typical of the process; (2) the attitudes of the entrepreneur—and inventor —mentality, at the time of the event; (3) the financing problem-solution cycle, including mostly judgments that become increasingly less black and white, and more gray.

Before discussing alternate financing methods of the new venture and specific problems and possible solutions to those problems, let us look at the questions relating to potential cost and potential profit.

Potential Cost and Potential Profit

The first question a businessman must ask about a new-product venture is, "How much will it cost?" The second question is, "How profitable can it be?" He can then make a judgment balancing risk against potential gain.

From a cash-use standpoint, invention and innovation may be seen as an alternative to expansion of existing manufacturing and distribution or to investment in another proved business, or simply as a continuation of what you have been doing before.

In 1973, technology transfer companies and small and large companies spent over $20 billion for new product development and research and development. Only a fraction of this total was spent on basic invention, however. According to a U.S. Department of Commerce study, "Invention and Innovation," considerably less than 10 percent of total funds are devoted to advanced development or "conception": the invention sector.

The total cost, however, is of prime importance both to the businessman and the investor. It makes little sense to invest just enough to determine that an invention will work and then to discover that you cannot afford to tool for it or are unwilling to invest in a marketing organization to support it.

Innovation, Step by Step

The inventor is faced with making many decisions at each stage in the innovative process. Here are some guidelines:

One or another employee will suggest a product. A "seat-of-the-pants" judgment is that it can be made and can be marketed.

Someone suggests a technical approach, and if he is convinced that it is feasible, he is encouraged to work it out. Drawings are made, prototype hardware is tooled, and a breadboard prototype is built.

The total investment in this very first "idea" stage can range from the cost of a sheet of paper (and an hour's time) to several thousand dollars and many man-hours.

If the idea appears technically feasible, the new venture is faced with dual questions: "Is it patentable?" and "Is it worth patenting?" A novelty search will cost several hundred dollars. The initial United States and foreign patent applications will range in price from $2,000 to $5,000.

Additional questions must now be considered: Can it be made commercially? At what price can it be sold? How much of a market is there for it at that price? At other prices?

For design engineering, to test the technical feasibility of a product and its ability to be reproduced commercially, one company has spent as little as $12 in material. The second stage of development on another product, however, cost the same company six figures.

Beyond the second stage of new-product development, costs can be as much as 80 percent of total investment. Tooling and manufacturing engineer-may eat up the lion's share of innovation cash and time. Market studies and marketing start-up expenses can be twice that of the basic invention.

The range of cost for new-product development varies enormously. Often a licensee creates an entire new plant, or a whole new division, to manufacture and market a new product. Another company invested almost $100,000 in market research and in technical evaluation, and later turned down the product. On the other hand, for companies seeking new products within their existing manufacturing and marketing facilities, costs have been little more than required for simple retooling or design changes on existing products.

How does a company judge a product's technical and commercial validity, and whether and how much to invest? For that matter, how do relatives and friends, sophisticated investors, or the general public judge a new-product development company? If there were a final and complete answer to this question, none of us would have to work for a living. But a reasonable answer and analysis can can be made that provide answers that are better than a blind guess.

Many judgments of new-product development are *subjective*. The initial decision to invest time and money must be intuitive, so that the idea may work and that it can be commercialized. At later stages, despite careful market analysis and technical evaluation, the final test of a product's potential lies in the marketplace.

And even then, what is profitable to one company may be totally uninteresting to another. Some companies ask for a product that would add as little as $250,000 a year to sales. Others point out that if a new venture does not add at least $25 million in sales, it will be rounded out in their year-end figures. The kinds of products in which hundreds of thousands or even millions of dollars must be invested must have a potential that appears to be open-ended. The judgment need only consider the minimum potential. For example, "If it can do at least $10 million in sales, and $1 million in after-tax profits, within five years, then a venture investment of $600,000 is justified today."

There also are *objective* yardsticks by which to judge new-product development. One way to minimize risk in a high-risk industry, and to maximize the profits inherent in the inventions industry, is to set standards of performance at every level of development. Note how standards differ from those of established businesses.

First, the ability to survive. Invention requires repeated judgments of *which* products deserve *how much* of an investment, and there must be a high enough ratio of correct decisions. One or two bad ones may mean disaster.

Second, the ability to grow. Is the inventor or company really capable of innovating many new products? (An all-or-nothing risk on a single effort, by experimental odds, is an even worse risk.)

Third, independent verification of the inventor's judgments. Merely to get another company to agree to look at and judge the validity of an invention is a major feat. Many inventors have devoted a lifetime to worthwhile innovations they were unable or unwilling to disclose to those capable of commercializing them.

Fourth, the ability to communicate. There is a wall of misunderstanding and obstructionism, the "not invented here" syndrome; the mutual wariness among inventors, manufacturing companies, the financial community, and others interested in innovation.

Fifth, the ability to make a profit: The potentials for profit in innovation are very great. The potential for total loss of an investment is even greater. The understanding, balancing, and accurate judgment of each particular case is the heart of the opportunity and the problem from the standpoint of the new company and the persons or groups asked to invest in that company. As we have said, this is one of the three most difficult judgments in the venture management business. In order for either the company itself or outside interests to bet on the new product, many difficult judgments are required. Each question has its own cycle, relevance, and importance. Each is constantly evolving, never remaining static. Each is intimately or personally involved with the present and with the short-term, medium-term, and long-term future.

Consider just a few of the elements that must be analyzed, balanced, and in the final analysis, judged: competition; newly issued patents; pricing; how long the present money supply should last; how well each of the new employees is doing; how to go about buying office supplies; vendors; numerous decisions about whether to make or buy equipment; the new piece of literature; the trade show in Los Angeles; the accounts payable that do not want to wait ninety days; how to furnish your office a little better; the morale of your employees; whether a new secretary should get a raise after six months even though the company is still not making money; whether to make 50 items and sell them at a loss or take a chance and make 200; whether a decision was the right one; whether to borrow or sell equity; whether the accounting firm is prestigious enough; what things have to be done first class, and where compromises can be made; whether the customers will pay a little more to cover start-up costs; whether the new investors like what you are doing; whether you will meet the forecast; whether you are qualified for a certain job; whether all new companies have these problems; whether you should change that poor or mediocre manager, since you'll have to invest your time to train his replacement; whether you can really be making a profit by the first quarter; whether the financial climate is going to be better or worse next year; whether you should write to that guy or take the time to go see him; why you spent more than you had planned; which of the banks will give you the most attention; whether anyone else really cares as much as you do; why product development costs so much; whether you should have taken that new direction on the product development; how much that change will cost; whether you can sell to 1 percent of the people in that industry; whether that other company will wait until you prove a market and then come in and clobber you; whether the patent search is positive because no one else really cares about your widget; when you can relax and take *something* for granted; why you have to do everything around here; whether you have priced yourself out of the market; whether that is an important problem or a detail; why he is worried, when you're not; whether you can afford it; why the phone doesn't stop ringing; what's wrong since nobody called you; how you can return all those calls before the meeting; why everything takes so long; why "they" always treat you like the president instead of like one of the boys; why "they" always get pregnant as soon as they have learned what to do; who needs it; why your wife doesn't know you're working this hard for her, also?

A book this size could be filled with nothing else. Yet, patterns do emerge. Experience does make it easier. Progress is made, however haltingly.

Internally, you are judging the new company. Externally, you are being judged, on the basis of fewer factors, perhaps more experience, and certainly more stereotypes: You didn't do it the way company X did it, and company X made it big. Is that projection going to be met? When should you go public? Will you ever make it work? Should you invest again when they need money? Why didn't you get more of the company? You'll never go into this industry again. Without your money they wouldn't have even gotten this far. Should you borrow next time? Should you merge them with someone else? He's never run a company before. You really should spend more time with the company. You're in too many deals now. You should have bought more. There should have been more investors in this deal. Why does it take so long? When should you get out? Should you find them a company to buy, in case it doesn't work? Are you falling in love with this company? Next time you won't do it this way. You should have sold when you could. How many times your investment can you make?

In the new venture there is a continuing search for credibility, a persisting flourishing of hope and doubt. All the factors can be frozen, at any particular point of time, and analyzed and judged. They can be given priorities, so that the major elements are distinguished from the details. Pertinence and priorities lend themselves to timely analysis, and their judgment matures with time, success, and failure—in a word, experience.

Like all decision making, financing of the whole company, a project, a function, or a component is interrelated with what you do now, considering in a priority manner all your present opportunities and problems, with an eye on your future situation and opportunities. "Financial planning," it is called, and there *are* alternatives.

Alternative Methods of Financing the New Venture

Assuming that you are committed to go ahead, have not already met your angel, and are in a position where only a handful of people, in the whole world, care about your financing problem, you still have options.

On "day one" your first decision is whether to finance yourself or go outside. And if you decide to finance yourself, to what point? To the point where you can show credibility to the first stranger you ask to bet on you! If you cannot afford this outlay—even if you have to ask help from friends, relatives, or associates who will never let you forget their help—stop before you really start.

Assuming that you have reached a condition of credibility, you may have alternate choices of financing. In addition to selling equity in your new product or company, you can license, sell outright, or form a joint venture with an existing company.

License Agreements

Licensing products can be financially rewarding and reduce the risk of products development. But there can be problems. All decision making is put into the hands of the licensee; this is not always desirable or successful. Someone else may not really care as much as you. Or the internal salesman, in the licensed company, may leave the company or be transferred to a different function.

Chester F. Carlson and the Battelle Memorial Institute, the inventors and preliminary developers of the Xerography process, are reported to have received $600 million in royalties for their pioneering efforts. Whether or not that figure is accurate, they certainly made an eminently successful licensing arrangement with the Haloid Corporation, now Xerox. What other very successful licensing agreements can one think of? Not many!

Oil companies, chemical companies, and other large companies in basic industries have been successful in licensing and cross-licensing each other. Some of the agreements have been forced upon these companies by the Justice Department, concerned with monopoly practices. But these are very specialized and they give the right to make, use, and sell a product or process that fits into the existing operation of the licensee. Few small and embryonic companies have that opportunity.

For the inventor or the company based on a new product, with little or no ability to raise capital, licensing provides the advantage of having something rather than nothing come from the product development. This advantage may be a critical one.

Outright Sale

The licensing of a product is a form of sale, and in some instances, title to the patent actually passes on the day of the signing of the licensing agreement. This may provide tax advantages to the licensee. Whether or not title passes in a licensing agreement, the royalty or fee is usually contingent upon the success of the new venture in the hands of the licensee. This is probably as it should be.

In the outright sale the inventor or developer of the new product is not making himself a partner of the purchaser. He is not taking the same contingent risks as the purchaser. However, some new products have been sold outright to a company interested in pursuing its commercialization. On other occasions, the product along with its corporate organization has been purchased because it was more advantageous, for tax reasons, and the value of the company was essentially the value of product development within the company.

In one instance, the developer of a new product sold all the rights in the product to an entrepreneurial group for $500,000, which used it as the basis for starting a new company. This new company, in the facsimile machine business, has been able to raise tens of millions of dollars to finance itself over the years and seems to be doing well.

Approaching a company or a group for the outright sale of your product usually appears negative to the buyer. After all, goes the prospect's thought, the seller should be the one most interested in his own invention or new product. Why does he want to sell it? What does he know that you, the buyer, do not know? Why should you give him a lump sum now, when purchasing the new product from the buyer will require that you add so much more money to commercialize it?

By and large, outright sale of a new product by an embryonic company has been rare, primarily because, on the one hand, the buyer fears the large additional investment he must make after the purchase, and on the other hand, the seller values the product on the basis of a high future expectation.

If the seller is willing to take only a few thousand dollars, he can sometimes make an outright sale to companies who will buy it strictly as a speculation.

Realistically, almost all purchasing companies would prefer a licensing agreement in which their investment will be owned by their company, as it is in an outright sale, but their payments to the inventor are contingent upon the success of the product.

Joint Venture

Another means by which many inventors and companies exploit their products is a transaction in which the new company becomes the partner of an existing company. Typically, the new start-up company will opt to market the product itself and to have someone else make it. Or, the new company will manufacture the product for an existing marketing organization. In either instance, the new company reduces its financial needs by limiting its activities.

The classical type of joint venture is rarely available to the small or embryonic company. Two large companies share know-how, expenses, and profits in a particular project, and the project is limited to a single business venture, usually within a short and predictable time frame and with a very specific goal. Joint ventures have been popular in the construction industries where, for example, a construction firm in one geographical area is able to receive a contract for a building job in another geographical area. Rather than project managing in an area with which they are not familiar, they join with a company already in the area within which the construction will be done.

The joint venture, as we call it, involves finding an existing company which believes it will make a profit by becoming your part-time or full-time partner, in either an active or a passive way. Sibany has used this financing technique on numerous occasions. These citations will provide an insight into the several formats that can be used.

FINANCED FUNCTIONS AS VENTURE CAPITAL

Normally, Allied Chemical (discussed in Chapter 9) is not a supplier of market research. They perform the function only for their internal departments. Sibany traded Allied an option for a license or joint venture in consideration of some cash and a market survey. Both companies had to believe they would make a tangible or intangible profit on the transaction, *whether or not* the license or joint venture agreement was later consummated.

Sibany has charged interested companies for the disclosure of a product development, usually $5,000 to $10,000. Sibany then used the income for working capital and at the same time had provided an additional qualifier of the interested outside company. The outside company was willing to pay the charge as part of the process of deciding whether to acquire the new venture from Sibany.

The new venture or company can not only finance by spending money to accomplish a goal, but also by having the function accomplished by another company and then owning the function. This approach in numerous formats is very common.

SUPPLIERS

The transducer, a major element of the Metrodyne system, is a flexible rubber mat. Almost all its development costs were sponsored by several major rubber companies. Their incentive is to gamble now, and to be the supplier later if and when Metrodyne has high volume requirements. They also are interested in experimenting with the mat technology, which may lead to other new products. Metrodyne had to sell these suppliers as hard as one would sell a customer, or an investor. They are investors in the new venture.

A common variation of this approach is a manufacturer who evaluates the new company and decides to invest his own money to provide production engineering, tooling, and sometimes even the inventory, until the new company is established. The manufacturer's payback is usually in the form of ownership in the new venture or by adding to the selling price to the new company on the first series of products purchased, or both.

Service functions are often provided to new companies in return for partial ownership and a nominal amount of cash. Many service vendors consider it an important part of their business to invest in the future, by taking a percentage of their income as stock. Typically, these include patent attorneys, corporate counsels, advertising agencies, consultants, and members of the financial community. The new company receives a service with a minimum cash outlay, and at the same time gains the sense that the work is being performed by a partner instead of a disinterested participant.

TRADING SERVICES   One or more employees may have abilities that can be traded with another accomplished company for a job required. "Will you do this for me, if I do that for you?" Bartering under such arrangements has to be balanced against the use of that employee's time in the company's basic business.

EARLIER-THAN-USUAL INCOME   The new company usually has "assets" that are not immediately obvious, and certainly will never appear on its balance sheet. These can be sold to an outside company, for prepaid income. These transactions can include: the franchise to distribute in, for example, the state of Illinois; the right to get delivery of the first ten units to be manufactured; the exclusive right to make or sell the product; the option to do all the company's financing, for a period of time; the right of first refusal to all of the inventor's inventions for a period of time; the right to use the company's activities as a continuing "window," or educational process; and, if the new company is engaged in high technology, high risk—the opportunity to "spice" the life of the outside interest.

THE SERVICES OF RETIRED PROFESSIONALS   Most retired or semiretired professional people and businessmen are bored, afraid they have been thrown on the trash pile by our society. They are frequently available and almost always have invaluable experience and "contacts" for the start-up company. They often have the added advantage of requiring little or no cash income; they will bet with the new venture.

MOONLIGHTING BY PROSPECTIVE EMPLOYEES   One of the common denominators in the process of selection of employees by the new company is the question of measuring in advance the commitment of the prospective employee. "Will he work as hard, care as much, as I do?" "Is he qualified?"

Assistance in answering these questions, as well as getting help in the performance of a certain job, can be accomplished by asking the prospective employee to work for you at night or on weekends. It is an excellent qualifier. But there is a danger. The prospective employee may be violating his contract in working for you.

We have seen that the financing of a new venture involves more than raising venture capital. It also includes alternate means of accomplishing tasks, functions, and jobs that the new venture would otherwise have to spend its own money to perform. Unless financing of the new venture is *quickly* accomplished, the whole process is in doubt. *Momentum* is vital to the new venture, and momentum is a psychological factor, rather than an objective analysis of results.

Assuming that the start-up company is successful in financing its business plan and the concretization of its plan, what other financial problems does it face?

Continuing Financial Problems

The financing of the business plan and its implementation is a continuous problem, as may be seen from the AT&T case. The operating company is always in the middle of a number of plans, implementations, and shakedowns. The new company is also attempting to attract and motivate new employees, the second most important problem of the start-up company.

Attracting and Motivating New Employees

Far and away the largest amount of money required by any new company, and in particular the technology-oriented embryonic company, is for salaries. In most product development projects the cost of labor will run approximately 70 percent. In addition, the new company has difficulty competing with larger and more established companies because of the greater risks involved in employment. In 1967, a Commerce Department report described the problem as follows:

> There are few subjects less popular and perhaps less likely to receive favorable consideration than any proposal for the liberalization of stock options. And yet, our study of small technologically based companies indicates they and the pace of their innovation have probably been affected adversely by the tightened provisions of the 1964 tax revisions. We note in the following chart three of the major stock option revisions that were enacted in 1964.[3]
>
> The latter two changes pose, we believe, especially significant problems for the small company. We believe that at the time of the change, the major thrust of Congress' intent was to minimize certain abuses of *large company* option holders. We question whether there was adequate understanding, at the time, of the special impact of this change on the small company. But first, let us consider the small technically based company's need to attract and motivate experienced managerial talent.

3. *Technological Innovation: Its Environment and Management*, U.S. Department of Commerce, 1967, pp. 34–36.

**Some of the Major 1964 Revisions of Stock Option Plans
Entitled to Capital Gains Treatment**

	Before 1964	*After 1964*
Minimum Purchase Price of Stock	85% of Market Value	100% of Market Value
Maximum Time to Exercise Option	10 years	5 years
Minimum Holding Time Between Purchase and Disposition of Stock	6 months	3 years

Small companies tend to go through a growth cycle where, in the early stages, technical know-how is the dominant skill required. Then, commercial products are developed from this know-how. Initially, the number of customers is very limited. Later, as markets grow, new requirements develop: how to manufacture and market products on a broader scale and how to control increasingly complex operations. This stage requires managerial talents that are more likely to be found in larger companies than in the small companies.

The problem, of course, is how to attract these men from the larger companies. Stock options in the small companies are, relatively speaking, substantially less desirable than they were, and less desirable than many large-company options. There are at least two reasons for this:

—First, the absence of a broadly based public market for the stock of many small, technologically based companies increases substantially the borrowing difficulties of the sought-after employee (the stock can be offered as security on loans), especially over a three-year period.

—Second, the employee of a large company can limit his downside risks, in the event the stock market declines, by selling his stock *immediately* should the stock fall below a given point. The very limited market for the stocks of many small companies makes the downside hazard of the stock option of such companies much greater than that of a large company.

For reasons we have already expressed, it is our belief that there would be a net national gain in industrial innovation if these small technologically based companies could attract more skilled, *managerial* talent from the *larger* companies. Liberalized stock options for these small companies could be an important incentive.

RECOMMENDATION

We recommend a liberalization of the stock option rules for small technologically based companies by (1) extending the permissible option period from a maximum of five years to ten years, and (2) reducing the holding period required to receive capital gains treatment to less than three years, preferably to six months.

George Doriot, president of American Research & Development Corporation, a major publicly held venture capital firm, has said, "I would rather invest in a company with 'A' people and 'B' products than in a company with 'A' products and 'B' people." Both the Commerce Department report and General Doriot make the same point: Without good management no company has a chance to succeed.

There is another dimension not referred to in the Commerce Department report. What cannot be measured is the enjoyment that certain people obtain from working on something that did not exist before. Such pleasure, sometimes referred to as "psychic income, is certainly not universal and many people do not have a need for it."

Many persons, particularly between their thirty-fifth and forty-fifth birthdays, develop the need to prove that they can work in a smaller environment with a great deal more authority and scope of management than in the large company with which they are presently employed. For example, many persons in the management of IBM tell you that around your fortieth birthday you have to make a choice about whether you're going to start your own business, go with a smaller company, or stay with IBM for the rest of your working life.

It has been my practice not to entice prospective new managers by offering higher salaries than they are presently receiving. This is also a qualifier. The same salary is given, or in one case, an even lower salary, because the previous salary of a new president was too high for the embryonic company.

The financing of the plan, its implementation, and its shakedown are continuing opportunities and problems. Preserving good relations with present investors and possible future investors is also a never-ending process.

Communication with Present and Future Investors

Almost all states require an annual meeting. It is a formal opportunity for the investors and the management of the new company to communicate, in person. Many of the investors have been in touch with the company during the year. Those who have not done so have the ability to do so at the annual meeting. For the start-up company, the annual meeting should be communicative, detailed, and held in a convenient place.

The annual report issued by a start-up company is also a usual practice, because it is required by law, by agreement with the investors, or simply because it is good management.

A large amount of corporate activity occurs within the new company in a year, and therefore the company should communicate more often with the people who have bet on the new company. Two weeks may be like a year, in comparison with the established company.

The top managers of a new company are, in many ways, frozen in a particular direction, insulated from the outside world, at least emotionally. Regular telephone conversations and personal meetings should be scheduled with investors who are willing to give you the time. They gain the benefit of being better informed and you gain the benefit of a sounding board. For similar reasons, the board of directors of an embryonic company should include outside board members. Non-board members should be invited to meetings regularly, to add insights on particular subjects, and to add to their knowledge of the activities of the company. While the management and board of directors of the company are responsible for making the final decision, insulation from the outside world is critically to be avoided.

Even when the company cannot afford all the jobs it would like to perform, a mailing list (a supplement to the shareholders list) and regular mailings are an excellent investment. When in doubt about a particular addition to the mailing list, remember that the cost is only a few cents, and add the person or company to the list.

During good financial times and bad, use of financially oriented public relations counselors is recommended. Sometimes the public relations counselors have to be paid in cash, but sometimes they will take stock. Left to its own devices, the new venture will communicate poorly and look unprofessional. A professional letterhead, calling cards, and literature provide an aura of competence. In general, the individual or company, knowing nothing else about your company, will judge you on the basis of what little information he has.

Press releases are an inexpensive method of telling your story to strangers and to potential future investors of money or services. Advertising, on the other hand, when you can afford it, has the advantage of being written by you, exactly as you want to say it. Press releases, which are professionally written and professionally distributed, are printed, usually in capsule fashion, by a pleasantly surprising number of publications. They are not doing your company a favor; they are providing a service to their readers.

Occasionally, you may have the opportunity of a feature article in a magazine or newspaper. It is usually a profitable investment of your time. In the suburbs or small towns, it is relatively easy to get the local newspaper to do a story on your company, or to print a press release.

A package of recent material on your company is a good way to satisfy letter or telephone requests for information on your company. The material should be selected according to what is up to date and should be collated periodically, in advance, to avoid hasty decisions about what to send.

Copies of your business plan are a good method of telling your entire story, to prevent outsiders from taking information about your company out of context. For reasons of communication, as well as internal management, the business plan should be regularly updated.

Regular meetings and memorandums to employees should be a part of the program of keeping those who are betting on you informed. In a very direct way, the motivation of your employees is based on their good will, and good will is based on the sense of knowing what is going on.

Fact sheets, regularly summarizing the latest information on the company, may be chosen by your public relations firm, on the basis of regular meetings with security analysts that follow your industry. These are formal methods of communicating with expected levels of competence and should be done well, or not at all, even more so than other parts of the routine of disseminating information.

Properly handled, your informal or formal public relations program can keep good relations with your present investors and add a large number of potential future investors, at all the levels at which you will require investment.

If enough credibility and operating results are attained by the new company, it is likely to become a public company, sooner or later.

The Problems of the First Public Offering

If you have not found honest corporate counsel, auditors, employees, private investors, and reputable people to occupy all the other vacuums of a new company, you will have discovered it long before you are a public company. This chapter need not tell you how and why to do it. There are a number of fine references, including the Bible, that deal with the subject very competently.

The creation of the Securities and Exchange Commission in 1933 has assisted in the problem of the dishonest person at the several levels of relevance to the public company. The creation of and evolution of the venture capital industry, with the explosion of sources of capital, have mitigated the temptation of the entrepreneur and inventor to deal with, and thereby sustain, the dishonest operator. The computer and other modern technology have increased the amount of information, and decreased its cost, on over-the-counter companies. The National Association of Securities Dealers (NASD) has established professional standards for and guidelines to the dealings of stockbrokers with investors in new issues and other over-the-counter securities.

Yet despite these favorable trends, the investor, particularly, the small investor, is essentially in the hands of the top management of the company and stock brokerage firms, as they contemplate investment in the new company that is going public. Rumors, misinformation, and half truths are inevitable despite policing by the SEC and NASD.

The new company, incomplete and insecure in so many ways, is in the hands of its angels—the underwriter who handles a public offering and the market makers in the over-the-counter trading of the new company's stock.

A few cautions: Many members of the financial community will tell you that a Regulation A exemption (Reg. A) public offering is far less desirable than a full registration of your company's securities. Perhaps; but with the problems of selling investment stock ("letter stock") and the increase in the size permitted, under a Reg. A, from $300,000 to $500,000, they are becoming more popular. In general, the expenses to the company, without regard to the discount to the underwriter, are $10,000 to $25,000 for a Reg. A, and $50,000 to $125,000 for the full registration.

A public offering by a new company can be self-underwritten or underwritten by an investment banker, on a firm or best/efforts basis.

The clause in an underwriting of a firm commitment public offering typically reads: "...to purchase *all* of the shares offered hereunder, *if any* are purchased." Until the SEC has made final allowance for the printing of the offering circular (Reg. A) or prospectus (full registration), there is not a final and signed underwriting agreement. During the period of months that the company is waiting for an action by the SEC, of suggested changes, the underwriter has an option to purchase *all* the shares, *if any*, but does not finally bind himself until the last minute. With a disreputable underwriter, this fact can become the basis for a syndrome of "promise them anything, to get the business, and deliver little after the public offering is effective."

As the effective date for the offering draws closer, a disreputable underwriter may tell you that he cannot continue on a firm-commitment basis. The company will have to change the agreement to a best-efforts basis. Changing the underwriter or changing to a self-underwriting will delay or perhaps eliminate the ability of the new company to even accomplish the public offering. Delay will necessitate the updating of the financial statements, a long and expensive step. To avoid a vicious cycle, the company usually agrees to the change.

The clause in an underwriting of a best-efforts public offering typically reads: "Although there is no firm commitment on the part of the underwriter to purchase any of the shares offered hereby, the underwriter is required to use its best efforts to sell such shares as agent of the company." Who can read into the mind and actions of the underwriter whether or not he has used his best efforts? In the final analysis, employees and others who have an interest in the company, will direct purchasers of the company's stock to the underwriter, in a manner analogous to a self-underwriting. The underwriter will receive the same discount and payment of his expenses as if he had sold all the stock himself. He may even sell very little of the stock through his own firm and depend on the company to make the primary effort.

There is no attempt in this chapter to suggest the direction of the decisions of the new company in becoming a public company. There are too many variables that are peculiar to the individual company and the particular timing of the financial climate. However, like other venture management decisions, this area lends itself to consultation, fact finding, and analysis. For example, an underwriter who has never done a firm offering before is not likely to start with your company.

What have been characterized as problems can also be stated as positive factors. You will find many valued friends for the company while selling stock directly to investors. A change in either the financial climate or the new company's situation can *honestly* require the switch of an underwriter from a firm to a best-efforts basis, and cooperation from the company can result in a grateful and helpful underwriter. And most important, the stock brokerage industry is conducted, almost totally, on the basis of good faith. In how many other industries are transactions valued at so high a price handled on the telephone, with so few failures to perform in fact? It is this factor that makes the dishonest stockbroker seem so paradoxical. In an industry that deals with so much money and so much temptation, it is perhaps astonishing that so many are honest.

Other Financial Problems

One important problem relates to the sequence of approaching venture capitalists and underwriters: "Should I deal with more than one firm at a time?" "Whom should I go to first?" The answer to the first question is likely to be that dealing with several firms at the same time, at the beginning, is accepted. However, after any one firm has indicated serious interest, dealing with other firms, until that transaction is completed or fails is inappropriate. Therefore, encumbent upon the president of the new company is the duty to learn to qualify the intention of the potential investor, as soon as possible, and move on the next prospect.

The answer to the second question is to avoid prejudging. The buyer and the nonbuyer are rarely distinguishable early in the procedure. Therefore, it is suggested that potential investors be handled chronologically.

Keeping a perspective when one is involved in the new venture company is probably easier for the person involved than for their families. After all, he knows that because of many considerations, the price of the stock of his company quoted in the paper is academic. The controlling person is subject to numerous actual and expected rules of behavior, but to his family, these considerations are less actual and more intellectual.

In Chapter 7 Richard Nixon was quoted as saying, "The real emotional pitfalls lurk not in preparing to meet a crisis or in fighting the battle itself, but rather in that time immediately afterward when the body, mind, and spirit are totally exhausted and there are still problems to deal with."[4]

In the middle of negotiations, there is often a time when it seems apparent that you are going to make the sale. Any letdown at that time can be devastating for the frail new company. The same thing is true in other negotiations that are protracted. A similar danger occurs at the time the new product seems to be working.

In general, these danger periods are characterized by what seems to be a solution to a critical problem. It is almost axiomatic that the solution, if it really is a solution, will create its own problems and they will have to be solved. In any case, relaxation is not the appropriate posture, for very long, in the new venture.

As a private or public company, the top managers of the new company and the managers of the venture capital of other investors are engaged in an election campaign without an election date. The never-ending nature of this continuum is often burdensome and occasionally almost overwhelming. It is the opposite of sitting in Madison Square Garden and watching one tennis player lose to another. Tomorrow the loser has another opportunity against the winner. To a great extent, his loss is a self-contained event, whereas your business is never-ending.

Philosophy professors explain, in very convincing terms, that all effects have a cause. Effects, each with a cause, each with its own logic, and each interrelated with other causes and effects, are never more obvious than in the new venture. When related, as in this case, to money, income, the egotism of betting on the right horse, and the other factors of financing, each cause and each effect is particularly graphic and has a deep emotional quality.

The seminar outline of AMR International in Chapter 4 provides an additional checklist of the financial problems of the new venture.

Simply stated, any company can be thought of as consisting of people, a business format, and money. Without any one of these three ingredients in appropriate quantitative and qualitative amounts, no business can succeed.

4. Richard Nixon, *My Six Crises* (New York: Doubleday & Co., 1962), p. 19.

To a small company just getting started, money is its lifeblood. It lacks credit and the goodwill of suppliers, customers, and others. It has few assets that a banker will recognize for making a loan. In many ways, no one in the world except a few insiders really cares.

Fortunately, our economy has provided a means of rewarding both the employees and investors in embryonic new ventures with the potential for a high return, tangibly and intangibly to counterbalance the high risk, if they are fortunate enough to pick a winner. Hundreds of companies have brought substantial rewards to thousands of people who bet on the firms' futures. These success stories cover the instances of firms that have made it. As is well known, this is a rare rather than a majority fate.

How and what is the bottom line? What tells interested parties whether they have a hit or a bust? This is the subject of the last two chapters.

Chapter 11

The Bottom Line: Financial Success of the New Venture

"We survive," replies one president of a new venture company in answer to, "How's your firm doing?"

But there are other answers. Another executive gives as his description of a successful company one that can boast, "experienced, motivated, well-organized and trained people *plus* market acceptance of a product line or service *plus* adequate investment capital *plus* timeliness *plus* some cash reserve—*that equals* a successful company."

Unlike a good receipe, the proportions of each ingredient cannot be defined, exactly. They vary from one business to another, from one industry to another, from one set of circumstances and one time to another. And since we cannot determine by insight or consulting a reference book or taking lessons from an expert the exact importance of each element, we had better try to do a good job with all the elements.

Despite the difficulty, judging a new venture is a function of those managers inside the company and the venture capitalists and others outside the company. To the entrepreneur and inventor, the cycle of judging begins with the initial idea. To the venture capitalist it begins later, when there is more information and more tangible evidence to consider. As has been stated, the process is a continuum. Entrepreneur-inventor: What will I plan? How well am I doing? Venture capitalist: What did he plan? How well is he meeting his goals? Both: What is the score of our investment?

How to keep score is the substance of this chapter. This topic will be discussed in terms of the need, the problems, and the methodology. The less tangible facets of the judging process will be discussed in the final chapter. What is a successful investment? From whose standpoint? Is *my* definition of success the same as *his?*

Interpreting the Bottom Line

For those planning employment or investment in new ventures, a word of encouragement: Our economy abounds with new needs. However, attempting to start with a product or service concept and to take it full cycle to a profitable operating company remains business's highest area of risk. The mortality rate of new ventures is great. Whatever your definition of success, it has to be very much a matter of degree. On the other hand, failure is more abrupt and ends the whole business. Does the product or company go down with a bang, exploding into economic disaster, or (to quote T. S. Eliot) "with a whimper," slowly deteriorating to leave its supports with only a vestige of viability.

From an outsider's view, new business venturing may seem to finally yield one of two results: marvelous or horrible. However, for those intimately involved, bottom-line results develop with almost imperceptible slowness. Success can be measured only after many individual and small occurrences add up over a period of time. On the other hand, the realization that the new effort is failing often comes too late, after much money and effort have been expended.

Early action may be triumph, of a kind, because stopping a company or product development that is getting nowhere commercially is better than sending good money after bad. Distinguishing the difference between successful and unsuccessful entrepreneurship, inventing, and venture capital investing, in the shorter term, requires a special sensitivity. Those who are successful seem to have a sixth sense, a kind of extrasensory perception, that others don't seem to possess. Most people invest their time or money according to their comfortableness with the venture. At the risk of stereotyping, the degree of comfort is usually higher when it is traditional, predictable, and established and lower when it is a new venture.

Traditionally, a successful company is one that is profitable. The more profitable, the more successful. Later, it should rise in price and pay a dividend. The more dividends and price appreciation, the greater the success. This is the attitude, and because of their situation, it is the appropriate attitude of the major portion of established investors. During periods of bear markets, it is also the opinion of many less established investors, attempting to weather the storm. But new ventures are rarely profitable in the first year.

The established investor or the investor who has been scared to death is pertinent to new business ventures only when he is acting out of character. Before the investment, their definition of success is having a great deal of information, relatively easy to analyze and judge, and confirmed over a period of years. To the established or fearful investor during and after the investment, success is a profitable company, dividends, and a long-term capital gain on the investment.

Tradition is also reassuring to would-be investors. It is the subject of the how-to books. And even when a subject factually is not appropriate for a how-to book, it is still handed out as *How to Make a Million Dollars in the Stock Market* or *Art Appreciation in Six Easy Lessons*.

Established Firms versus New Companies

In a mature business, the effort to evaluate the bottom line is much simpler, which is perhaps the reason that such a large majority of people choose it as a place to work or invest. Profits that are growing are a sign of health. Other indicators are used to provide forewarnings of sickness. For example, sales dollars divided by inventory dollars result in a ratio that, depending on the industry, the company, the goals and objectives of the company, and various other factors, should be within a certain known and historical range. If the ratio increases (that is, if sales are increasing relative to inventory), the management is put on guard to ensure that inventory levels are maintained or possibly even increased to correspond to the increasing sales. If the company does not maintain or increase inventory, they may lose sales because there are not sufficient goods in inventory to satisfy the needs of the customer.

If the ratio decreases, inventories are building up more rapidly than sales and excess dollars are being tied up in goods that are sitting on the shelf and are not needed to fulfill incoming orders. Special efforts are then undertaken to reduce inventory.

Using these ratios and dozens of others, a mature company can constantly take its own pulse at all levels of its business activities. In the computer age, predicting and controlling these activities have become more scientific because computers can handle and process a great deal more information and have it available almost instantly.

Such ratios are only of academic interest to the person who tries to evaluate a start-up company. While they are less scientific and objective, the managers of a new ompany and those outside must also have methods for measuring the performance of the company.

"Incompetent but Better Organized"

On Day One, the operation actually starts in a garage or the equivalent. Perhaps the father of the product or service is the only worker. Somewhere along the way he develops a business plan with overall corporate goals along with departmental goals and functional goals. In comparison with a larger company; he is incompetent but better organized.

The report by Stefflre Associates provides an excellent summary of the problems of starting a new business and coming to grips with finance:

> A business is really a machine for multiplying resources—for creating resources. The purposes to which these newly created resources can be put are multifarious and multitudinous. The legal contraints on the use of these resources allow great flexibility and seem to the layman to boil down to the fact that newly created resources can be used in any legal way management and the IRS feel may create more resources and keep the corporate resource multiplication moving.
>
> Whenever one starts a business in pursuit of one dream, or in rejection of another, as a way of life, as an attempt to make money, or as an attempt to change the world, the actual complex nitty gritty of creating a small machine that works (in the sense of creating at each stage as much as it uses in the way of financial resources) is quite difficult.
>
> We have sveral observations to make regarding this point. (1) The man who starts a new business is almost never qualified to do all the jobs he is going to have to do to keep the firm afloat. (2) The man who starts a new small business is only as strong as he is in his weakest area (finance, marketing, production, organization).
>
> Many aspects of business do not get simpler as businesses get smaller. The man who starts a small new business is responsible for areas (functions) that in larger businesses are the collective job of groups of specialists. Our hero is not a professional in each of the areas he must make professional judgments in. By these standards he is incompetent. The differentiation and specialization of the large corporation results, however, in a loss of perspective on the part of many of the participants in modern corporate life. Our hero has fewer of these problems the smaller his organization is. As a one man organization his only intra-organizational problems are intra-psychic ones, and more easily resolved.
>
> Our hero is then, in comparison with a larger company, incompetent but better organized. The problem is that the business will fail if he mishandles any of the functions badly enough . . . even though performance of the others is adequate.

In designing a multi-person organization it is frequently recommended, and sometimes possible, to design the interrelations of the several people so that each finds a position such that their strengths add. In this kind of situation it is not a man's weakness but his strongest point that determines his worth to the organization.

The founder of a small new business, however, is in a position where his business is only as strong as he is at his weakest.

This is a somewhat extreme position but we are inclined to believe that it is a useful perspective from which to view the problem of starting a business.

FINANCE IS MOST IMPORTANT

Since most small new businesses are started by men specializing in marketing or production, the area of greatest importance in business, its jugular vein, seems to be finance. Finance breaks down into two very different types of functions: (1) The ability to talk to bankers, investors, creditors, and underwriters in a manner that induces them to provide the incipient entrepreneur with cash, credit or whatever to facilitate successful development of the enterprise; and (2) the ability to realistically project costs and revenues of the business into the future under varying contingencies and to measure the performance of the firm and portions thereof quickly and accurately in comparison with the original projections and in comparison with generally accepted standards.

Thus, finance breaks down into its persuasive function and into *projection, control,* and *score-keeping* functions.

The devices we feel generally applicable for these functions are cash flow projections, standard balance sheet and profit and loss statements, subsidiary analysis of project and/or cost functions, and the simple daily cash position report.[1]

SCORE KEEPING

The focus of the man starting a new business should be short-term, with the realization that procedures, once established, are likely to continue and therefore should have the flexibility of being expandable. Therefore, procedures should be set up to provide room to grow so that the initial approach does not have to be redone again because of growth.

A flexible approach takes foresight and planning at a time when the new venture has many other problems. However, it is basic that the financial goals be targeted and met.

1. Stefflre Associates, Inc., *The Small New Business,* report prepared for the Office of Economic Opportunity, Executive Office of the President, p. 6–9.

The new company can adopt the techniques of larger companies to keep track. Then it can continually determine where it stands. How fast is outgo exceeding income? How many months are left before the money is gone? Where are the greatest expenditures taking place? Are they necessary? Could they be reduced without harming the company? Is the money being spent in the best way to achieve the company's goals?

It is in the area of information that many new companies seem to do the worst job, and yet it is paradoxical that finance and accounting are the most written-about functions of a company. Services are available by the dozens to provide systems. Still, accounting and other information is almost always lacking in new ventures. An evaluation of the new venture provides the answer to this paradox.

THE ACCOUNTANT

The disciplines and attitudes of the accountant, inside or outside the company, are almost exactly opposite those of the other employees of the company. The accountant is factual and realistic while the entrepreneur and inventor tend to be vague and intuitive. For a time, sometimes for a long time, a new company spends more money than it takes in, which goes against the grain of a person who has voluntarily chosen a professional career that involves working with numbers. The accountant is looking for specifics in a situation where the venture manager can only guess at what he has and where he is going.

It seems safe to say that the accountant in a new venture has to review and revise many of his attitudes because the nature of the situation is not likely to change as much as he will have to change.

FORECASTING

Starting the first day, the new company and each of its departments is continually forecasting. Early forecasts are almost totally without a factual base. Assumption is piled upon assumption to create a company on paper, implement it, and shake it down. The dream is found to be on the top floor of a building with a flimsy foundation. This is inevitable, and everyone has to learn that, in the world of new ventures, forecasting will not become a science. In fact, a better ability to forecast could preclude taking advantage of immediate opportunities.

THE FEAR OF KNOWING WHAT IS GOING ON

Those attracted to new ventures seem to feel an ecstasy in operating by the seat of their pants. Facts and reality are treated as if their use would be unsportsmanlike. You can almost hear the entrepreneur or inventor thinking, "Anyone can succeed if he has information or uses systems; the challenge is to succeed without them."

THE NEED TO BELIEVE

Those involved in starting a new venture have a need to believe and often do not want to be confused by the facts. In a sense, this *must* be the case because few new ventures would be started if the entrepreneur-inventor or the investors were totally realistic. The mountain has to be climbed because it is there. Either you understand that or you don't. "One can live out his life in the 20th century without ever learning whether or not he is a coward," said G. K. Chesterton.

OTHER WAYS OF EVALUATING

One of the most confusing aspects of judging new ventures relates to the items that cannot be quantified. In starting a small drugstore, a daily cash report and a monthly profit and loss statement is all the information needed. But broader-based businesses with higher expectations have to be evaluated in many other ways. Though the opportunity to invest in a new restaurant can also be exciting, the business of venture management and the essence of its most difficult problems relate to the broader business.

Beyond the systems and cash-flow projections, evaluating new companies involves your own perceptions and the opinions of the others watching the evolving process. The other investors of time and/or money.

The crucial problem in making your own judgment and questioning others is the same as that of the poll taker. Ensuring as much objectivity as possible; forcing yourself and the other person to rank all of the alternatives to eliminate intellectualizing; and forcing yourself and others to answer seriously by requiring the answer in writing.

New Venture Problems versus Profits

We have discussed some of the problems of the new company that tend to work against the company's becoming profitable and how they can be combated, first by understanding them, and then by a continuing program of acquiring as much information as soon as possible.

There are other problems and conditions of the new venture that are important and not necessarily obvious.

NO PLACE TO HIDE

The new company has a lot of people who have bet time and money on it, and many people have the right and duty to tell you what to do. Most people are traditional and not engaged in new ventures. They assume that the logic of their own business situation should automatically be carried over to the new venture. This creates a tendency for many outside people to expect too much too fast, and for the inside people to feed those expectations with good news or faster-than-appropriate results. The result may be short-term euphoria and longer-term problems.

The reverse is a problem for the investors. In the absence of operating results, the management of the new company may imply that the outside person is ignorant, to avoid admitting to a poor performance.

MANY ROADS TO THE TRUTH

A new venture requires a large diversity of people inside and outside the company who are willing to bet on it. Their diversity creates its own problem. They communicate with each other in ways that are misunderstood or only partially understood. Because of their attempts to be polite or because they simply do not have the time, they let this lack of understanding go uncorrected.

The same information will be interpreted in different ways by diverse people. Their effort at coming to a mutual understanding is as likely to be like the Tower of Babel as it is to be successful.

Statistics on the one hand are a function of the rules that are established to provide them and on the other hand the specific information. Unless each of the diverse people understand the same rules, the resulting statistical information will be either unuseful or distorted.

SELECTIVE INFORMATION

Compare the *New York Times* with a local newspaper. The *Times* attempts and to a great extent succeeds in printing "all the news that's fit to print." The local newspaper of necessity is much more selective. The new company tends to be more like the local newspaper. To some extent this is necessary because there are always many more important things to do in a new company than anyone has the time for. But in addition, each participant has a vested interest in making his own activities as successful as possible, actually and from an appearance standpoint.

Most people, being reasonable, expect less information from a new venture and assume that the little information they receive is a representative sampling of all of the information they might receive if the new company had the time. Often, this is not the case.

THE STAKES ARE HIGH

Whether your philosophy of life assumes that people are basically honest or not, in a new venture they are likely to be tested more than in other situations. The stakes are much higher. Few people will disagree that people invest their time and money for high leverage profits, and the intangible profits of stimulation and enjoyment.

New business ventures usually include opportunities for a greater profit and greater stimulation and enjoyment. In that environment the temptation to hang on as long as possible may cause people to commit acts that in less tempting situations they would not commit. The most difficult problems of the new venture that mitigate against profits relate to the fact that to the investors of time and money, profit is only one of the yardsticks for measuring its success. This apparent conflict of terms will be discussed in the last chapter.

Chapter 12

Other Bottom Lines of the New Business Venture

If happiness is the most misunderstood concept in the world, *success* is in second place. Success and happiness are so elusive because, like all human responses, their existence or nonexistence is entirely *relative* to the satisfaction of a particular person's needs at a particular *time*. Change the person, and the level required to inspire the feeling of success changes. Change the time frame of the same person, and the sense of success will be realized only when different *goals* have been attained.

Therefore, to judge whether a new venture is likely to be successful, is presently successful, or was successful, one has to consider the viewpoint of the venture manager and his individual goals.

The Goals of the New Business Venturer

Most companies and investors enter into new products or other new ventures for the tangible reasons normally associated with the subject: to avoid obsolescence and to retain their market share; to increase average profit margins; to increase the rate of sales and profit growth. During the past twenty years, increasing the price-earnings ratio has become a common goal.

A company associated with product development and technology will often carry a higher price-earnings ratio than another company that does not have the same reputation. The expectation is that "technology companies" will grow faster and have an edge over companies which do not spend money to stay modern.

An example of this phenomenon that we might cite here occurred several years ago when Sibany had licensed a communications device to a listed company on the American Stock Exchange. The licensee's stock had closed at a price of $19.50 on the day the new product was introduced at a press conference at a Manhattan hotel. The story appeared in the *Wall Street Journal*, the *New York Times*, the *New York Daily Mirror*, the *New York Daily News*, the *New York Post*, and the *New York World Telegram and Sun*. The next day there were so many buy orders that trading was suspended for about an hour and the stock finally opened at $22, up 2½. The profit for a theoretical *one-day* investor, including the payment of brokerage commissions, was equivalent to *two years* of interest earned in a savings account. The licensee's corporate status had not essentially changed, but the company *looked* like a more successful company and investors were willing to increase the company's price-earnings ratio. Investors were betting on the future on the basis of a present intangible. To the theoretical investor, his 10 percent return on a one-day investment was as tangible as any other successful investment he made.

The tangible goals of new ventures are more obvious. The problem is that when your assistant or boss, or an outside entrepreneur or inventor, walks into your office with a business plan, he may not define success on the basis of attaining ordinary tangible goals, and neither may you. Here are some other reasons that investors go into new ventures:

To Enable a Manager to Move up in the Organization   An enterprising executive somewhere in the lower echelons may try to use new ventures as a rung, or several rungs, on his career ladder. This explains the "internal salesman," the man who is almost as zealous in promoting a developer's offering inside his company as the developer himself.

In at least one instance the new product mystique created a temporary and amusing sales appeal. A $300 million chemical company was called on by a company selling new-product development services. This particular company's wares were examined by the chemical company, evaluated, and turned down, probably for perfectly sound reasons. But even though there was no sale, each of three successive regimes, within the chemical company, solicited the company—and in each case, also turned down the proposal. Apparently it had become a tradition for the manager of product developmnt in the chemical company to invite this particular company in, entertain its proposals, and then reject them.

For Internal Morale   People like to feel that they are working for and betting on a winner. Often companies will go into new ventures to build up the enthusiasm of their employees.

Any reader of the classified personnel advertisements in the business section of the Sunday *New York Times* knows that participation in modern technologies is a leading factor advertised by firms to attract engineers, and others, to apply to their company for employment.

To Hide Earnings   A few companies are engaged in businesses where profits are inordinately high as a percentage of sales or investment. A commonway of hiding earnings, and avoiding competition, is to spend large sums for new-product development and research and development. At the same time the company is able to stay ahead of potential competitors in technological matters.

The Sense of Participation in Modern Technology   Many company presidents, particularly self-made men, have achieved a great deal, often everything in sight, and are looking for new worlds to conquer. Those who are not college graduates, particularly, may feel a lack in their background and like to control people who have many degrees and seem to be sophisticated about modern technology. One way to control such people is to hire them as consultants or staff members. But then they have the problem of giving these highly qualified and experienced people something to do, and sometimes they start a new-product chain in spite of themselves.

The mass media may also contribute to the frustration of these people, particularly those in routine and relatively slow-changing industries. The media give such people the sense that the computer and other technological breakthroughs are taking over and they themselves are not participants in tomorrow—that all they are doing is making money. In a sense, one has the feeling that they are legitimatizing themselves philosophically and sometimes socially.

Impressing the Wife, Children, Family, and Neighbors   Many companies go into new things in order to give the top man and some of his assistants more credibility in the eyes of their contemporaries. In the United States it is almost a fad to do something new, whether or not it is constructive.

Some companies market a new ingredient and a renamed product every six or nine months even though no new performance advantage can validly be claimed for the item. Social and professional prestige may be the motivation behind the move. Gaining a reputation as a front-runner may also explain such moves.

In the garment industry it is sometimes a status symbol to have a scientist or engineer on the payroll. One can visualize wife A telling her husband that she was humiliated that afternoon because wife B's husband's company hired an engineer and her husband has not gotten around to it yet.

THE HEIR MAKES HIS MARK   In some companies, a key purpose in going into new products is for the son or grandson of the founder to be able to point to the additions he has made to the company

A traditional story told in the legal field dramatizes one kind of possibility. A lawyer's son completes law school and enters the father's firm. Noting that his father has not taken a decent vacation in a long time, he suggests that his father take a trip around the world. With reluctance, the father agrees and takes four months away from his law practice. The major client of the law firm is a railroad company involved in litigation for twenty-five years, which by now has been subdivided into three separate cases, each in various stages of appeal to state and federal courts. The law firm has been receiving fees averaging more than $40,000 per year. Upon the return of the father the son admonishes him for failure to keep up with modern practices. "This firm has been fooling around with that railroad litigation for twenty-five years, and because you have not kept up with modern legal practices, you were not able to settle the claims. You go away for a few months and I settle each of the cases."

Such an instance nevertheless may be a sound business move, as many grandfathers and fathers are less sophisticated than their children about technology, less well attuned to the wave of change. Often this kind of top man is not vitally involved in the everyday activities of the company and merely has the title of top man while other executives are actually keeping the company together. In this case, there is a double advantage: the top man stays out of the way of the active line executives, and also runs the chance of coming up with something worthwhile.

A variation on this theme is older brother and younger brother each trying to upstage the other. A new and successful product to the credit of one or the other can be a major victory.

TO AVOID A TAKEOVER   Until the recent "bear market," many companies were preoccupied by fears of being taken over by other companies. One of the methods used by lawyer-specialists knowledgable in the way of such business strife was to have the takeover candidate announce new technologies being worked on. The assumption was that this would increase the appearance of success of the company to the shareholders and cause them to not turn in their stock to the pursuing company if a takeover bid were made.

A generally accepted rule of thumb is that a company not investing at least 3 percent of its sales in research and development is not keeping up. Many companies charge questionable items to their R&D budgets to get themselves up to 3 percent. At many annual meetings the subject of new-product development and the new technologies that the company is involved in is often the leading subject. As in so many cases, the quantitative factor becomes an end in itself, with the qualitative factor lost. The quantity, rather than the quality, of innovations is given major emphasis, to create a favorable reaction from shareholders. In fact, some companies stress the number of patents granted during the year rather than how many of those breakthroughs resulted in successful products.

To TAKE THE SHAREHOLDER'S MIND OFF BAD NEWS   The company that is about to release a quarterly statement showing that it is losing money or that its profits are down sometimes announces a new program heavy with newness. Such a move is intended to show that though the company lost money it is right in there, the management is doing a good job, and the company is successful.

One company licensed a product from a developer and made the announcement about the license just prior to the announcement that a previous product development that they had trumpeted was about to die.

The chief executive officer of another company stated, "I'd rather keep losing $10,000 a month on this project than announce to my shareholders that our investment of over $1 million has gone down the drain."

And one tale, possibly apocryphal, tells of a paint company not known for its innovation-mindedness, deciding that it had to do something spectacular for an upcoming fiftieth anniversary. It hired a consulting firm to which it paid several hundred thousand dollars to develop a perpetual organic paint. The consulting firm invented several paints that were perpetual and depended on the life cycles of bacteria, fungi and other minute animal life for their color. This was taken by the trade to be one of the most ingenious developments of all time, and yet the product to date has never reached the market. Perhaps it does not really work, but it was an expensive anniversary cake for the company that apparently had nothing else to tell its shareholders. It certainly was an effective distraction from the firm's otherwise undistinguished innovation record.

To MAKE THE COMPANY MORE SALABLE   From time to time companies pursue product development to burnish the company image prior to a sale. Normally, the company may be ill-equipped to handle technological developments and manage them even if it is capable of spending the money to hire the managerial and development talent. This approach invariably fails because the investigation that the buying company makes determines that the technology is entirely new to the company, it is being poorly managed, and the managers of the company are unable to discuss the new product with perspective.

PSYCHOLOGICAL BENEFITS   New products can provide almost all the psychological benefits of life itself: adventure amid untold perils; gambling at high stakes; commitment; and the opportunity to sponsor a new fledgling corporate endeavor. And with success comes a sense of achievement and security.

The peripheral benefits of new-product activities are both personal and corporate. The existence of such an effort proves to its participants (e.g., workers, cash investors, suppliers, and customers) that the company is not moribund or dormant, but aggressively striving to become even better in the future. In many ways new products are an extension of man's higher striving and signify his desire to reach and become something better than he already is.

The psychological motivation of entrepreneurs is to some extent according to the stereotype, but with important differences. According to Treadway C. Parker:

> To begin with, the successful entrepreneur is not a gambler. He is likely to seek out and work best in situations that have some risk attached to them, but he is very intelligent about the matter of risk. He prefers situations which have a moderate amount of risk and which offer him the clear possibility to affect the outcome, through his own personal actions. If he judges the outcome to be based on chance, he won't be interested because he can have little effect. On the other hand, if the outcome is largely predictable by following a set of relatively routine actions, he won't be interested because the results will not be affected by his personal activities.
>
> The entrepreneur prefers situations in which he can reasonably feel he possesses the successful solutions and they can be clearly traced to his own personal abilities.
>
> In regard to physical activity level, the entrepreneur has the capacity to be very active. However, he will not constantly exhibit a high degree of activity but will tend to reserve his bursts of activity for those situations in which he sees the definite possibility of a payoff. While many businessmen are action-oriented, they often act without thought. The entrepreneur acts strenuously, less often, on a more selective basis.
>
> The entrepreneur's work activities tend to be a personal matter in which he sees himself as attempting to master challenging situations through the use of his . . . personal skills. He needs and desires personal independence to sink or swim on the basis of [those] skills. Thus, he desires enough decision-making and

action freedom so that the results which he achieves can clearly be attributed to him and not to circumstances or to the decision of others.

This need has given rise to the popular notion that entrepreneurs want freedom for freedom's sake. This isn't the whole picture. Personal independence is only one of the instruments by which he can connect his own behavior to the results. If results could be associated with his abilities with less personal freedom, he wouldn't really care.

The clearest indications in the research literature is that entrepreneurs are results oriented. They have a strong need to know the impact of their own actions on the situations with which they are dealing. They are not content to just act, they want to know what happens as a result of their actions. Their main interest in the results is personal. They simply want to know how they are doing. Are they winning the game or losing? They aren't particularly concerned with what the spectators might think. They are likely to set high standards for themselves.[2]

Like the college professor, many scientific employees of companies seem to get turned on to a much greater extent by recognition than by financial reward—for example, the issuance of a patent in their name, or the publication of a book, or the opportunity to deliver a paper at a conference. Similarly, it would be difficult to convince managers of even the most profitable companies with the highest price-earnings ratios that they were employed by successful companies if they did not enjoy the job they were doing.

Karl Marx may have been most wrong when he assumed that either capitalists or employees were motivated entirely, or even mostly, by economic gain.

Even in the financial community, the need to find a "winner" seems at least as important as making an investment that appreciates. The financial community almost never admits to any motivation except financial gain. Only when the entrepreneur-inventor or new investor has been around a while and has been taken into the confidence of the money manager does he learn of the intangible motivations. In short, membership or identification with a winning team can be a prime motivator.

THE GOVERNMENT SUBSIDIZES 50 PERCENT   New companies, not yet profitable, invest gross dollars in new ventures. Established companies are subsidized 50 percent in their new ventures by the federal and state governments because the 50 percent would have been paid as a corporate income tax. This situation would suggest that the government believes that profit-making companies are the best source of innovation. As indicated ear-

2. Treadway C. Parker, Ph.D., is a consulting industrial psychologist in the areas of management selection, management training and development, and performance improvement programs. Extract cited by permission.

lier, the history of the 20th century proves that this contention is, to a great extent, incorrect.

SUCCESSFUL FAILURE   To the investor, a successful company is one whose stock price increases in value, whether or not the company makes a profit or, for that matter, whether or not the company continues. The stock of Viatron Computer Systems Corp. rose in value several hundred percent during 1970, while the price of IBM stock was going down. Though Viatron later filed for bankruptcy, the investor who originally purchased Viatron at its new-issue price of $15 and sold it at $30, $40, or $50 certainly considers Viatron a successful investment. Venture management success is, therefore, the satisfaction of the goals of the new business venturer, including, but not limited to, profits.

Adam Smith in *The Money Game* suggests that only one out of five investors invests just to make money. On the face of it, this seems a preposterous statement. But is it? Look at how many investors do not sell their stock in a company whose value has tripled in a few months—or gone up 10 or 20 times in a year. Perhaps such investors are greedy, and it is certain that many are. It is also possible that finding a company whose success they can so immediately identify with is more important to many of these investors than the tangible profits they could make. Is that good or bad? Neither! There are neither good nor bad reasons for new business venturing until you examine the goals of the individual making the judgment. Good goals are those that are the same as yours. Bad reasons for new venturing are those that are different than yours.

When your assistant or boss, or an outside entrepreneur or inventor walks into your office with a business plan, find out whether his goals are the same as yours. Do not assume they are the same, simply because you are both in a business office. A new business plan could be the beginning of a profitable or a horrible relationship. In new business venturing it is not likely to be in between.

When you are evaluating the ongoing new company, or any company for that matter, consider all its investors of time and money as a source of information. If each of them has also ensured that the goals of the other new ventures was the same as his own, success is much more likely.

Other Factors Relating to the Bottom Line

Armed with a better understanding, we can proceed to other factors relating to the bottom line. The expenditures of a technically oriented start-up company begin at the bottom, and with time gradually widen from this base into an upside-down pyramid.

The expenditures of a new company are a function of how sanguine they are about each part of their business. Knowledge and experience increase confidence and in all respects the new company *deliberately* expands, or decides not to expand, even when it does not appear that way. In particular, the passage of time dictates an increase in the number of activities whether or not they are objectively called for. Therefore, the entrepreneur-inventor will feel the necessity to do more things simply because six months or a year has passed. The investor may see many new activities and be lulled by a quantitative rather than a qualitative growth in the number of employees or other aspects of the company in which he has invested.

Less discussed in the measurement of the status of a company is the company's popularity with others. Ideally, the entrepreneur-inventor would like the thrills of participating in a new company with the possibility of great intangible and financial rewards.

So would the investor. But the persons starting a new company and their investors have to live with the reality that what they are doing involves a high degree of financial risk and in many ways is unpopular.

If you quit the highly responsible job you have with Union Carbide, you are a threat to your neighbor who has decided to spend the rest of his working life at the Shell Oil Company. He may have a vested interest in disturbing you or a psychological stake that shows up in his secret wish that you not succeed.

Your stockbroker may discourage you from investing in a company in the over-the-counter market because the transaction is somewhat more difficult to accomplish than if you buy a stock on the New York Stock Exchange. He may even be concerned that you will blame him if the riskier investment does not pan out.

Your bank will not lend you money if the collateral is the stock of a company of which they have never heard.

Your wife and children may think you don't love them as much because you're working the number of hours required by your new company instead of what had been a regular work week. Your friends may think you are no longer one of the boys because you have switched from bonds and blue chip stocks to putting a few thousand dollars into the private company of a crazy inventor down the street.

All across the board, not only are there people who are doing and those who are not doing, but also those who are not doing have a vested interest, they seem to think, in your not rocking the boat by being employed by or investing in an untraditional vehicle.

If you deviate from the ordinary, you even have the statistics against you.

Staying at Shell is likely to be more financially safe. How are you going to explain to your neighbor—or your wife, for that matter—about the gratification you are receiving from a job that has really turned you on for the first time in ten years?

We come now to the loneliness of the new business venture. At a cocktail party, who is going to understand why you are buying your own paper clips? In the board room of a stockbrokerage firm, how do you justify that your over-the-counter stock is down a half-point while the Dow Jones Averages were up 11 points in heavy volume? Or even that there is no way to place a financial value on the investment you made in that private company with a machine that can convert red paint into white paint?

Defining success is therefore simple or complex, depending on how you make it. Presently, it is closer to simple than to complex. If you are employed in or invested in a high-technology company, you are likely to be deemed stupid. In 1968 you were crazy as a fox. While the future is not certain, there are indications that managing or investing in new ventures will get much better before it gets worse.

The Myths and Realities of New Business Venturing

One of the major problems of venture managers is to distinguish between myth and reality. We learn as children the difference between a truth and a lie. But many of us go to the grave without realizing that much of our lives, personal and professional, has been based on myth. While illusion may enrich our personal lives, it tends to make us poorer businessmen. But without illusion there would be no new business ventures.

Edna St. Vincent Millay tells us that "Euclid alone has looked on Beauty bare." To paraphrase, you alone can look on venture management in its real and most utilitarian guise when it is demythologized, denuded of its falsities of belief and assumption.

To some extent this has already been touched on in the course of this book. The line between myth and reality is in fact so thin, in new ventures, that no discussion can avoid it, because we *are* dealing with an *art form*.

As an art form, some of the most interesting and profitable insights relating to venture management cannot be organized in a manner that will adequately communicate. In some cases they are paradoxical. In others they violate beliefs that have been held for a long time. In all cases, they are in the category of those little tidbits that one reads and never forgets or are those rare occasions when the "light bulb" flashes in your mind and you see a particular situation clearly and stripped of its normal clothing. For the author they are insights that have been retained and cannot necessarily be explained logically.

They have been set down here without justification, are stated nakedly, and are unashamedly without supporting material and will either light your bulb or not:

BREAD-AND-BUTTER BUSINESS   Without a bread-and-butter business providing adequate cash income, the high-technology new venture is putting all its eggs into the basket of the health of the American economy and the whims of individuals in the financial community.

THE PH.D. SYNDROME   The "Ph.D. syndrome" is the phenomenon of being mainly concerned with the cleverness of a new product or technology instead of the business of the company. It exists among technicians and engineers as well as most technologists with a Ph.D. degree.

ACCOUNTING AND MANUFACTURING   Concern about manufacturing and accounting are becoming the lost arts of technical new ventures.

TIME   The factor least understood and most poorly planned is how much longer everything takes than anyone thinks it will.

CONTINUITY   Planning, organization, shakedown, marketing, and financing are a continuing function of both the start-up company and the mature company and can never be thought of as being over.

ADVISERS   Everyone has better advice for you than you have for yourself; and if you follow their advice and it does not work, they will forget your name and who you are.

COMMITTEE DECISIONS   Anytime you are faced with a decision by a committee, you can assume either that the answer will be no, or that they have not yet come to a decision.

MORALITY   The difference between large brokerage firms and small brokerage firms, and between large venture capital firms and small venture capital firms, is entirely size and not morality.

STUFF IN THE PIPELINE   On February 13, 1971, few people cared about the headlines in the *New York Times* financial section: "New Issue Market Posts Eighth Advance on Heavy Turnover." The Dow Jones Industrial Averages, the most popular barometer of the status of the financial community, had recovered more than 70 percent of its losses from the spring of 1969. In the previous week, the volume of trading on the New York Stock Exchange included the two busiest days (to that time) in the history of stock trading. On the editorial page the *New York Times* was a warning that the Securities and Exchange Commission or somebody should do something now to avoid the many problems associated with more paperwork than brokerage firms could handle. In other sections of the newspaper, one also read:

> The Federal Reserve Bank had just lowered the discount rate for the fifth time in four months confirming that the nation's banks had a lot of money to lend, there really was a great deal of unemployment, and the Federal Government was very concerned about the recession.

In the beginning of the "New Issue" article, the writer emphasized the transitional nature of the receptivity for the stock of new companies or companies that were not previously known to the financial community:

> The new issue market bounded ahead in heavy trading this week, posting its eighth consecutive advance.
> "People were taking stuff this afternoon like it was going out of style," one specialist in shares of companies recently offered to the public for the first time declared yesterday. "Orders were simply pouring in."
> Despite the sharp pick-up in this sector, the number of companies going public continues small. The pipeline, empty for so long, has not yet been refilled.

NEW VENTURE PROMOTION

The article then went on to suggest the strongly promotional nature of the financing of new technology.

> The Environment/One Corporation marketed 275,000 shares at 14½ after negotiations with the First Hudson Securities Corporation. The shares, which began trading Tuesday, finished the week at 14¾—15¾.
> Environment/One, based in Schenectady, are producers of monitoring systems and pollution-control equipment.
> Ground Water Industries, Inc., a Liverpool, New York, company that markets a broad line of products for the distribution and treatment of water, sold 110,3300 shares at 8½ through Shaskan & Co., Inc., on Wednesday. Yesterday's close was 9¾—10¼.

The promoters of new issues, those Wall Street brokerage firms that specialize in these companies, had waited for the climate to be right to offer any new issues at all. As the market for established companies began to get better, they were planning for new issues most likely to be accepted by the general public. The mass media was in effect advertising the pollution and environmental control industry and there was a bandwagon forming. The catchwords were environment, earth, water, pollution control, and so on.

One could begin to project the names of existing companies whose names would be changed and new companies that would be formed: "Climatation, Inc."; "Electronic Pollution Controls"; "American Pollution Controls"; "North American Pollution Controls"; "Pollution Control Corporation of America"; "National Pollution Controls"; "International Pollution Controls"; "The Laboratory for Pollution Control"; "Advanced Pollution Controls"; "Automatic Pollution Controls"; and "Pollutronics Corp."

NEW ISSUES MEASURED

The article then went on to point out that the indexes were definitely up:

> Despite another round of profit taking among a dozen relatively higher-priced issues, New Issue Outlook declared, "The average share price of the 417 most recently offered new issues jumped 34¢ to $8.55 in the week ended Wednesday."
>
> This was the sharpest dollar advance since the trade service began recording this figure in mid-1970.
>
> The current new-issue share average is now up 74% from its lows last July. The Dow Jones Industrials are up 40% from their lows of last May.

EARLY AND LATE PLANNING

There are those who read the article in the *New York Times* and were prompted to start planning right then. Others had been making their plans for months and read the article as confirmation of their views. Still others would not start planning and committing their plans to actions until the sixteenth week of advance, or the thirty-second or the sixty-fourth week.

Those who plan early will later be described as "visionary" or "promoters" or "captains of industry" if they are successful. If they are not successful, they will later be called "stupid" "wheelers-and-dealers" or "vultures".

Those who do their planning (investing) much later in the cycle will be victims of the "greater fool theory": If you get on a bandwagon early enough, there will be a sucker later on who will be willing to pay more than you paid.

There are many people in our society who have never really been challenged. They wait to die. They grow up, go to school, and work in one or several jobs gaining fair or excellent results without ever committing themselves to anything. In a society that tells every man from the time he is a little boy that he must make a living, what is he to do? For the imaginative and the brave, the message that we live not by bread alone has special point. For them the excitement and the room for faith that exists in new ventures has special appeal and reward. Living, instead of waiting, precedes death.

THE MEANS ARE AS IMPORTANT AS THE ENDS   Success for the entrepreneur-inventor is always different from that of the traditional businessman. It is only in the long run that the starters of new ventures and those with traditional standards will have the same needs and motivations. In the short term, those associated with a new venture relish the trip.

THE SEC   The Securities and Exchange Commission is no better or worse than any other government agency.

THE BUCK STOPS HERE   The man who has had a great deal of responsibility in another company still faces a different situation when he has to operate his own company, where the buck stops at his desk.

THE PROBLEM STATEMENTS   Refining the problem to be answered is much more difficult than inventing the answer.

NEW VENTURE ORGANIZATION IS MOSTLY MYTH   New ventures are concerned with practical dreaming. They are unanalyzably, unpredictably, unauthoritatively, *unbudgetably* subjective. Their roadmarks are hints and not *directions*. Their schedules are faint hopes, and not the basis for *planning*. *Supervision* is often the blind leading the blind. *Communication* is necessarily a flat gray in a society of people and institutions trained to make judgments from black-and-white evidence, or to force the evidence into black or white pigeonholes.

"THEY ARE CRACKPOTS" IS A MYTH   Leonardo da Vinci may have had the greatest mind in the history of Western civilization. He was an inventor and an innovator. A business or country or institution or art form or technology moves sideways or drifts down until a da Vinci. Then it suddenly makes a big jump. But the business or technology is made up of many patterns, and at a given moment, to the beholder, most patterns are moving sideways, some are drifting down, and a few are making big jumps. Who is allowing it to drift down and who is making big jumps? Whom should one bet on?

It is an "answer" that all the individuals and little groups in all their garages and euphemistic garages are crackpots. Most large companies are compelled to say this. It is a more appropriate answer that in these garages are the cavemen who first grew grain and invented the wheel, along with George Westinghouse and Edwin Land.

A new venture is a long-term commitment. The dynamo-leader-pragmatist-politician who becomes head of the company usually likes to command those matters where the results of his efforts are relatively short-term. He can see relatively short-term results when he borrows money, goes through an underwriting, buys a company, or changes a manager. He knows it takes a long time from the product idea to the commercial product. So he leaves new-product development to a group he has inherited or a new group he creates.

Myth or Reality?

The function is called planning, corporate development, product development, venture management, or whatever. Old Joe, the vice president of a certain company, claims thirty-seven years' experience in this business (he actually has one year's experience thirty-seven times). Old Joe has been busy staying alive for thirty-seven years in the rat race. He's about eight years from retirement and the last thing he wants to do is bet on anything.

If Old Joe gets egg on his face within a year or two, he faces six or seven years of trouble. One of the best ways to avoid this is an elaborate committee called a team. Old Joe has almost patriotic fervor toward "my boys," his team. Old Joe and his team report to Old Joe's boss and Old Joe is on his boss's team. In thirty-seven years of playing the game, Old Joe has developed a twinkle in his eye when he's scared to death, a knowing smile when he does not know what someone is talking about, a knack for taking both sides of an issue, and other credentials. Armed with these credentials, his team effort, and the fact that Old Joe's boss's team meets three or four times a year, Old Joe can avoid getting to the heart of the matter for six months or a year, anyway. This stretch-out is not even noticed by Old Joe's boss, because Old Joe's boss knows that product development takes a long time.

In any decent-sized new-product development effort you can always count on the loss of one or two key people to blame a lot of things on, and you can blame subsequent mistakes on the fact that the new key people take time to be trained before they know how to think. Also: the computer can be programmed wrong, a supplier can fail to deliver a part on time or can make it wrong, the machine shop can go on strike, the budget can be inadequate to do the job, or any one of thirteen department heads can fail to cooperate in an important matter.

Stretching the new project two or three years is relatively simple. Old Joe can now show a business plan on Yetta's, which, the plan from his team shows, is twice as good as Zilch's. After two or three years of Yetta stretch-out, Old Joe can switch to Xerob's, which gets him to retirement, and replacement by New Joe, the man Old Joe's boss moved up to get new blood.

If Xerob's, Yetta's, and Zilch's work out, Old Joe is home free: Corporate Development Man of the Year. If one or all do not work out, Old Joe can explain about what the younger generation is coming to.

New Joe has a different set of problems. If Zilch's, Yetta's, or Xerob's work out, they were great products and anyone could have done it. If they do not work out, well, he's young and all that. If handled properly, being young can be stretched out into one year's experience, thirty-seven times. It gives New Joe the time to learn the twinkle and the knowing smile, to play both sides of the street, and to build his own team.

EXPAND NEW VENTURES IN BAD TIMES   New ventures are most profitably bought when others are selling. Entrepreneurs and inventors should be hired when others are not hiring them. You may get a better crop.

LIVE WITH THE NEW VENTURE   A new venture cannot be understood by report. You have to live with it every day.

BETTING   New-venture financing is a two-way transaction where a bet is made when there is often little or nothing to show.

VENTURE MANAGEMENT OPERATING COMPANIES   There will come a day when a large established company will promote itself as one of the first of the "venture management operating companies." They will regularly budget a portion of their earnings for venture management working capital. The common stock of profitable new ventures will be distributed to their shareholders as a regular part of their dividend policy. Other types of venture capitalists cannot successfully compete with a large company making a full commitment of its resources to a new venture.

PSYCHOLOGY OF THE INSTANT   One of the best times to judge the new venture is during those occasional instants, when the customary pretenses and defenses, behind which we all hide, are momentarily unguarded.

HIGH RISK IS BETTER   During a fair or good climate for venture capital, the higher the risk of a new venture, the more money is available and the more money can be justified.

HAVE NOBODY   In a small company it is far worse to have somebody who is not doing a job than to have nobody.

MISCELLANEOUS MYTHS AND REALITY   People are more important than things. Good news is more newsworthy than bad news. Almost all people are responsible, honest and honorable, when given half a chance. Fear can be overcome. Good businessmen do not always wear nice clothes and cut their hair. Creativity can be harnessed and understood. Most companies treat new ventures as a necessary evil. Manliness does not require making quick and decisive decisions. Reliance on application blanks, psychological tests, and interviews leads more to hiring worse people than allowing a prospective employee to openly seek his or her own level. Naiveté provides answers and insights that sophistication hides. Experts do not exist, merely better-informed and less informed people. Scientists treat their employer as a granter of aid and their project as a toy. Computers are not holy. Turning on an unproductive employee provides an atomic explosion of productivity. People rise to the occasion as soon as they think someone cares. An expert is a guy you have rationalized and barely know. An idea can be made profitable after a great deal of hard and clever work. Large companies are inherently stiflers of creativity and initiative and small companies use creativity and initiative to become large companies and then stiflers.

The Last Bottom Line

This book has resorted to overgeneralizations, stereotypes, and simplifications. The foundation and each story can be faulted on one score or another. Venture management is a new industry and its ideas are to a large extent still untested by time. Only after the fact can you be certain.

I believe that certainties are relative. My belief in this conflict in terms has been strengthened through twelve years of new venturing. Many of today's conflicts in terms are tomorrow's definitions. All absolutes are changed by time. Even the items that are selected to be communicated have to be frozen in time, to get them on paper. Therefore, many of them begin as a partial distortion and are never quite up to date.

If you have found one or more elements in this book that you can recognize and apply, the book is successful. My intention was not to offer a complete plan for what to do with and about new ventures. The book contains attitudes, rules of thumb, insights, and dreams: the substance of venture management.

Index

Index